MAGNA
CUM LAUDE

MAGNA
CUM LAUDE

HOW FRANK STRONACH BECAME
CANADA'S BEST-PAID MAN

WAYNE LILLEY

McCLELLAND & STEWART

Library and Archives Canada Cataloguing in Publication

Lilley, Wayne, 1943–
    Magna cum laude : how Frank Stronach became Canada's best-paid man / Wayne Lilley.

"Douglas Gibson books".
ISBN 10: 0-7710-5291-X
ISBN 13: 978-0-7710-5291-0
1. Stronach, Frank. 2. Magna International Inc. – Biography.
3. Businessmen – Canada – Biography. 4. Industrialists – Canada –
Biography. I. Title.

HC112.5.S76L54 2006   338.092   C2006-901909-6

We acknowledge the financial support of the Government of Canada through the Book Publishing Industry Development Program and that of the Government of Ontario through the Ontario Media Development Corporation's Ontario Book Initiative. We further acknowledge the support of the Canada Council for the Arts and the Ontario Arts Council for our publishing program.

Typeset in Berkeley by M&S, Toronto
Printed and bound in Canada

A Douglas Gibson Book

This book is printed on acid-free paper that is 100% recycled, ancient-forest friendly (100% post-consumer recycled).

McClelland & Stewart Ltd.
75 Sherbourne Street
Toronto, Ontario
M5A 2P9
www.mcclelland.com

1 2 3 4 5   10 09 08 07 06

To Shawn and Jay

Contents

AUTHOR'S NOTE

I first met Frank Stronach when I was assigned to interview him for a magazine article in the late 1980s. My editor had been intrigued by the notion of a curly-haired auto-parts executive who hung around his own Toronto disco. Stronach was gracious when he met with me in Magna's Markham, Ontario, office. Projecting a professorial air, he insisted on beginning the interview by using felt-tipped markers on a flip chart beside his desk to illustrate Fair Enterprise, the management theory upon which he structured Magna, and to which he attributed its success. The composition of the drawing seemed overly simplistic, doodles almost, but there was no denying the fervour in Stronach's accompanying commentary, delivered with an Austrian accent. When he was finished, Stronach tore off the sheet, rolled it up, and advised that I should take it with me, suggesting that one day it would be valuable.

I doubt that the drawing would have any intrinsic value today, had I held onto it. Stronach diagrams Fair Enterprise for everyone he meets, so there are far too many similar graphics to make any single one of them unique or valuable. But adherence to the principles of Fair Enterprise has undeniably made both Magna and Stronach worth, as Stronach might put it, "a lot of moneys."

In a sense, that was the genesis of this book. In the years after that meeting, Magna evolved into one of the most successful industrial enterprises in Canadian business annals, a global auto-parts company with sales of nearly $23 billion (U.S.) in 2005. Yet there existed no public record of that remarkable growth. Nor was there a biography of Stronach, one of the best-paid executives in North America.

Journalists, like nature, abhor a vacuum.

One reason for this particular hole in the universe was that it was widely perceived as impossible to tell the Magna story without the co-operation of its enigmatic founder. Sure enough, regrettably, I found that despite repeated interview requests, Stronach was not interested in contributing to a project over which he did not have full control.

I don't know if Stronach's collaboration would have made *Magna Cum Laude* richer. But I am certain that this book would have been impossible were it not for those who assisted me in my attempt to prove that the sprawling Magna story could indeed be told without Stronach's input. I leave it to readers to determine whether the effort has been successful.

I am indebted to the current and past employees of Magna who spoke with me, in many cases despite being bound by non-disclosure agreements as part of their employment contracts. Significantly, even those who related nothing but positive experiences at Magna, and who showed total admiration for Stronach, often requested anonymity. Their wishes, of course, have been respected.

Secondary sources were of considerable value to me in piecing together almost half a century of corporate history. The staff at the Toronto Public Reference Library was unfailingly helpful in tracking down documents related to Magna's early history. So too was the staff in the records department of the Ontario Securities Commission. It was fun looking at actual paper documents, as we used to in pre-electronic days (even if paying rather a lot for access to public documents seemed beyond the pale.)

I was greatly assisted as well by the press coverage that Magna and Stronach have received over the last forty years. Few Canadian companies have generated so many words, often written by my friends and colleagues, who must at times have shared my frustration at Stronach's and Magna's predilection for secrecy. I'm just as sure that, like me, they've considered themselves fortunate to cover Canada's most fascinating corporate figure.

Particularly helpful has been the reporting by Greg Keenan of the *Globe and Mail* and Tony Van Alphen of the *Toronto Star*, automotive-industry beat reporters who have followed Magna for years. Their impressive grasp of the complex Magna empire provided a useful background of events. The reportage and insight of Andy Beyer of the *Washington Post* and Bill Christine of the *Los Angeles Times* was invaluable for its perspective on horse racing. Canadian journalists Martin O'Malley and Don Rumball, both of whom worked on authorized biographies of Stronach (books that their subject cancelled in midstream), added pieces to the puzzle, as did Peter Broecker and Henner Löffler, who assisted by translating material from its original German. John Partridge and Chuck Davies, friends whose indefatigable reporting and fine writing I've admired for years, both offered welcome comments on the manuscript.

I have been doubly fortunate from the outset in undertaking this project. Don Sedgwick and Shaun Bradley of the Transatlantic Literary Agency believed in the book and have been supportive throughout. More importantly, they introduced me to Doug Gibson of Douglas Gibson Books at McClelland & Stewart, who surely must be every writer's dream editor and publisher. It is hard to imagine any writer working with Doug without regarding him as a valued friend.

Peter Jacobsen of Bersenas, Jacobsen, Chouest, Thomson Blackburn LLP deserves a special mention. I'd had the privilege of working with Peter in vetting magazine articles from a legal perspective and was delighted that he was able to lend his experience and discerning eye to the *Magna Cum Laude* manuscript to ensure that no legal boundaries were crossed. In addition to his acute understanding of the law pertaining to publishing, and his talent for spotting inconsistencies, Peter brought to the task a wit, patience, and support that turned a potentially stressful experience into a reassuring one.

My thanks, as well, to Doug Gibson's assistant, Trena White, for shepherding the manuscript on its route toward publication, and to copy editor Lynn Schellenberg, another member of Doug's crack team, whose efforts saved me much embarrassment. Any errors or omissions that have escaped their vigilance are mine alone.

The person to whom I owe the deepest debt on the most counts is my wife, Mary Partridge. The banker's boxes full of carefully tabbed files and documents in our shared office support the even bigger electronic archives on our computers, and are a testament to her organizational talent. As first reader of the manuscript, fact-checker, and office whip-cracker, she kept the project on track, always with her customary good humour and patience. I am blessed that, having completed this journey with me, she remains my best friend.

Finally, I would be remiss in failing to mention the role played – however unwittingly and unwillingly – by Frank Stronach. Had this book been fictional, creating Frank Stronach would have demanded a major suspension of disbelief. By merely being himself, Frank has been the most colourful, innovative, and intriguing personality I've encountered in more than thirty years of business journalism. Like many who have followed his career, I thank him for being, well, Frank.

1

SHAREHOLDERS' REVOLT

On the morning of May 4, 2005, Frank Stronach was gearing up for a big fight at the shareholders' meeting he'd be addressing in a few hours. This was to be the last of three annual meetings of Magna-related public companies that Stronach would chair in as many days, and the public showdown would be unprecedented. For Frank Stronach wasn't typically intimidated by shareholders. As chairman of Magna International Inc., then a $21-billion (U.S.) auto-parts colossus, he'd had perhaps as much experience addressing share-holders at annual general meetings as anyone in the world. His control of Magna and its publicly traded subsidiaries was (and con-tinues to be) so dominating that his regard for ordinary shareholders has tended toward disdain rather than respect. Despite his seventy-two years, Stronach wasn't concerned about fatigue or the possibility of fluffing his lines, either. His belief that he was at his folksy, enter-taining best when wandering around a stage delivering impromptu speeches is mostly unjustified – and not necessarily shared by his own executives or the stockholder audiences. But he'd been doing it that way, his way, for nearly forty years. In Stronach's mind, appear-ing to work without a net demonstrated his entrepreneurial, risk-taking persona.

He'd used the spontaneous technique in the earlier sessions that week, first at the AGM of Magna Entertainment Corp. (MEC), his money-losing company that owns racetracks throughout North America, then the next day at the meeting of the very profitable Magna International Inc. After his walkabout routine, if any shareholders challenged him on anything, Stronach's stock answer was that they could sell their shares if they didn't like the way he was running their company. As a result, few shareholders bothered to raise their voices. The muttered complaints of institutional stockholders – pension and mutual fund companies – had grown louder in recent years, but their worst sanction so far had been to withhold their vote for the slate of directors proposed by management. It had been a decidedly ineffectual protest given that Stronach, through his multiple-voting shares, had the votes to place anyone he wanted on the boards of any of his companies, at any time.

This drizzly spring morning Stronach intended to deliver his usual off-the-cuff, state-of-the-company address to the shareholders of MI Developments Inc. (MID), the third company of which he is chairman and controlling shareholder. (Figure 1.1) But Greenlight Capital Inc., a New York hedge fund that owned about 10 per cent of MID's shares, had become what Stronach feared most – an uppity shareholder that was less interested in *his* performance than in that of the company. Greenlight had already shown a year earlier that it wasn't about to approve of his every whim. In the summer of 2004, Stronach had proposed that MID, Magna's real-estate subsidiary, purchase the shares in the racetrack and gaming business of MEC that it didn't already own. The plan would have effectively privatized MEC, nestling the loss-making racetrack business, a pet project of Stronach's, under the wing of cash-rich MID. Greenlight had objected noisily and had spearheaded a shareholder revolt, complaining that it had bought shares in a solid industrial real-estate company, MID, that had a sound tenant for its properties, Magna. It was *not* interested in owning racetracks, especially unprofitable ones.

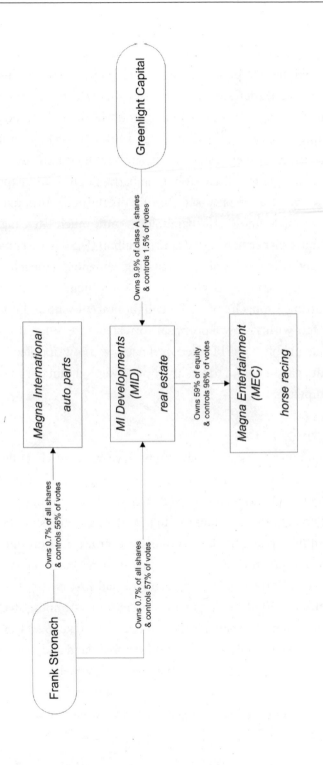

Figure 1.1. Magna Company Structure (2005)

Stronach, though used to shareholders' complaints, wasn't in the habit of paying them any heed. Despite the fact that his own executives opposed the MEC privatization, he had ignored the Greenlight-led insurrection. Underestimating the strength of the protest proved a mistake. The objections grew louder until, in the end, Stronach had grumpily abandoned the idea. But not before MID's high-profile chief executive, former Canadian federal cabinet minister and Newfoundland premier Brian Tobin, embarrassingly – and expensively – resigned after only six months on the job. Although it wouldn't be made known to shareholders until much later, maintaining Tobin's silence had cost MID $1.2 million (U.S.) in severance.

After caving in to Greenlight's irritating demands, Stronach had figured his attacker would go away. No such luck. Not satisfied with thwarting Stronach's plan, Greenlight brazenly showed up on his doorstep with its own proposal to restructure MID. Already angry at having his plans blocked, Stronach was now apoplectic at Greenlight's gall in daring to tell him how it wanted him to run one of his companies.

THE GREENLIGHT PLAN

In other circumstances, Stronach might have admired Greenlight. Founded by David Einhorn in 1996, its principals, all of them less than half Stronach's age, had showed an affinity for spotting promising investments and a willingness to take risks and challenge convention. In nine years, the New Yorkers had grown its portfolio to more than $3 billion (U.S.) in assets that it managed on behalf of institutions and private clients. Greenlight had first crossed paths with Stronach in 2000 when it invested in racetrack-running MEC at the time of its spinoff. Then, in 2003, it bought a stake in MI Developments Inc. As its name implies, MID assembles land and develops factories that it then leases to Magna. This is a very big business. Rents collected from 104 of the car-parts company's 280 facilities around the world have made MID Canada's second-largest industrial real-estate company. The extent of its holdings, as well as the quality of its biggest tenant, Magna, makes it profitable. But Einhorn and his partners at Greenlight reckoned it would be a lot more so if the 59 per cent of MEC that MID owned wasn't there to be a drag on earnings. Hence the first of Greenlight's recommendations to restructure MID: instead of buying the portion of MEC that it didn't already own, as Stronach had wanted, Greenlight thought MID should peddle its investment. Secondly, Greenlight wanted MID to convert itself into a real-estate investment trust (REIT), a structure similar to a mutual fund that pays out the bulk of its income to its unitholders.

Stronach had no appetite for either plan. Since he controlled MID through a relatively small number of multiple-voting shares, he didn't stand to gain much by improving the lot of the shareholders who theoretically owned MID through their single-vote subordinate shares. The fact that he paid himself extraordinary fees – more than $40 million (U.S.) in 2004 – showed that spreading every last dollar among shareholders did not appear to be his top priority. The proposal to sell MEC was a non-starter with him as well. The racetrack business was part of his plan to resuscitate the sport of horse racing, his great passion. Selling MEC was the furthest thing from his mind. In fact, his rationale for including it in MID's portfolio in the first place had been so that he could pump more of Magna's money into it. He couldn't do so directly because he'd promised Magna International shareholders he wouldn't invest in non-automotive ventures. But Stronach knew very well that MID was under no such embargo. Since MID generated most of its revenue from rent that Magna paid, he saw it as a conduit through which Magna's cash could be used indirectly to pay the bills of the spendthrift racetrack business, in some cases by paying inflated rents.

Affronted by Greenlight's impudence, Stronach had given short shrift to its proposal to sell off the racetrack business and had tried to blow off the New Yorkers. But he had again underestimated Greenlight's determination. Instead of disappearing into the background, as previous dissatisfied shareholders had when rebuffed by Stronach, Einhorn and his partners had launched a proxy battle, soliciting support from other shareholders. Greenlight had also petitioned the Ontario Securities Commission to "requisition" a special meeting, to be held at the same time as the 2005 annual general meeting, at which its proposals would be made to shareholders and a vote would be held.

Greenlight was under no illusions that it could ever win a vote to force the issue. Stronach controlled the Class B shares, each of which carried five hundred votes. Though there were far more Class A shares, each carried only a single vote. When all the votes from both classes were combined, Stronach controlled 56.5 per cent of their voting power. But Greenlight hoped that a massive show of support would at least force Stronach and his management to take its proposal seriously.

For Stronach, the certainty that the proxy vote would go his way was small comfort. The very fact it was being held infuriated him. There were bound to be negative optics if he were shown to be ignoring a majority of MID's shareholders, the actual owners of the company's equity, if not the controllers of its votes. Another source of concern was that those shareholders, and especially those institutions who had been complaining for years about his management, but who had remained docile, now had in Greenlight a champion.

None of this was good news for Stronach as he prepared to drive to the elegant King Edward Hotel in downtown Toronto for the showdown with Greenlight at the MID annual meeting – and the infuriating, requisitioned special meeting. It wasn't supposed to be this way. He had intended Magna to be a monument that would at once define his life and become a dynamic legacy confirming his status among history's thinkers and doers. He'd created in Magna an empire that sat astride myriad far-flung colonies. As its emperor, he so closely identified with Magna that he had become it, as it had become him. In attacking one of his companies, the upstart Greenlight was assailing him and all his values. As his car left the Magna compound in Aurora that May morning, Stronach had more important things on his mind than the arrival of spring.

ALONG MAGNA DRIVE, PAST STRONACH BOULEVARD

Nothing better symbolizes the fusion of Frank Stronach and Magna than the huge compound in Aurora, about fifty kilometres north of Toronto, in which he has painstakingly assembled everything that matters in his life – family, Magna, and horse racing, though not always in that order. The size of a small town, the corporate campus has the look and feel of a theme park in search of a coherent theme. The massive home that he built for himself and his wife, Elfriede, is on a street he named Adena Springs. A slightly less imposing house nearby is home to his daughter, Belinda, and her two children, Frank Jr. and Nikki, fathered by Don Walker, Magna's current co-chief executive. Farther along is the home of his son, Andy, and Andy's wife, Kathleen. Nearby, the Magna Golf Course features a clubhouse with soaring ceilings and five-star service that inspired no less a golfer than Vijay Singh to declare it the most magnificent in the world.

Barely visible behind a knoll some four hundred metres from his front door, Canadian flags mark the site of Stronach's Adena Springs North stable, his Canadian thoroughbred breeding centre. Though its white rooftop cupolas give the building a touch of artifice, an affectation intended to mïmic the iconic style of world-famous stables in Kentucky's bluegrass region, Stronach is no pretender where horses are concerned. His Adena Springs location in Midway, Kentucky, a two-thousand-acre farm, is one of the state's largest spreads. Adena Springs South, near Ocala in central Florida, is even more expansive. Stronach owns an estimated one thousand thoroughbreds – not even he knows the exact number – and they include some of the most celebrated money-winners in North American racing history.

But it is the buildings along Magna Drive, past Stronach Boulevard to the east of his home, that matter most to Frank Stronach.

One is a factory that makes parts for car seats. Next to it, as abruptly inconsistent with their surroundings as is Kentucky barn-gingerbread in Ontario, we find hulking stone buildings with green slate roofs hunching over a reflecting pond that separates them from Stronach's home a short walk away. The buildings are the headquarters, administrative offices, and research centre of Magna International Inc., the globe-spanning automotive-parts and auto-assembly behemoth that Stronach founded in a Toronto garage in 1957. In 2005, it boasted 82,000 employees in 224 manufacturing plants and 60 product development and engineering centres in 22 countries. Altogether it generated sales of $22.8 billion (U.S.) and a profit of $639 million (U.S.), making it the fourth-biggest auto-parts concern in the world. With more than 6,000 product lines, it is the most diversified automotive supply company on the planet, with customers that include virtually every automaker in the world.

THE RAGS-TO-RICHES LEGEND

The various elements of the Magna corporate campus define a mythic life that has become part of Canadian business lore. More than fifty years earlier, at the age of twenty-two, Frank Stronach had arrived in Canada intent on making his mark in the business world. By the late 1950s, he had already established a prosperous tool-and-die business in Toronto, which later moved to York Region, a vast, largely agricultural area north of the city. There had been solid economic grounds for moving his company to the area, but the location had also meshed with his social ambitions. The discreet lines of maples and elms that hid tennis courts and swimming pools behind the handsome century homes hinted at the area's gentility. And the three-rail fencing that veined the surrounding hills revealed the local landowners' expensive preoccupation with horses.

There Stronach recognized a world of dusty money that – in his mind, anyway – would balk at accepting an arriviste tool-and-die maker with a thick Austrian accent. With the purchase of a farm,

Stronach could, at the very least, claim real-estate equality. His original vision had been to build a comfortable country homestead where he and Elfriede could raise a family. But an introduction to thoroughbreds, by a farmer from whom he bought a riding horse for six hundred dollars in 1962, changed everything. By applying to the raising and racing of horses the same determination he'd demonstrated in business, he saw an opportunity to earn the approbation, if not necessarily the acceptance, of local high society. That horse racing also seemed a potentially lucrative pursuit, and one at which he could demonstrate his superiority, was all it took to turn it into a lifelong passion.

As for the lore about his business life, the legends abound. Most of them are true. In business, Stronach's credo has always been that only perfection is acceptable. The quality of Magna's products, combined with Magna's flexibility in meeting the most particular customer's demands at a competitive price, was an early hallmark that Stronach has striven to maintain throughout the company's history. To do so, he has demanded the same commitment to excellence in his employees, gaining their confidence by giving them the opportunity to manage autonomously, unfettered by bureaucracy. He has also given them a strong incentive in the form of a share of the profits for which they were directly responsible.

Job satisfaction at Magna has been so high over the years that it has constantly frustrated efforts by the Canadian Auto Workers to unionize the Magna plants. The difficulty of organizing the small units in Magna's decentralized structure has been one obstacle. Magna's subtle, and sometimes not-so-subtle, resistance has been another. But the union has admitted that employee benefits such as a deferred profit-sharing plan, the company-sponsored recreation area, and its daycare facilities have created a contented workforce. Shareholders, especially those who've been investors over a long period, have mostly been content, too, since Magna's compound annual growth rate of about 20 per cent has boosted the value of their shares many

times over. An investor who spent $100 (U.S.) on Magna shares at
their low of $2 in 1991 would have seen the stake grow to almost
$5,000 (U.S.) by 2005. Investors like that sort of thing.

Which isn't to say there haven't been rumblings of discontent.
Stronach has also demanded of employees unalloyed loyalty and
adherence to *his* word. Directors of Stronach-controlled companies
may be more generously rewarded than those at other companies,
but it's clear that they serve more at the pleasure of their chairman
than as representatives of shareholders at large. The board consistently approves Stronach's compensation, which just as consistently
tops the list of corporate executive pay packets in Canada. His paycheque is so frequently cited as a scandal by corporate-governance
mavens that he routinely pre-empts queries about it at annual meetings by bringing it up himself. To put his annual stipend in perspective, in 1997 it was noted that he alone earned as much as the chief
executives of Ford, General Motors, and Chrysler combined. But
Stronach defended it, as he generally does at shareholders' meetings,
on the grounds that he's smarter and more innovative and works
harder than his corporate peers. If entertainers and athletes are worth
salaries that look like long-distance telephone numbers, he's fond of
suggesting, then surely he is worth at least as much.

Shareholders have also expressed concern that Stronach, a self-
proclaimed visionary, will become subsumed by some of his more
quixotic inspirations instead of taking care of business. It's happened
before. In the late 1980s, Stronach attempted to launch a magazine
and multimedia empire, build a ski resort development, establish a
restaurant chain named after his daughter, Belinda, and run for
Parliament. These unsuccessful diversions were blamed by some for
pushing Magna to the brink of bankruptcy. To avoid it, Stronach
engineered one of the most spectacular turnarounds in Canadian
business history. All part of the lore.

Now, in 2005, so far as Greenlight Capital was concerned,
Stronach's attempt to grow a racetrack and gambling business within

MID was evidence of his continuing inability – or his unwillingness, take your pick – to separate Magna's affairs from his own hobbies. More to the point, it was a diversion from the real-estate business it thought it had invested in.

A TALE OF THREE MEETINGS

As Stronach headed through the cream and gilt stylishness of the King Edward Hotel and into the MI Development annual meeting to face his challenger, he could look back with satisfaction on the two earlier Magna AGMs he'd chaired that week. Monday's meeting of MEC had held the potential to be contentious, since Stronach had introduced Tom Hodgson as CEO to shareholders for the very first time. There was nothing wrong with the former banker's credentials. But the fact that Hodgson was Magna Entertainment's fifth boss since 2000 spoke to the difficulties the company had experienced.

MEC had spent heavily to build the biggest portfolio of racetracks in the world. But efforts to execute its somewhat incoherent business plan had gone badly. Very badly. After initially making money, MEC had begun hemorrhaging it. The phlegmatic Hodgson, the latest CEO to try to stem the flow, hadn't had much good news to report to shareholders at the meeting. On top of losses of $215 million (U.S.) over the previous three years – at least $10 million of which had been spent on U.S. lobbyists – Hodgson forecast another losing year in 2005. Even so, shareholders had accepted that management had seen the light and was cutting costs. There had been few challenges from the floor.

One AGM down and two to go.

The much larger meeting of Magna International the next day, attended by about five hundred in Toronto's Roy Thomson Hall, the elegant dove-grey home of the Toronto Symphony Orchestra, had gone better still. Admittedly, for the second year running, institutional shareholders, including one of Canada's biggest pension funds, defiantly withheld their vote for the management-proposed slate of directors. They were protesting the $40-million (U.S.) consulting fee that Stronach received from Magna in fiscal 2004, without indicating what he had done for the money. But as had become his habit, Stronach shrugged off the complaint, and gave his considered opinion that he was worth *even more* as the creator and protector of Magna's unique corporate culture.

If shareholders objected to his compensation, or anything else about Magna's corporate governance, he offered his customary response: sell your shares and invest elsewhere. As at the MEC meeting, there were few questions.

Two down, and one to go.

THE GREENLIGHT GAMBIT

A trim silver-haired man of medium height, Stronach likes to sit alone on stage prior to annual meetings as though collecting his thoughts. As he did so on the morning of May 4, he was aware that the annual meeting of MID's shareholders, due to start in a few minutes, was not likely to go as smoothly as those of the previous two days. For one thing, it had the special proxy meeting tacked onto it. And for that, he could thank the three Greenlight executives, who entered the room quietly. In previous encounters, Greenlight president David Einhorn, chief operating officer Dan Roitman, and vice-president Vinit Setha had conducted themselves respectfully. In fact, when they'd made what they'd known were demands that Stronach would reject outright, they had seemed almost too polite, their deference almost mocking. The politeness was not returned. Someone at MID had seen fit to reserve for Greenlight – whose 10 per cent of MID's shares constituted a stake worth about $160 million (U.S.) – seats that were near the back of the room and almost out of Stronach's sight behind a pillar.

If MID thought it had won a small victory of nerves when the New Yorkers obligingly accepted the awful seats, that idea evaporated when David Einhorn stood to give his scheduled address to shareholders to outline Greenlight's dissident proposals for MID and to criticize the company's management. The floor microphone he'd been expected to use, he pointed out to Richard Crofts, an MID lawyer chairing the special meeting, was invisible to most of the audience. Einhorn suggested innocently that shareholders would be better served if he delivered his address from the podium on stage. Temporarily flustered, Crofts looked to the scowling Stronach for direction, then acceded to the request. Strolling to the podium, the lanky Einhorn was careful not to gloat at the ease with which he'd turned MID's cheesy manoeuvre to his advantage. ("What was Frank going to do?" he asked later. "Say, 'No, the plan was to have you stand over there behind the post when you deliver your speech'?")

Stronach was still steaming at being trumped when Einhorn launched into a speech from the podium – *his* podium – that excoriated Stronach and MID. He accused Stronach of treating the company as though it were his personal property when in fact he had considerably less money invested in it than ordinary shareholders did. As a capper, Einhorn compared Stronach's iron-fisted control of MID to the despotism of Cuban dictator Fidel Castro.

Of course, Einhorn knew very well that the best orator in the world would be unlikely to sway Stronach, just as he knew the proxy solicitation would fail. Stronach held enough votes to bury those of the dissidents. And when all the speeches were over, he did just that.

Even so, the experience had been discomfiting for him. He had never had to actually vote his shares in the past; that he *could* had been enough to discourage dissidents. No Magna company had ever before faced a proxy challenge. But now a hotshot hedge fund run by kids only a few years out of Ivy League colleges had rallied about 87 per cent of MID's shareholders to tell him how they wanted their company run. They wanted it run a lot differently.

It was only a matter of weeks before Stronach received more bad news. Greenlight announced, in June 2005, that it was suing Stronach for "shareholder oppression." A judgment against him could be catastrophic. It would be bad enough if MID were forced to peddle MEC and turn itself into a REIT that transferred most of its profits to unitholders. But what made the situation even worse was that each of the public companies in the Magna empire is structured identically. If he lost this challenge to MID, it might be only a matter of time before MEC, and possibly even Magna International itself, were similarly challenged.

It struck some observers as ironic that to defend himself against the charge of shareholder oppression, Stronach would have to reveal in court information about the company that he'd never previously given to shareholders.

2

STROHSACK TO STRONACH

Frank Stronach has been eager to become the subject of a biography. In fact, he has gone so far as to commission, and pay in full for their literary labours, three different writers to be his Boswell. Journalists Martin O'Malley, Don Rumball, and Rod McQueen all took a crack at it. But after co-operating with the writers, Stronach abruptly abandoned the projects in mid-tale when he lost interest or found the results inadequate, and invoked non-disclosure agreements to prevent their publication. And so, Stronach's life story, as he told it, sits in three different versions on a strong shelf somewhere, and three paid-off authors sit silenced.

Nonetheless, bits and pieces have emerged to support the rags-to-riches image he has cultivated. Toronto writer Martin O'Malley remembers Stronach recalling his first visit back to Austria as a twenty-eight-year-old in 1960, six years after he emigrated to Canada. Eager to impress his parents and friends with his success as an entrepreneur in his adopted country, he'd loaded his pride and joy, a new Pontiac Parisienne convertible, on a ship to Le Havre, France. Gigantic by European standards, the car drew the expected attention as he drove through France and Germany. Gazing down from a hill overlooking his hometown of Weiz in Austria, Stronach experienced

a rush of nostalgia as he sat behind the wheel of the huge car, before
steering the Pontiac triumphantly into Weiz to surprise his mother.
She was the person he wanted to see most, the one responsible for
his acquiring the skill and training that had been the foundation of
a new life in Canada – a life surpassing the most optimistic dreams
of his parents.

Stronach had to get used to hearing himself introduced to old
friends and new acquaintances as Franz Strohsack, the name on his
birth registration. In Canada he was accustomed to being called
Frank Stronach, the version he'd adopted believing it might mitigate
the foreignness conveyed by his distinct Austrian accent, and smooth
his integration into Canada's mainly English-speaking business community. If his friends ever kidded him, he could respond he hadn't
altogether sold out his heritage: Though "Stronach" might have a ring
of Scottish Presbyterianism to it, it also happened to be Austrian; the
village of Iselberg-Stronach in Austria's Lienz Valley, he could remind
them, is famous for its view of the Dolomite mountains.

Frank Stronach was once more Franz Strohsack (literally "straw
sack") during his visit with his parents, whom he was eager to thank
for much of his good fortune. His mother, Eva Strohsack, was especially gratified that her efforts to raise him didn't appear to have been
wasted. She'd had reason for concern when she gave birth to Franz
in September 1932 in the village of Kleinsemmering, near Weiz. The
political confusion that had plagued Austria following its defeat
in World War I had deepened the country's economic woes, and
the worldwide Depression had not helped. Eva and Franz's father,
Johannes Adelman, unwed when their son was born, had jobs in a
local factory. But as custodian of the family finances, Eva was aware
that the extra mouth to feed – they already had a two-year-old
daughter, Elisabeth – would strain the family's meagre resources, not
to mention her relationship with Johannes.

In 1938, the year the German *Anschluss* led to the unopposed
occupation of Austria, Eva and Johannes did marry, but not to each

other. Under Austrian law, children of unwed parents were registered under their mother's surname. Franz, then six, and Elisabeth, eight, went to live with their mother. Their basic schooling in Austria was under the Nazi regime, but Stronach has always maintained that the impact was neutralized by the influence of his father, whom he has depicted as a fervent Communist whose anti-fascist activism led to frequent arrests during World War II; not everyone with such a record was fortunate enough to survive, and the story, as told by Frank, is one of remarkable courage.

An able student, the young Franz was also a talented athlete. He dreamed of a professional soccer career amid talk of the sport's recovery following a wartime suspension. Eva Strohsack, however, had a more practical career in mind for her son. At the conclusion of Franz's formal schooling in 1946, she trotted him along to ELIN, a local manufacturer of electrical products. It was accepting apprentices to train as machinists as Austria geared up for its industrial recovery after the war.

It was a defining period in Franz Strohsack's life. In four years at ELIN, he became a tool-and-die maker, the possessor of a valuable – and, more importantly, a portable – trade. As a soccer player of some local renown, he took a tool-and-die job in Bern, Switzerland, in 1950 while weighing his prospects of playing in a new semi-professional league. In Switzerland, he experienced for the first time life in a country relatively unscarred by war and economically stable compared to postwar Austria. And he could see that countries that hadn't suffered as Europe had from the war – Australia, the United States, South Africa, and Canada, for instance – were booming even more. Returning to Weiz, he applied for visas to immigrate to all four. When Canada responded first, twenty-two-year-old Franz Strohsack cobbled together his savings to buy a one-way train ticket to Rotterdam, and passage on a ship bound for Montreal. Disembarking in Quebec in the spring of 1954, Franz had forty dollars in his pocket.

Or was it two hundred dollars? The oft-repeated story has its variations, occasionally provided by Stronach himself. But the actual amount could have been much more without diminishing the dramatic effect of the near penniless immigrant arriving in Canada. Within a month or so Franz Strohsack turned himself into Frank Stronach. Within a few decades his restless energy and ambition turned his new persona into one of Canada's richest industrialists.

DISHWASHING AND OTHER EARLY JOBS

Still struggling with English, Stronach launched his business career inauspiciously in Quebec. Through an employment agency, he accepted a job picking up golf balls on a driving range and got on a bus to go to work. But he'd misunderstood the directions, and in any case thought that he would be looking for a golf course; driving *ranges*, still relatively new in Canada, were non-existent in Austria. He never did find his would-be employer. Thinking that his heavily accented English would be less of an impediment to employment in Ontario than in Quebec, he spent what was left of his money on a bus ticket to Kitchener, about 100 kilometres west of Toronto, where he hooked up with another Weizer.

Stronach bunked with his compatriot, and took a job washing dishes in a Kitchener hospital to replenish his savings and practice his English. Within a year or so, he and his friend were joined by another Weiz-born tool-and-die maker, Anton "Tony" Czapka. As German-speaking bachelors, the young Austrians found another benefit to living in Kitchener. Populated in the 1800s by German immigrants, the city had been called Berlin until World War I, when the name became an unpatriotic liability to local merchants. But a considerable German-speaking population remained, and the young Weizers found it convenient at dances to meet girls with whom they could communicate in their native language. Although Stronach's job at the sink was hardly impressive, it left his hands cleaner and softer than they'd ever been. When he told girls that he worked at the hospital, they assumed he was a medical intern. He would admit later that he enjoyed the new respect he received, and didn't always bother to set the record straight.

The agreeable social life in Kitchener did little to blunt Stronach's ambition to ply his trade. He and Czapka spent hours talking about some day opening their own business. When Czapka left Kitchener for work in Hamilton, an hour's drive southwest of Toronto, Stronach took a job in an aircraft plant near Toronto's airport. He left that job for a position with a small toolmaker who promised to make him a partner. He was on his way! Disappointment replaced elation, however, when the shop owner reneged. "I'd keep asking him when he was going to make me a partner," Stronach recalled. "He'd always answer, 'Soon.' But he didn't offer his people a raise, and I could see that he was taking home most of the money."

THE FIRST FACTORY

It is understandable, perhaps, that the tale of Magna's near-heroic ascent from that point nearly half a century ago to its iconic stature today in Canada's industrial history has meandered occasionally from fact to fable. In Stronach's version, the shop owner's perfidy helped shape his own future belief that an employee's contribution to a business should be rewarded. In the shorter term, the sense that he was being led on brought out his combative side. He quit.

Supplementing his savings with a thousand-dollar line of credit from the Bank of Nova Scotia and an investment from Tony Czapka, Stronach bought some used equipment and opened his own shop, Accurate Tool and Die, in a garage on the property of American Standard, a Toronto plumbing-fixture firm, near the corner of Dupont and Dufferin streets in the heart of Toronto's industrial district. In addition to tooling work for American Standard, there was potentially more at the nearby farm-implement manufacturer Massey-Harris, and at Inglis, a white-goods company that made stoves, fridges, and washing machines. Czapka, still working in Hamilton, helped Stronach on weekends.

The image of Stronach that emerges is of an entrepreneur driven to succeed. Working from blueprints, toolmakers fashion precision tools that are used as components for equipment that will mass-produce parts to be used in manufacturing. American Standard was so impressed with Accurate Tool and Die's work that it doubled, then tripled, its orders. Accurate grew to keep pace. "The first year in business I had sales of about $13,000 and did most of the work myself," Stronach recalled in 1995. "After one month, I hired somebody. After a year I had about 10 people; after two years about 20 people." All were inculcated with Stronach's single-minded determination to fulfill orders faster than any other shop and to a quality standard that exceeded customer specifications. "It meant long days," Stronach has said. "I had a cot beside the machines where I slept so I could work long after dark and still be in the shop before the sun was up." He admitted later to the occasional wistful pang when he noticed couples strolling by on summer evenings while he was bent over a machine trying to ensure exact tolerances of a part he was making. But at twenty-five, he had achieved his goal. "I was using my skills and running my own business. The area it was in wasn't so hot, but I was in heaven."

Stronach's frustration at the treatment from his previous boss, the story goes, only made him more determined to become a benevolent employer. He spent most of his time in the shop or looking for business, and lived frugally. Czapka had income from his Hamilton job. "Tony [Czapka] and I didn't need much money," Stronach said, "so we kind of agreed to use most of it to give the guys in the shop a little bonus and the rest for new equipment."

It's not surprising that Accurate's subsequent growth into Multimatic and thence into Magna has since become part of Canadian business legend. Somewhat like Apple Computer and Hewlett

Packard, it is Canada's own Horatio Alger, garage-to-multinational tale, elevating Frank Stronach to the pantheon of Canadian business titans.

Stronach no doubt deserves the stature conferred on him and time excuses the story's embellishment to mythic proportions. Yet Stronach has oddly failed to extend to Burton Pabst, his 50 per cent partner for more than two decades, the respect that he extends to his employees. It's entirely possible that Stronach would have eventually created Magna on his own, without Pabst. But it's virtually certain that Pabst played a major role in the formation of Magna International, a fact that Stronach rarely acknowledges.

THE FORGOTTEN PARTNER, BURTON PABST

Stronach had reason to envy Burton Pabst when the two first met in 1956. A Detroit native born the same year as Stronach, Pabst had already achieved some of the career objectives that Stronach had set out for himself. He'd worked in the auto-parts business following college, eventually joining Trim Trends Inc., a hometown company that primarily made parts for Ford. While still in his early twenties, he'd supplemented his education to become what he describes as "a half-assed engineer." Trim Trends, a 350-employee company, was small enough that he was thrown into the thick of activities, learning such things as how to approach buyers and meet manufacturing deadlines. By the mid 1950s, Trim Trends was confident enough in his ability that it sent him to Canada to reorganize its Canadian subsidiary, a plant that had a contract to supply parts for Ford's Canadian-made Meteor, a variant of the U.S. Mercury model. Pabst did the job so well that when he was just twenty-two, the company promoted him to plant manager – the same year that Stronach crossed the Atlantic to start his new life.

Given the chance to run his own show in Canada, Pabst quickly proved a capable manager as well. "I learned all the ropes," he says. "I had to do all the sales myself. All the design, production scheduling and a lot of things." Trim Trends was the main beneficiary of his effort. In his six years with the company, he expanded the Canadian subsidiary from fifty to three hundred employees and had it operating so efficiently that it was more profitable than the parent company's three U.S. plants.

In his capacity with Trim Trends, Pabst had occasionally contracted out tooling work to the company whose owner had promised Stronach a partnership. Impressed with Stronach's work ethic and entrepreneurial bent, Pabst helped him with the design of some tooling that he was trying out. Pabst, who hankered to go into business for himself, kept in touch with Stronach after he opened Accurate, and they talked about a partnership. But rather than forgo his salary at Trim Trends, in 1959 Pabst instead used his company bonus of fifteen thousand dollars to buy half of Stronach's Accurate Tool and Die – the best investment he ever made, Pabst now understates. They created Multimatic Investments Inc. as the vehicle for the joint venture; the suffix "matic," at the time, was being attached to all manner of things to signify modernity or ease of use (somewhat as "solutions" would find its way into the technology lexicon in the 1990s). Although Pabst didn't join Multimatic immediately, he put his auto-industry contacts to work generating orders for the company. Business only got better after he moved to Multimatic full-time in 1961 and they relocated to a new plant in Richmond Hill, a town just north of Toronto.

"It was seven days a week, but we had a lot of fun," Pabst says. "And we always made profits. There was no such thing as 'It took a few years to be profitable.' We were profitable right from the beginning." The two entrepreneurs, barely out of their twenties, and unencumbered by wives or family responsibilities, revelled in their new wealth as men about town, Pabst says. But they were never anything but serious about Multimatic. The partners' roles in the business were practically self-defining. It made sense, they agreed, that as the "outside guy" who wrote the new-business orders, Pabst should be president, "because he [Stronach] thought it would reflect a better image to customers," Pabst says. Stronach became vice-president. "At the time, his [Stronach's] English was not that good," Pabst says. "But I didn't make more money. It was an equal thing."

Impressed with Stronach's energy before they created Multimatic, Pabst was even more awed afterwards by his partner's obsessive drive for perfection. Most customers would accept or repair minor flaws in parts they received. But flaws were unacceptable to Stronach. He'd go so far as to go to a customer's plant to file off an imperfection that only he had noticed. "The customer had been more than happy but Frank wanted it perfect," says Pabst. Stronach was just as compulsive about everything else he tried. Aware that Pabst had been on his college track team, Stronach insisted on challenging his partner to noon-hour sprints in front of the Multimatic plant. Stronach always won. "Frank is a great athlete, and he was just as determined to win at tennis or anything else he tried," says Pabst, who spent part of his youth on a farm in Michigan. "The only thing I could always do better than him was ride a horse. I'd grown up riding to school every day."

For all their competitiveness, the partners' talents dovetailed perfectly. In expanding the business to make parts with their tooling, their guiding principle was that a manufactured part is only as good as the tooling used to make it. Convinced that European technical training was superior to North America's, Stronach looked to the German and especially the Austrian diaspora in Canada to assemble the best teams he could find. He oversaw their rendering of the tooling designs into production equipment, then supervised the manufacturing of finished products made with the equipment. "He had a great talent for pulling together people, future tool makers, managers and [people] of that type," recalls Pabst, whose role was booking business, costing out orders, and assisting with production scheduling and design work for the tooling.

The goal from the beginning was to break into the auto-parts industry. U.S. import duties made their products uncompetitive with those of U.S. suppliers selling to U.S. auto plants, so Pabst used his contacts among Canadian automakers' purchasing agents and buyers, and in 1960 Multimatic got a breakthrough contract to supply General Motors in Canada with sun-visor brackets. The $30,000 amount of the contract wasn't earthshaking. Hundreds would follow that were bigger and more profitable for Multimatic. But it was a win for Multimatic that Stronach has since cited as a defining moment in Magna's history and in his own rise to become an auto-parts magnate.

The fact that Stronach scarcely mentions that he had a partner at all, Pabst says, is entirely in character, and isn't the only instance of Stronach's readiness to revise Magna's history. Pabst, now seventy-four and living on his farm near Magna's Aurora headquarters, is more bemused than indignant that Stronach seldom bothers to mention his role in that first contract and in Magna's early years. Pabst says a picture was taken to commemorate Multimatic's first auto part. The original photo featured him and a machinist alongside Stronach who was holding up the part. But he's since seen the picture on television with only Stronach in it.

"I was next to him when he took that," Pabst says, but somehow he was cut out.

BETTING ON THE PLANT MANAGER

As Multimatic continued to grow, Stronach developed a strategy to counter the paucity of skilled tradesmen in Canada. Keeping good ones already on the payroll, he figured, was easier than finding new ones. But simply paying more would quickly escalate the company's cost structure, and even then there was a risk that someone else would offer his good tradesmen more money. He would later tell interviewers that he came to believe that giving top performers a piece of the business would not only discourage their jumping to another job, but would also tie their income to the company's performance, giving them an incentive to work harder and smarter. He got a chance to test his theory shortly after Multimatic landed the GM contract.

Herman Koob, one of his foremen, had hinted that he was thinking about setting up his own shop to do similar work. Stronach liked
Koob, and even admired his entrepreneurial spirit. But he also recognized that losing him would hurt Multimatic. "I told him, 'Look,
why don't we open a new factory,'" Stronach recalled. "You'll own
one-third of it." Koob took the deal and became one-third owner
and manager of Speedex Manufacturing Ltd., a new plant two-thirds
owned by Multimatic. Koob was responsible for such things as its
business plan and a compensation approach for his plant's employees. Although his base salary wasn't as big as what counterparts were
paid at other companies, he received one-third of the profit after
expenses. Multimatic got the rest.

As Pabst found contracts with customers ranging from aerospace
companies to the government, Multimatic replicated the strategy.
Plant managers had what was, at the time, unusually broad authority to make decisions affecting their own operations. Stronach
insisted that a plant operated more efficiently if the manager knew
every machine, employee, customer, and job, and was accountable
for all of them. The prescription put a natural limit on optimal plant
size, which he initially pegged at fifty employees but later determined to be about one hundred. And if any plant manager believed
a new plant was required, and could justify it with a sound business
plan, Multimatic built it. The manager could either manage the new
plant or his existing one, but in any event got a share of the new
plant's profits, in addition to those from his original one.

The approach, which has become part of the DNA of Magna and
which Stronach has taken credit for developing and later fine tuning,
proved successful from the beginning at Multimatic. Within a year
or so, it had three plants, each managed by an entrepreneur who had
a clear incentive to keep a lid on costs and maximize profits. Most
did. After Speedex was created, Stronach's old pal Tony Czapka
became one-third owner and plant manager of Unimatic Ltd. A third
plant, called Dieomatic Metal Ltd., was managed by Klaus Bytzek.

Significantly, all three men – Koob, Czapka, and Bytzek – remained with Multimatic and its successor companies and became very wealthy as a result. Multimatic, of course, prospered as well. "It was very successful," Stronach told *Success* magazine in 1995. "So I took another foreman, and another one, and another. All of a sudden I was a young guy who had a whole bunch of factories."

Actually, he was a 50 per cent partner with another young guy, Burton Pabst, who now chuckles and shakes his head at Stronach's apparent forgetfulness about how Magna's structure came about, and why. Trim Trends, he says, had had production and profitability problems in the U.S. when it operated one big, heavily unionized plant while he was there. He'd seen it improve immeasurably after it broke up into smaller, non-unionized units in different locations. "The only thing they didn't do was carry it far enough so there was an incentive so the manager could profit-share," says Pabst, who otherwise regarded the Trim Trends' model as an exemplar. When the 1965 Auto Pact promised to boost business dramatically, Pabst remembered the Trim Trends experience. "Frank wanted to build a big plant, and I convinced him to have small plants with a general manager with an incentive," Pabst says. "So we went that route, and that was one of our keys to success."

THE FIRST NON-AUTOMOTIVE VENTURES

Pabst, who admits to having been by far the more conservative of the partners, spent a lot of time trying to rein in Stronach's fecund imagination, which all too often tended to generate new business ideas based on his personal interests. A skier, Stronach at one point wanted to go into the business of making fibreglass skis, although "there was already somebody making equipment with it [fibreglass] that was huge," says Pabst. "He was always getting off on some tangent and I would bring him back to our bread and butter, which really was automotive and to hell with that [other] stuff."

But Pabst concedes he wasn't always successful. Stronach saw himself as a generator of big ideas that would have an impact on society or industry. His enthusiasm for a business idea could appear and vanish with astonishing speed, as ski manufacturing had, and as another hobby-inspired idea, the tennis-equipment business, would. At the same time, he could become inexplicably fixated for a longer term on other no-hope projects that had little to do with auto parts. His fervour for a process that purported to extract bitumen – low grade crude oil that can be upgraded into more valuable products such as gasoline – from Alberta's Athabasca oil sands using a minimum of water was typical of the grand ideas that attracted him. "Some guys brought in a cylinder and you put the goop [extracted oil sands] against a wheel and the friction would separate it into pure bitumen," Pabst recalls. "But it wasn't practical. When you scaled it up to a huge drum, it took more power to extract the oil out of the sand than it [the oil] was worth." Still, Stronach insisted on carrying on developing the process and Pabst resignedly indulged his partner. "It wasn't hurting us much," he says.

The partners may have been very different guys, but they enjoyed each others' company, and rode the same wave of adrenalin while building Multimatic. Young and single, they had plenty of money and played as hard as they worked, Pabst says. But then he married and started a family before Stronach, which changed his view of the nightlife. "I couldn't see causing a lot of crap being out on the street when we were in business," is how Pabst puts it. "And I had a lot more [family] responsibilities than he did." Though never a drinker beyond the odd glass of wine, Stronach carried on enjoying a reputation as a lady's man, without any apparent loss of energy on the job. "He's always been like that, from the day I met him," says Pabst. "He doesn't need the sleep I do, I know that."

One of the strengths of the partnership of Stronach and Pabst was their mutual trust and the fact that they worked from the same office. Still, it wasn't always easy to stay out of the line of fire when Stronach was launching personal plans, Pabst remembers. They'd

more or less agreed when setting up Multimatic that instead of big
salaries they'd pay themselves bonuses. But there had been little
mention of an extra-big payment in the mid 1960s when Stronach
surprised his partner. "We were making money and all of a sudden
he said to me, 'I've bought a farm,'" says Pabst. He emphasizes that
Stronach was perfectly entitled to money that they'd been leaving in
the business, and though initially annoyed, Pabst thought Stronach's
real-estate idea was a good one. "I thought, 'Shit.' Then I said, 'Okay,
you bought a farm, now I get that money [from the company] too.'"
Ultimately Pabst not only saw merit in Stronach's purchase, he used
his own money from Multimatic to buy an eleven-acre corner of
Stronach's farm on which the original farmhouse sat. "He wanted to
tear down the old house," says Pabst. "I bought the piece of property and had enough left over to restore the old house."

Typically, Stronach's plans for the balance of the one hundred or
so acres he'd bought were much bigger. He named the property
Beechwood Farm and intended to build a home on it in preparation
for starting a family of his own.

TIME FOR A WIFE

In 1960, when Stronach had taken his first trip back to Austria with
his Pontiac, he'd been eager to show off his wealth from the New
World. But he'd also had another agenda: having decided that it was
time he married and had a family, he was on a scouting mission for
a suitable bride.

As an entrepreneur, Stronach was not averse to taking business
risks. But in his personal life, he wasn't about to leave to chance – and
certainly not to passion or romance – something so important as the
taking of a wife. On his visit back home, he'd met Elfriede Sallmutter,
daughter of a prominent Weiz furniture maker. That she was blonde
and pretty was important to Stronach, who had then, and would
continue to have, an eye for attractive women. But the fact that her
mother was equally handsome, and of an agreeable disposition, was

just as important, he confessed to the writer of one of his unpublished biographies. Perhaps foreshadowing his later fascination with the breeding of thoroughbred horses, in addition to his genuine affection for her, Stronach came close to choosing his wife, the future mother of his children, for her genetic pedigree. On a second visit to Austria, in 1961, he proposed to Elfriede. They married in Toronto in 1964.

In 1966, on a return trip to Austria to recruit skilled tradesmen for Multimatic, Stronach had something more than his wealth to boast about; he had pictures of his new baby daughter, Belinda, to show to her grandparents. Two years later, his son, Andy, was born. Although he stayed in touch with his father and mother, both of whom had their own families with their new spouses, Frank felt closest to his sister, Elisabeth, who eventually followed him to Toronto, where she opened a crystal shop.

BUILDING THE STRONACH STABLE

As well as being partners in business, Stronach and Pabst shared an interest in horses, though Pabst favoured hunters and jumpers rather than thoroughbreds. Since the head office had moved to Richmond Hill in 1961, Multimatic's expansion had been in that same area. Driving from one plant to another in the region, Stronach inevitably noticed that horses were very much a part of the local culture. In 1961 he bought a riding horse from a local farmer who agreed to stable it for him. Although he didn't know much about riding, he showed characteristic grit and determination to become a competent rider in a short time. "When Frank decides he's going to do something," Pabst observes, "he won't sit still until he does it better than anyone else."

While visiting the stable, he became interested in the racehorses owned by the farmer who'd sold him his riding horse. It only took a single trip to the track, with his host explaining what was going on and how to read the racing form, for Stronach to turn his attention from riding horses to horses you owned and hired someone to ride in races. In 1963 he paid seven hundred dollars for his first thoroughbred, a yearling named Miss Scooter. To his delight, Miss Scooter turned out to be an excellent purchase as racehorses go. In 1965, she went on to win three claiming races (designed to ensure a level quality among horses entered, by making any of the entries eligible for purchase at a set price) and enough in purses to earn out her cost and turn a tidy profit.

Stronach was smitten by everything he'd so far experienced about racing, and felt that he had an instinct for picking horses that could win. Finding time to indulge in his new hobby wasn't always easy, but his rising income from Multimatic permitted him to raise his sights. That Elfriede shared his interest in thoroughbreds was further encouragement, and he began expanding his Beechwood Farm. In 1967, he bought two horses at an auction for a total of $5,700, more than a first-year teacher's salary in those days. But Stronach enjoyed the image of a high-rolling thoroughbred owner and mingling with prominent business and society figures. Menetic, one of the horses he bought, had been bred by Windfields Farm, the famous stable founded by industrialist E. P. Taylor, a legendary figure in both the business and racing worlds.

He also loved the deference owners got at the track – especially those who found themselves in the winner's circle. "Frank discovered that you can make millions of dollars cranking out motor mounts for Chevys and nobody knows who you are," says one who worked for him in the years in which he was establishing his stable. "But the owner of a winning horse worth a couple of thousand dollars gets his picture taken and his name in the paper. I think he liked that."

THE AUTO PACT CHANGES EVERYTHING

In fact, Stronach was beginning to be noticed in the business pages as well. By 1965, Multimatic consisted of five divisions with a total of four or five hundred employees in the Toronto area. To go with the GM contract, Pabst had added a few others in the automotive sector. But most car-company buying decisions were still made in the United States, which protected its domestic auto-parts companies with high duties on imports. So Multimatic, like other Canadian car-parts makers, was always on the outside, looking in. In 1965, following a Royal Commission into the auto industry, that would change dramatically.

Until the 1960s, Canada's automotive business mainly consisted of assembly plants owned by the Big Three U.S. companies, General Motors, Ford, and Chrysler (with American Motors playing a smaller role). But the companies did virtually all their design, engineering, and manufacturing in the States, giving American auto-parts suppliers a huge advantage. Although U.S.-owned Canadian assembly plants didn't have the capacity to meet the Canadian domestic demand, they were disinclined to expand their capacity in Canada, which would have meant exporting well-paying auto-plant jobs as well. Forced to import cars from the south, Canada had developed a massive automotive trade deficit, which it countered with a 17 per cent import tax on cars, upsetting the automakers.

The Canadian–U.S. Automotive Products Agreement signed at the beginning of 1965 (soon popularly known as the Auto Pact) broke the impasse. It eliminated tariffs between the two countries, effectively creating free trade in the auto sector, and permitting automakers to integrate their U.S. and Canadian production into more efficient units able to serve both markets. Canada benefited immensely from the agreement. In addition to gaining tariff-free access to U.S. markets, its domestic market was protected from a flood of U.S. imports by a provision that bound the Big Three to produce one dollar's worth of car in Canada for every dollar's worth it sold there. The impact on the Canadian economy, in which the automobile business accounts for about 12 per cent of the gross domestic product, was both huge and immediate. Prior to the Auto

Pact, a mere 7 per cent of Canadian-made cars were exported to the U.S.; by 1968, the export number had risen to 60 per cent, and only 40 per cent of the cars bought in Canada were made in the U.S.

The Auto Pact changed Frank Stronach's life. In retrospect, it's clear that the Pact made it possible for him to build a profitable small business into an empire. The feature of the Auto Pact of greatest interest to Stronach and Pabst at Multimatic was its requirement that automakers source a minimum of 60 per cent of each Canadian-made vehicle's parts and labour in Canada. A codicil further demanded that Canadian parts-makers' quality match that of their U.S. counterparts; its intent was to force Canadian suppliers to improve their production methods and quality control. But this was no problem at all at Multimatic. "We could already make whatever they needed," Stronach later said of the Auto Pact. "Now we could go after automakers' business without having to worry about tariffs."

And they did. "Being from Detroit, I scrambled down there right away and got familiar with the buyers down there," says Pabst. "I knew damned well if we didn't get at least one part from each automaker, and do a good job, we couldn't grow. We had to get at least one part or two parts." Pabst was singularly successful. In 1965, before the Auto Pact kicked in, Multimatic was doing well enough with sales of about $1 million. By 1968, with the Auto Pact in place, contracts with Ford, General Motors, Chrysler and American Motors swelled sales to nearly $4 million. Now the sky was the limit.

3

MAGNA TAKES OFF

By late 1968 Multimatic had reached a crossroads. Though confident they could grow the company, the partners were short of capital. Aware that a downturn in the notoriously cyclical car business could reverse their fortunes in a hurry, they were disinclined to load up with debt. Even in good times it was occasionally difficult to manage cash flow. It was the nature of the business that Multimatic had to spend heavily on tooling in the spring to get ready for the fall production period, and then hope that the new car models it was making parts for were a success. But the company's relatively small line of credit didn't leave much margin for error. "The tooling caused cost accumulations," says Murray Kingsburgh, a former Clarkson and Gordon accountant hired by Pabst in 1967 to handle finances. "I would have to go to GM in Oshawa and sit and wait for the cheque and bring it back to the Richmond Hill bank so we could get under our line of credit."

One route to growth was to become a public company. An initial public offering (IPO) of shares would mean giving up equity in the company to gain access to shareholders' money for growth capital. A more interesting option appeared when Magna Electronics Inc., a

Toronto-based manufacturing concern that was already a public company, offered to buy Multimatic from them.

FROM MULTIMATIC TO MAGNA

Magna Electronics was run by its founder, Jack Warrington, a flamboyant promoter/financier, and appeared similar to Multimatic in structure. It had interests in everything from aerospace and industrial electronics to machine shops, located in separate plants around Toronto. Magna intended to let Stronach and Pabst carry on operating Multimatic as Magna Electronics' automotive-parts division. The partners liked that. They liked the money Magna was offering, too; at the end of November 1968, it paid them $2 million, of which $800,000 was paid in cash and the balance by the issue of 100,000 common shares, for Multimatic. They knew they'd no longer possess Multimatic as their own. But that was okay because they'd own a large stake in a bigger company that included Multimatic, and whose diverse holdings offered them more opportunities as manufacturers.

Newly enriched from selling their company, Stronach and Pabst worked apart from each other in offices in different locations for the first time since they'd started Multimatic. They were both made vice-president and director of Magna Electronics, while Warrington remained president. Stronach's primary responsibility was running the Multimatic division in Richmond Hill, north of Toronto, as before. Pabst, based in Scarborough, east of Toronto, oversaw the rest of the company. As he set about assessing Magna's various businesses, he began to worry. He'd liked Warrington, an entrepreneur who shared Stronach's readiness to take a flyer on ventures that captured his imagination. But unlike Stronach, whom Pabst had been able to talk out of his wilder ideas, Warrington had apparently had no one checking his at Magna Electronics.

The evidence was the grab bag of operations that made up Magna Electronics. In addition to Multimatic, there were a couple of much smaller divisions making car parts, a flimsy electronics operation, and something it billed as a defence-industry group with contracts to make components for the Canadian Forces. It also had an aerospace division that listed NASA as a customer. To go with those, however, Warrington's mishmash of outfits also included one that used a sandblasting process to make patterned wallcoverings out of plywood and another that applied Teflon coating to pots and pans. Warrington had deemed the coating operation sufficiently promising that he'd incorporated a line-drawn illustration of a saucepan into Magna Electronics' 1969 annual report. Pabst and Stronach, used to the testosterone-fuelled world of auto parts, were aghast at being portrayed as tinkers who fixed pots and pans. The coating unit was one of the first that Pabst shuttered before trying to make sense of the rest of the hodgepodge. "We weren't even sure what some of the stuff did," Pabst says.

As he began to appraise each product line on the basis of its likelihood of generating a profit, he was quick to spot what some didn't do, which was make money. He cut the money-losing divisions, even if they were in the auto-parts business. For example, Motor Specialty Corp., a piston manufacturer whose equipment was ageing, was lopped. Others seemed about to slip into oblivion of their own accord. Prospects for the impressively named aerospace division were diminishing daily as the Viet Nam war sucked cash out of the U.S. space program. Pabst had also come to the conclusion that the second half of the name Magna Electronics was a misrepresentation. The electronics division "was nothing about electronics," he says. "It was hardware – avionics boxes and torpedo shafts and torpedoes and hardware for electronics." Worse, he says, its products were made to be stockpiled. He shut down the electronics division as well.

Pabst and Stronach, meanwhile, were beginning to understand why Warrington had been so keen on buying their company: the Multimatic division's $5 million in sales in 1969 accounted for nearly 74 per cent of Magna Electronics' total of $6.8 million. It was also by far the most profitable division in the company. Warrington and his management had made money on Magna Electronics' stock in the past, says Pabst, but the company had run down and was "losing money and sucking us [Multimatic] down too."

The Multimatic partners looked for a way out of the dilemma. Pabst found it in the structure of the merger with Multimatic. Unbelievably, Magna Electronics had partly paid him and Stronach in shares that, if combined, gave them control of Magna Electronics. Pabst still can't explain how Magna's board had failed to see that it was giving them control, "but thank god they did," he says, "Warrington would have sunk us." In the end, Pabst recalls, "I said to Frank, 'They don't have controlling interest. We have more shares than they do.' So we made a reverse takeover and threw Warrington out."

A BAD START AT MAGNA

As it turned out, there was a hidden cost to gaining control of Magna Electronics. With Stronach focused on the auto-parts business and Pabst, now president, sorting out all the other divisions in Magna, they were working more independently than at any time since they first came together in the late 1950s. Pabst believes this opened a fissure between him and Stronach that never quite healed. Once Pabst had winnowed the company down to the point that divisions besides Multimatic were making a profit, he fully intended to return to the automotive group, his real love. In the meantime, Magna Electronics' business may have been confused and problematic, but he and Stronach recognized opportunities that its status as a public company presented, if it were well run. They could raise capital by selling more shares, for example, or use shares as currency to make acquisitions without using up cash.

To shore up their inexperience in running a public company, Pabst and Stronach leaned on the expertise of John McCutcheon, a McGill engineering professor who was on Magna Electronics' board, and whom they made chairman. Unfortunately, McCutcheon's engineering and corporate knowledge was not infallible when it came to business analysis. In 1969, McCutcheon suggested that the company invest in Digital Systems Associates, an Ottawa firm that had developed computerized design applications based on a minicomputer. It appealed to Pabst and Stronach that Digital Systems had a somewhat bigger technology component than the soupçon they'd found at Magna Electronics' existing divisions. Besides, it seemed cheap: Magna Electronics got a 49 per cent interest for only $23,000 in cash plus 10,000 Magna common shares (worth $15 each, or a total of $150,000 at the time). Magna also made a commitment to advance the company working capital and to put up stock to secure an option on the other 51 per cent of its shares. "Frank was sitting there [at the board meeting] and he approved it," says Pabst. "And I did. And we went with it."

But the acquisition was a disaster, the partners' first big mistake in business. Pabst admits his due diligence was lousy. When he finally visited the Ottawa operation, he was appalled: "The managers were driving Cadillacs, plush offices, no revenue coming, no profits and no *sign* of profits . . . I closed it up." Magna ultimately wrote off the Digital Systems investment in 1970, taking a $350,000 hit.

TO SELL OR NOT TO SELL

The financial loss caused by the Digital Systems fiasco was bad enough (especially since a GM strike had hurt the automotive business). Pabst also blames the mess for widening a little more the split that was developing between him and Stronach. "Frank never saw it [Digital Systems], but he approved it, and [then] he blamed me [for the loss]," says Pabst. Meanwhile, though Stronach and Pabst were equal partners, Stronach was becoming the dominant one. Perhaps he was ready to go it alone in business. Or perhaps he wanted out from under the control of the board and shareholders. For whatever reasons, he told Pabst he wanted to sell Magna Electronics. Pabst agreed. They'd already pocketed $400,000 each when they sold Multimatic. If they could get a decent price for Magna Electronics and cash in their shares, they'd enjoy a second pay day. Both still under the age of forty, they had time to start again, either together or separately. So Pabst went looking for a buyer and lined up Continental Can, a multinational container-maker headquartered in New York that operated in Canada through a subsidiary.

Before the sale was executed, however, Pabst and Stronach had a change of heart. Neither recognized it at the time, but the unravelling of the deal, which left them still the controlling shareholders of Magna Electronics, changed the course of Canadian business history.

REFOCUSING MAGNA ELECTRONICS

Turning their attention and energy back to restructuring Magna Electronics, the partners figured that their automotive assets, thanks to the tailwind that the Auto Pact provided, was their best hope for high-flying growth. First, there were some loose ends left over at Multimatic that they had to clear up. When Magna Electronics bought Multimatic, Tony Czapka had joined the company as a one-third owner of Unimatic, one of Multimatic's plants. Multimatic had owned the rest. After the Magna Electronics takeover, Stronach and Pabst bought Czapka's share of Unimatic for $100,000 and 7,000 Magna Electronics shares, then worth about the same as the cash. Czapka, in addition to being rewarded in cash for his role at Unimatic, was now a significant shareholder in Magna Electronics. He stayed on as an employee, running the Unimatic operation.

With the aroma of the Digital Systems debacle still hanging around, they had to be very careful with the acquisition of Unimade Industries Ltd., a structural steel fabricator and erector that also had real-estate assets. To complicate matters, Stronach and Pabst had privately invested in the company and each held a 26 per cent interest. Their friend Robin Sloan held 25 per cent and Ruth Storey, wife of Magna director William Storey, owned the balance. Unimade's ability to handle the construction of plants, a growing number of which Magna Electronics needed, made it a worthy purchase. But as a public company, Magna Electronics had to avoid overpaying Unimade's principals with shareholders' money. In other words, Stronach and Pabst could not be seen to be paying themselves, and Sloan and Storey, more for Unimade than it was worth.

The deal they came up with eliminated any chance of that and also reassured Magna Electronics' shareholders that Unimade would contribute to earnings. They offered $120,000 in cash and a discounted number of Magna Electronic shares – only 42,000 – for Unimade. But the agreement included a provision that would award Unimade's owners – Stronach, Pabst, Sloan and Storey – more Magna Electronics shares if Unimade's pre-tax profit exceeded $250,000 within three years ending July 1973. It met the challenge a year early.

In 1972, Magna departed from its practice of dealing mainly with original-equipment manufacturers (or OEMs, as automakers are called) when it began to make mufflers, and air-conditioning and heater motors for the replacement, or "after" market. But as Pabst turned more of his attention back to the automotive business, now with the assistance of full-time sales staff, he also added to the Multimatic division's product line. By the end of 1972, he had contracts for interior- and exterior-trim parts, oil strainers, motor mounting brackets, instrument panels, and bumper guards. It all added up.

R&D PAYS OFF IN SPADES – AND IN PULLEYS

Stronach's ardour for new business ventures was proving an asset when channelled into research and development. An employee proposing a new way of doing things who could demonstrate that it would improve production or quality could count on Stronach's support – and a share of any profit or cost savings that might result. The value of the approach was exemplified after Pabst learned during a sales call to General Motors' Oldsmobile division in the early 1970s that it was having quality-control problems with pulleys. Recognizing that belt-driven add-ons such as air conditioning, power steering, and power brakes were becoming standard features on cars, and that serpentine belt systems would increase the number of pulleys under the hood, Pabst promised to solve the problem if he were given a blanket order for all the division's pulley business. One minor problem: Magna wasn't in the pulley business at all at the time. But Stronach was all for investing in R&D to get into it.

They assigned the task of exploring pulley manufacturing to Klaus Bytzek, a toolmaker Stronach had recruited as a plant manager. The imaginative Bytzek, a race car driver in his spare time, found a German manufacturer that had developed a method of manufacturing pulleys by spinning sheet metal. Back in Canada, Bytzek developed his own metal-spinning machine that made stronger, lighter pulleys for less money than previous casting methods. Stronger, lighter, and cheaper was an amazing triple play. "It was much better than [the German one] and we were in the pulley business," says Pabst. "It took maybe a year, but we came through. It was a great business." Magna's pulleys rapidly became the industry standard around which Magna developed entire systems of self-tensioning devices and belts, based on Bytzek's patented manufacturing methods.

MAGNA GOES INTERNATIONAL

In 1973, the complexion of Magna Electronics changed on a number of fronts. For one thing, Stronach and Pabst changed the company name to Magna International Inc., to reflect the breadth of the business's ambitions. They also relocated the head office from Scarborough to Downsview on Toronto's northern fringe, a move that was both practical and symbolic: Downsview was closer to Multimatic's factories in York Region, north of Toronto; Scarborough had been the headquarters of Magna Electronics, not much of which had escaped Pabst's pogrom. "Out of Magna Electronics, we were left with two plants that were profitable," he says. "And when I say profitable, they sure as hell weren't profitable like automotive was. But they quit losing." Also in fiscal 1973, a shuffle at the executive level saw Stronach add the title of CEO to the chairmanship he'd held since 1971 as he began taking a greater interest in overall management. The move reflected Stronach's eagerness to take a more active role in directing the whole company's fortunes, and Pabst's recognition that his partner's commitment to Magna was stronger than his. Pabst moved to vice-chairman and gave up the presidency to a new hire, Helmut Hofmann, but remained a majority shareholder in Magna.

By this time, the pieces of Magna were falling into place as planned, and the results were excellent. In 1973, sales of $23.8 million constituted an 83 per cent rise over the previous year's $13 million, and profit of $808 thousand was up from $432 thousand. Magna continued to expand, buying some small tool-and-die operations including P & F Tool and Die Inc., as well as Vernomatic Ltd. But "without seeking to limit growth in the auto sector," Stronach wrote in the 1973 annual report, Magna was also eager to diversify beyond the manufacture of auto parts. In August 1973, the company paid $1.2 million for Paul B. Helliwell Ltd., an Ontario heavy-stamping company whose product line included tractor cabs, stove panels, and refrigerator doors. A new plant in Iowa that targeted the appliance and farm equipment markets, Stronach said, showed Magna's intent to build on the basis of economics rather than national considera-tion and to extend its skills beyond the automotive sector. But while this diversification was prudent, it would have been difficult for Magna to escape the disruption triggered by an energy crisis, whose tremors began in countries few North Americans could correctly place on a map.

THE ENERGY CRISIS CRUSHES CAR-MAKERS

The industrialization of the West following World War II floated on the availability of cheap oil. In turn, low-cost energy transformed North American society. As cities sprawled into vast suburbs, commuters increasingly relied on cars. Encouraged by a growing network of highways, a population becoming more and more affluent in the postwar industrial boom responded eagerly to automakers' marketing. Television stars like Dinah Shore encouraged viewers to "See the U.S.A. in your Chevrolet." Ed Sullivan extolled Ford's Mercury as "The Big M." The automobile evolved from a utilitarian device, to a luxury, then to a commodity, and then to an important status symbol. If you didn't have a good car, you were a failure. Fuelled by low-cost energy and raw materials, car companies cranked out ever-larger and more powerful products; unconcerned by fuel costs, buyers snapped them up, turning the North American car business into one of the most profitable industries in the world.

In the twenty-five years following the war, Western nations (and Japan) became the most profligate users of energy in history, consuming more oil than the entire world had used to that point. Not surprisingly, as the leading industrial nation, the U.S. was the biggest consumer: though it had only about 6 per cent of the world's population, it was gobbling up about one-third of the world's energy. In turn, that made the West in general and the U.S. in particular, dependent on the Middle East, the world's biggest source of oil.

U.S., British, and Dutch companies benefited mightily from the increasing consumption of their product; they paid producing nations a pittance for oil in exchange for exploration and development rights to oil fields around the world. But by the 1960s, thirteen oil-producing nations – including eight Arab nations in the Middle East – had formed the Organization of Petroleum Exporting Countries (OPEC) in an effort to wangle a bigger cut of the profits from their resources, and more say in production levels. OPEC had begun flexing its muscle in earnest in the early 1970s. But matters came to a head when Egypt and Syria triggered the Yom Kippur War in October 1973, attacking Israel in an attempt to reclaim land it had annexed six years earlier. U.S. support for Israel infuriated the Arab-led OPEC. It promptly cut oil production, embargoed shipments to the West, and demanded a dramatic price increase from oil companies operating within their territory.

As the biggest user of oil, the U.S. was the country most affected by the crisis. Motorists accustomed to low-priced gas suddenly faced rationing of supply, and a doubling of the price at the pump when gas was available at all. Overnight, the big, gas-guzzling North American cars seemed destined to become dinosaurs. The U.S. interstate highway network (which President Dwight Eisenhower commissioned following the war as a defence measure and which had become one of the world's best high-speed freeway systems) changed dramatically as huge cars and trucks wallowed along under the nationally mandated 55-mile-per-hour maximum imposed to reduce fuel consumption.

OPEC eventually lifted its embargo in 1974, allowing oil prices to decline. But the crisis had focused attention on the inefficiency of North American cars and highlighted the opposite qualities in the cars from Japanese companies such as Toyota and Datsun. Developed for a domestic market smaller than the U.S., and cautiously first exported to North America in the 1960s, the low-cost, fuel-frugal Japanese cars had shed their reputation for being underpowered and had found a new popularity. During the 1970s their innovative production techniques and steady quality control (by North American car production standards) led to an increasing penetration of the home markets of the Big Three car companies.

Economic and political events of the day did the rest. Inflation that followed U.S. efforts to counter the oil shock crimped business growth. The evacuation of Americans from Saigon, a symbolic end to the United States' costly and controversial involvement in Vietnam, cast doubts on the global hegemony and a demoralizing pall on the American public. The Watergate scandal leading to Richard Nixon's resignation only added to the angst, roiling financial markets and laying bare the political faults of the world's most important economic power.

MAGNA DEFIES THE ODDS

Amazingly, Magna seemed to soar above it all. A bad time to be trying
to sell auto parts to North American companies? You couldn't tell
from Magna's growth. In 1976, its balance sheet was strong enough
that it added two new divisions, Benco Manufacturing and Power
Motion Manufacturing. The Japanese had a lock on innovation?
Not judging from the success of Magna's flourishing new pulley-
manufacturing operation. Its success only reinforced Stronach's commitment to R&D. True, no joint venture or government assistance
had materialized to move the oil-sands bitumen-extraction process
any closer to adoption, but Magna was on its way to sales of
$81 million and a profit of $4.1 million in 1977. And although the
results were largely attributable to its automotive division, it hadn't
given up on the possibility of defence and aerospace contracts, especially after Canada reaffirmed its commitment to the North Atlantic
Treaty Organization.

Nor had Magna's job-generation record escaped the attention of
governments. Ottawa and the Nova Scotia government, which had
become joint owners of Hermes Electronics Ltd. of Dartmouth, Nova
Scotia, primarily to preserve jobs at the company, were eager to privatize it. Pabst, having dumped the electronics business inherited
with Magna Electronics, wasn't fussy about getting back into it. But
he and Stronach recognized that the governments needed Magna
more than it needed Hermes. They persuaded Ottawa to sweeten the
privatization by throwing in a contract to repair sono-buoys and took
over 53 per cent of Hermes. The company's profitability wasn't up
to the standard of Magna's automotive factories, Pabst allows. In fact,
it was non-existent, "but we got it for a song." It didn't hurt, either,
that Magna had done a favour for government and might reasonably
call the chip in at a future date. It would discover, though, that while
quid pro quo arrangements with government can yield benefits,
unwelcome controversy often comes with the deal.

REAL ESTATE – MAGNA PERFECTS THE "MARKHAM MOVE"

Even when operating outside its manufacturing expertise, Magna seemed to have the golden touch, especially when it came to real estate. By the mid 1970s, Stronach and Pabst were looking for larger office quarters. And they thought Markham, in the region of York, would be a fine location. In addition to being close to many of Magna's plants (and to Stronach's farm), Markham had amenities, such as Buttonville Airport, a regional facility that accommodates corporate jets, and plenty of undeveloped land, still zoned agricultural, with which it hoped to attract tax-paying, job-producing businesses.

Magna filled that bill. Accordingly, when it bought a fifty-acre site in Markham, a few minutes from its existing offices, for $1.8 million in 1977, and announced that it planned to build new headquarters on it, the town enthusiastically fast-tracked a change in zoning from agricultural to commercial and industrial, nearly doubling the value of the land. But, within a year, Magna claimed that it wasn't as suitable to its purposes as it had thought and, lo and behold, flipped the property to Allstate Insurance for a $1.3-million profit.

The property deals increased when the real-estate-savvy Tony Czapka, Stronach's long-time friend, joined the head-office team as a director and vice-president of administration. Having seen in the Markham move how it could leverage its power as an employer and taxpaying corporation to have land it had acquired re-zoned to suit its "needs," Magna used the Markham gambit in at least three other municipalities, blaming its change of plans on constantly changing demands due to its rapid growth: "Corporate functions have to be augmented to properly assimilate our increased business activities," the company piously explained. But that didn't persuade the communities Magna had left at the altar, who believed they'd been duped into creating a speculative profit for Magna. In the 1990s, when Magna finally decided on land in Aurora that it actually *did* want to build on, the municipality was disinclined, due to the pattern it had seen play out elsewhere, to cut the company much slack. To Stronach's great irritation, Aurora forced Magna to clear more regulatory hurdles than it otherwise might have faced.

THE FAIR ENTERPRISE MANIFESTO

As Magna's 20–30 per cent compound annual growth established it as a true juggernaut, Stronach's profile rose with it. His special claim to fame was as the inventor of the business model to which Magna owed much of its success. Labelled Fair Enterprise, his version of "free enterprise" held that business operated best when the interests of employees, management, and investors were balanced. Magna's small, decentralized plants, each with a manager whose compensation was tied to its performance and whose workers were partly compensated in shares, created just such an entrepreneurial culture. Stronach believed that owners worked harder than employees, so he made all workers at all levels into owners by including them in a share-ownership program. As Magna grew, their shares rose in value. It also helped establish employee loyalty, which reduced worker turnover and discouraged trade unions from sniffing around Magna plants.

Neither the first nor the only company to offer employees a share-ownership program, Magna was a leader in allotting a portion of pre-tax profits to employees in the form of cash bonuses and shares. The actual percentage was unspecified until 1979 when it was set at 7 per cent. By the mid 1970s, Magna was also apportioning 20 per cent of after-tax profit to shareholders in the form of dividends, 7 per cent of pre-tax profit to research and development, and an unspecified amount of pre-tax profit to social causes.

Magna's executive team, which set the long-term strategy that plant managers executed in the shorter term, profited as well, of course. Though not eligible for the employee share-ownership plan, executive management received salary-supplementing bonuses out

of pre-tax profit, so they could decide for themselves whether or not
to buy Magna shares.

MAGNA AND THE UNIONS

Magna salaries were modest by auto-industry standards, and the
company's contention that its share-ownership plan combined with
an annual cash bonus elevated its pay scale above the rest of the
industry was difficult to verify. It kept its pay structure close to the
executive vest lest the Canadian Auto Workers union (CAW) use it as
a weapon in any battle to organize its plants. Not wanting to pick a
fight, Stronach constantly professed to having no quarrel with organized labour, while at the same time observing that its guiding principles ran counter to free enterprise and democracy.

Burt Pabst made no attempt to hide his dislike of unions. He
had seen unions nearly choke Trim Trends to death before it restruc-
tured into smaller plants. Having persuaded Stronach to organize
Magna similarly to ward off labour organizers, he wasn't about to
undermine the strategy by attracting them to Magna's factory gates.
"I used to discourage the managers even from putting signs on
plants telling people who the hell we were," he says. "We didn't need
to advertise . . . The commodities we were making had nothing to
do with the public."

His biggest challenge in attempting to keep Magna off labour's
radar, he adds, was his partner. "I used to give Frank hell for wanting
to advertise and shooting his mouth off too much," Pabst says. "He's
always been a hound for publicity – anything to get in the limelight.
Right from the beginning that's one thing I never cared for."

The CAW repeatedly complained that Magna, unlike most companies in the auto sector, didn't have an employee pension plan and
that there were risks in Magna's share-ownership scheme. For Magna,
the amount invested in shares held for the employees' retirement fund
was cheap capital. As Magna's stock price rose, it made employees

rich, at least on paper. But the union argued the reverse could be true. Even if Magna's management performed flawlessly, events beyond its control – a car-industry downturn, say, or another energy shock – could sink the stock price. There was some irony, in short, that Magna as a corporation sought to diversify to spread risk, but was asking its employees to concentrate their retirement funds in a single security, rather than in a diversified portfolio in the hands of a pension manager.

THE MAGNA WAY – ONE TRIUMPH AFTER ANOTHER

But slumps never seemed to happen at Magna. Between 1971, when Stronach and Pabst had decided not to sell Magna Electronics, and 1976, the company's sales had soared from $10 million to $55 million. In the same period, profit increased from $43 thousand to $2.8 million. Shareholders were pleased, too: the share price had quadrupled from $5.50 in 1971 to $21.50 in 1976.

The more Stronach was identified as the originator and custodian of the Magna model, the less he bothered to acknowledge that it had been at least based on, if not entirely derived from, someone else's idea. As well as Pabst, Jack Warrington disputed Stronach's claim. "Don't let me steal old Frankie's glory," the founder of Magna Electronics told the *Globe and Mail* in 1985, "but . . . that strategy was in place long before he was even in Canada and it was working very well . . ."

What was never in dispute was the fact that it all worked and that Stronach's dedication to its application was crucial. Rightly or wrongly, by 1976 Stronach had unreservedly taken ownership of the Magna Way, which he'd come to regard as the spiritual core of the company. By extension, he'd come to think of Magna as *his* company, despite the fact that he did not control a majority of the shares. Only a few years after he had considered selling Magna, he had now become preoccupied by the prospect that he might lose it. Or, tantamount to the same thing for the independent Stronach, that shareholders might infringe on what he believed was the founder's right to make all decisions affecting the company.

Stronach spent the next two years altering Magna's ownership structure to ensure that neither of these terrible things ever happened. In the process, he added to his self-claimed role as creator and custodian of Magna's guiding principles something more important – absolute control of Magna's physical assets. The combination would make him unbelievably wealthy.

4

FRANK GRABS THE REINS

Under the original incorporation of Magna Electronics, Magna International's total authorized equity capital was one million common shares. By the end of its fiscal year in July 1976, Magna had only issued 580,599 common shares, including those owned by management insiders, those sold to the public through the Toronto Stock Exchange, and those paid to owners of companies Magna bought. In short, with just under half of its authorized share capital still in its treasury, Magna had ample room to sell more shares in order to raise capital or add worthwhile assets. But issuing more stock dilutes the value of existing shares, including those held by management and directors, and increases the number of shares required to make purchases. In 1975 Stronach had begun planning a capital restructuring, which he billed innocuously in 1976 as shareholder-friendly, demonstrating a new-found fluency in obscure corporate-speak. "On the basis of your company's past achievements and confidence in the future," he told Magna's shareholders, "your board of directors will recommend a new, higher-yield stock for your ratification. These adjustments will more accurately reflect the worth of your company."

In fact, Stronach was mostly concerned that spreading the company's shares too broadly exposed Magna to a takeover. To eliminate the possibility, he planned to create two classes of shares, one of which would have overpowering voting control over Magna. He achieved his goal wonderfully, converting the company's capital base into a dual-class share structure that set the stage for Magna's growth from a smallish manufacturer to the world's most diversified auto-parts company. Oh, one other thing. The fact that it also effectively disenfranchised common shareholders, and turned Magna into a publicly traded autocracy over which Stronach alone would hold sway for the foreseeable future, would generate huge controversy and make Stronach the target of corporate-governance activists for many years to come.

TWO SIDES TO DUAL-CLASS SHARES

The rationale behind a dual-class share structure is the belief that companies that manage to achieve their long-term goals ultimately create more value for their shareholders, and that having to react quarterly to short-term fluctuations can hinder reaching those long-term goals. Such things as capital expenditure for infrastructure (plants, tools, equipment) or marketing (to build a clientele), for instance, strain company resources and profits in the short term, which often results in a falling stock price and produces baying shareholders who demand that management address short-term profitability. Undeniably, as well, a lower share price can make the company attractive as a takeover target. Proponents of dual-class arrangements claim that giving voting control of the company to management allows managers to take a longer-term view without fear of being voted out of office by shareholders or takeover raiders. Opponents of the structure are quick to counter that it violates shareholder rights, discourages legitimate takeover bids that would generate a premium price for shareholders' stock, and entrenches management (or family) that can make decisions in its own interests.

In a typical dual-class structure, a company raises capital through sale to the public of common shares with one vote each. But *control* of the company resides in a second, so-called super-voting class of shares, mainly held by a founder, his family, management, or other insiders. There are usually far more common shares than "super" shares, but the super-voting (or multiple-voting) shares carry more than one vote each. The ratio of votes carried by the super-voting shares to those carried by the common ones may vary but the set-up is designed so that insiders will always be able to outvote common shareholders, although these luckless folks are the ones who usually have the most economic value invested.

The self-enrichment program allegedly conducted by Conrad Black and his cronies at Hollinger International is frequently cited by corporate-governance advocates as the epitome of what can go wrong with a dual-class system. But as undemocratic as the dual-class structure may seem, the idea is neither new nor shady. Notable companies employing it in the U.S. include Google Inc., Dow Jones & Co. (owner of *The Wall Street Journal*), The Washington Post Co., The New York Times Co. (controlled by the Sulzberger family), and Berkshire Hathaway Inc., the company run by Warren Buffett, considered by many to be the high priest of investors. In the automotive sector, the Ford family holds only 4 per cent of the eponymous automaker, but controls 40 per cent of the voting power with its super-voting shares, and Volkswagen is among the 20 per cent of European companies with two classes of shares. In Canada, about 22 per cent of the companies on the TSX (formerly the TSE) Index have them, including CanWest Global, Canadian Tire, and Bombardier.

Stronach never made clear his reasons for dividing Magna's stock into two classes. If it weren't for the fact that the process took place over a couple of years, the capital restructuring could be called a pivotal point in Magna's history. And by any measure, the restructuring qualified as a complicated moment.

RESTRUCTURING THE SHARES TO TAKE CONTROL

The restructuring was done in two steps (Figure 4.1). The first came in February 1977, when Magna split its 580,999 outstanding common shares two-for-one, giving shareholders one "new" common share and one new Class A special share for each common share held. Under the new arrangement, the common shares paid a dividend and carried one vote per share; the Class A special shares did not carry a vote but compensated by paying a dividend equal to 125 per cent of that paid on the common voting shares. That is, owners of the Class A special shares enjoyed a 25 per cent dividend premium over common shareholders.

At this point there was an equal number of common and Class A special shares outstanding. But during 1977 and 1978, Magna dipped into its treasury of shares to issue stock of both classes to raise cash, to redeem debt held in debentures, or to exchange for minority interest in a couple of subsidiaries. (One of the recipients of Magna stock was Stronach's compatriot, Tony Czapka, who received $100,000 in cash and 7,000 shares for his third of Unimatic, the plant he'd been managing.) By the end of its fiscal year in July 1978, Magna's capital stock outstanding consisted of 661,456 voting common shares and 768,499 Class A special non-voting shares.

Then, in December 1978, Magna executed the baffling second phase of the capital restructuring. First it converted the non-voting Class A special shares into Class A voting shares, which it then split on a 15-for-4 basis. That is, for each four Class A special non-voting shares held, a shareholder wound up with 15 Class A voting shares, each carrying one vote. This sounded good to the lucky shareholders.

Magna then turned to the old, single-vote common shares. They were renamed Class B shares and split three-for-one. Had things remained that way, holders of the new Class B shares would have

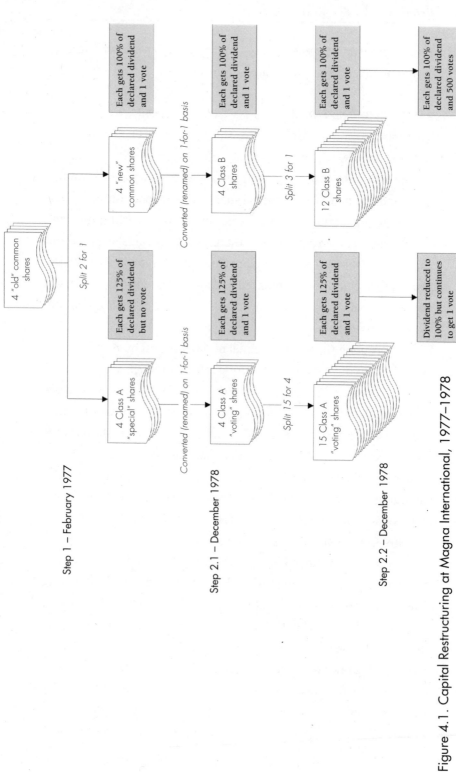

Figure 4.1. Capital Restructuring at Magna International, 1977–1978

been in an inferior position compared to holders of the Class A voting shares: following the splits, there were about two million issued Class B shares with one vote each and three million issued Class A shares also with one vote each and a 25 per cent bigger dividend to boot.

Clearly, Stronach and his executives – some of whom had been quietly collecting the common shares in anticipation of their conversion to Class B shares – were not about to leave it at that. First, the dividend was made equal for both shares. Next, Magna addressed the control issue, proposing that each Class B share would be entitled to 500 votes. Finally, to seal the deal, it proposed that the ratio of the number of A to B class shares could not change in the future and that no division or consolidation of either class could take place without the other class being treated identically. In other words, barring another restructuring, major Class B shareholders will always rule Magna.

Class A shareholders may have been somewhat befuddled by the new structure's complexity, but they voted for the change anyway. After all, their shareholding increased by 275 per cent, so the loss of their former 25 per cent dividend premium didn't matter much in real terms. They now collected the same amount as Class B shareholders, but multiplied by many more shares, which was excellent. If it dawned on them that they'd opted for financial gains over control, it didn't seem to bother many of them. More important to shareholders was that Magna should continue to grow, perform well, produce a decent profit and dividend, and attract investors who would raise its stock price.

On most counts, Magna didn't disappoint. Assisted by a $6-million federal government grant and $13 million in interest-free government loans spread over five years, Magna spent $24 million to develop plastics technology and enhanced its product line by adding polyurethane bumper facings, which automakers were increasingly using to replace chrome in their new car designs. The plastics activity was incorporated into the automotive division, whose segregated sub-groups already moulded and extruded plastic interior and exterior trim, stamped out body parts, spun pulleys incorporated into belt-drive systems, and developed electromechanical devices, all of which together accounted for 70 per cent of the $128.2 million in sales and $6.6 million in profit in 1978. The industrial products group that included Unimade's structural steel business and Hermes' operations in Nova Scotia, contributed the other 30 per cent. In 1979, Magna's total sales rose another 30 per cent to $166.3 million, the sixth consecutive record high.

AN UNUSUAL CANADIAN SUCCESS STORY

To an extent, Magna's performance was accentuated by the economic context. A growing perception among Canadians that Canada was destined to industrial inferiority wasn't entirely unjustified on the basis of historical evidence. The few homegrown industries in the 1970s that hadn't been crushed by multinational companies' economies of scale generally owed their survival to tariffs that discouraged ingenuity and productivity. Canadian manufacturers capable of producing goods suitable for export met countervailing duties that priced their goods out of the market. Those that didn't fold typically sold out to multinational owners, usually American, who managed them as subsidiaries to dodge Canadian tariffs, contributing to what a growing body of economic nationalists derided as a branch-plant economy. Ottawa responded to the chauvinistic fears with the Foreign Investment Review Agency in 1974 to vet takeovers, but in fact FIRA rubber-stamped most applications, becoming itself a symbol of the industrial sclerosis.

Magna, though, had defied the trend. It was on its way to stardom, and not just in Canada's minor league. Under the Auto Pact's free trade, Magna was proving itself to be a player, a serious competitor in the major-league U.S. market. Inevitably, Magna's success turned the spotlight yet again on Frank Stronach.

THE ENTREPRENEUR FROM CENTRAL CASTING

If Canadians were ready to embrace a new business role model, the trim, fit Frank Stronach seemed sent from Central Casting to oblige. His curly blond hair, dimpled good looks, and fashionable suits made him attractively different from the usual pin-striped, prim Presbyterian-banker types. Nor had he inherited stewardship of the usual boring rocks, trees, fish, or oil that anchored the Canadian economy. Magna, his creation, didn't simply reap the spoils of geography; it actually made things. His own story revived everyone's belief in the Canadian dream, an immigrant who arrived as a youth with forty dollars – or two hundred dollars or one hundred dollars, depending on the version he was telling – and a compulsion to succeed. Stronach, forty-seven in 1979, looked and acted at least a decade younger, displaying in business the same energetic daring with which he skied moguls or attacked the net on the tennis court. Even the immodesty of his self-description as a corporate visionary somehow seemed excusable, as though he'd adopted the role at the suggestion of the guys at the factory who'd intended it as a joke at his expense, only to have Magna's progress under his guidance validate the label.

And it did, at least in part. Stronach attributed Magna's success to the solid mix of free enterprise, profit sharing, and social responsibility that he (and Burt Pabst) had poured as its foundation. But if the form had been his vision, the qualities of persistence and focus that he'd showed after it cured were more often on display when he explained the result. With a habitual "huh" punctuating his statements, and a heavy Austrian accent reminding everyone of his immigrant background, Stronach never tired of regaling anyone who wanted to listen (and many who did not) with his theories ranging from how to create the perfect corporate structure (as he had Magna's), to why it is that the enlightened management of a work force (like, for example, his management of Magna's) produces superior results. "Frank seems arrogant, and there could be some of that in his attitude which turns some people off," says his former partner Burt Pabst, who was still Magna's vice-chairman in 1979. "But it's really more a matter of absolute conviction that he's right."

Stronach's brash belief that the perfect business model that he created at Magna would benefit other companies (and indeed, the entire Canadian economy) wasn't universally shared. Nor was there much evidence that his peers found anything particularly noteworthy in his self-proclaimed vision. As a relatively young, entrepreneurial CEO of a dynamic and very successful company, for instance, Stronach appeared to have the qualities that other companies would welcome on their boards of directors. None evidently did, perhaps reluctant to endure his endless proselytizing on how Magna's success might be adapted to their business, or wary of his unwavering confidence that he was always right. "He told me he had a reading of his hand [by a palmist] in 1958 or around then," says the former president of a Magna division, who was fired by Stronach for challenging him. "He was told he could do no wrong. And he believes that."

But he wasn't always right. Stronach could change his mind in an eye-blink, making and then rescinding decisions with dazzling speed: Marine Resources, a tiny Florida company he bought for $243,000 in 1979 to support Hermes Electronics' oceanographic business, was shut down and written off by 1980. Paradoxically, he could be exasperatingly stubborn in supporting impractical schemes whose broad scope appealed to him: his commitment to the oil-sands recovery process, first mentioned in a Magna annual report in 1974, never produced the gusher of profits Stronach had envisioned. For that matter, it never produced a dime and had soaked up plenty by 1981 when he quit touting it as a "promising" potential megaproject.

Stronach's quest to diversify into non-automotive fields puzzled many of his colleagues at Magna, not so much because of the specific ventures he selected, but for the fact that he considered any at all. Magna was excelling in the auto-parts business, which accounted for 70 per cent of the company's income. Stronach's contagious confidence and his ability to attract and keep the people that made it all work played no small part. To Stronach, though, motor mounts, power-window motors, and trunk latches were unglamorous bits and pieces of a vehicle, not the sexy finished product that people paid attention to. Research that developed a lighter car and saved fuel would add to his wealth, but it wouldn't generate the acclaim that, say, solving the riddle of the oil sands would. "I'd say 'Frank, we got it made, look at what we've made, we've got it made, we made good money,'" says Pabst of his efforts to redirect the errant interests of his partner of more than twenty years. "But he always wanted to go further."

FROM CAR PARTS TO PONIES

Stronach's confidence in his power of creation was tested when he set out to duplicate his success at Magna in the expensive world of horses. Since being attracted to racing almost by accident, he'd become enchanted by the thrill of owning and racing thoroughbreds, not to mention the hobnobbing with other business owners. Though other companies had ignored him when choosing their directors, he seemed to believe that those whose instincts in racing were sound would be worthy of Magna's board. Toronto stockbroker George Gardiner, a leading thoroughbred owner from whom Stronach claimed a horse in 1971, sat as a Magna director for a number of years.

Despite the initial racing success he'd enjoyed in the late 1960s, Stronach duly experienced the immutable truth that sooner or later confounds most sports-team owners: you can spend an enormous amount of money on training and on an environment that encourages success, but the natural ability of athletes, and luck, dammit, play at least as big a part in creating a winner. In racing, where the athletes are horses, winning is especially elusive, and the maintenance especially expensive. In the early 1980s, only about 10 per cent of the 40,000 thoroughbreds foaled each year in North America would grow up to earn money. In 1982, only 356 horses earned more than $100,000 in North America, and only 11 earned more than $500,000. According to the late Charles Taylor, operator of the famous Windfields Farm founded by his father, E. P. Taylor, a horse had to win at least two races to earn its keep, which he estimated at the time to be about $10,000 a year.

Horse racing, however, is a unique sport when it comes to the factor of natural ability. Serendipitous in human athletes, ability can actually be bred into horses. Matching a dam and sire according to pedigree, the theory goes, increases the chances of producing winning offspring. By the early 1970s Stronach had turned to breeding as well as racing thoroughbreds from his Beechwood Farm in Aurora. In addition to possibly turning out a winning horse for himself, breeding generated cash from the sales of horses to others, money that supported the development of the more promising keepers from among his broodmares' foals.

Stronach, ever the contrarian, added his own twist to his breeding operation, imprinting it with the quality-control hallmark that he'd placed on operations at Multimatic and Magna. Rather than sell yearlings (by convention, all horses' birthdays are considered January 1, regardless of their actual birth date) as others did, he elected to hang onto them until they were two-year-olds and in training. A one-year-old raced unsuccessfully before it was fully developed, he reasoned, would reflect negatively on Beechwood's stock in future buyers' eyes. Keeping his horses an extra year also gave him more time to identify a future Queen's Plate winner. But "I'd be just as happy if [one of my horses] won the Plate for someone else," he maintained. "Most of all, I want to build a reputation for selling a good product."

Still, the fun of racing was the spectacle, going to the track to watch your horse win. And Stronach was willing to spend for the privilege. In 1979, he celebrated his forty-seventh birthday by paying $270,000, a Canadian record, for a horse called Stellarette.

The same year, he approached trainer Gerry Belanger to take over the training of the seven horses he'd been stabling at Toronto's Woodbine Racetrack.

ENTER GERRY BELANGER, AND GLORIOUS SONG

They made an odd duo. Belanger, a Runyonesque raconteur, had practically been born at a racetrack and, except when supplementing his income playing pool and golf for money, has seldom been far from racing in his life. He'd worked his way through the ranks as hotwalker, groom, and owner before turning his horse sense to training. In 1977, his 20 per cent winning percentage, second-best on the circuit, while handling the stable of Toronto car dealer Ed Seedhouse, caught Stronach's eye. "I was a rising young star and Frank liked to win," says Belanger. "He partnered with Ed and me, and I took over some of his horses."

Belanger, who'd tried his hand at owning horses in 1961, initially welcomed the management he saw Stronach contributing. For all his track smarts, Belanger never won a race until 1973. "I wasted twelve years of my life with those horses because I didn't have the management skills to build the dream," says Belanger. The partnership got off to a good start in 1977 when a couple of Stronach's horses won. Belanger also recommended that Stronach spend $36,000 for a yearling filly named Glorious Song whose pedigree and looks Belanger liked. Stronach did, and the horse continued to show the promise in training that Belanger had spotted. Although Belanger says he and Stronach got along famously while winning, Stronach's impatient carping during one of the inevitable losing streaks that happen in racing began to grate. Belanger figures Stronach hadn't yet grasped that all the money and planning in the world can't guarantee winners. "He pushed, and I don't push very good," he says. Belanger abruptly quit and headed to a training gig at Santa Anita Park in California where he hoped his record would entice owners to send horses his way. They did – and one of them was Stronach, who, in an uncharacteristically conciliatory move, shipped Glorious Song out west to resume training with Belanger.

Belanger lost little time proving his initial judgment of the horse accurate. He trained Glorious Song to two Grade 1 stakes wins (races for horses of the highest calibre that offer the biggest purses). No romantic where money and horses are concerned, and all too aware of the afflictions that can befall a horse, Belanger negotiated through a broker to sell a half-interest in the horse to Texas multi-millionaire Nelson Bunker Hunt for $500,000. It was a great deal for Stronach; Glorious Song had already earned enough to be close to the record for Canadian-bred horses, and had returned his investment many times over. Now he was getting another huge return, and would still be entitled to half of future winnings. Glorious Song went on to become the first million-dollar Canadian-bred thoroughbred and also won the Eclipse Award, the highest accolade in the sport, as the best horse in North America. In 1981, she became the horse that kept on giving when Hunt paid Stronach $1 million for the other half of Glorious Song.

Shortly afterward, Belanger and Stronach parted company over an issue that Belanger no longer remembers. It was, he points out, one of the four times that Stronach-as-Steinbrenner fired him. But to Belanger, Stronach's handling of Glorious Song demonstrated that he had developed an instinct for the game. "The essence of his operation is that everything is well thought out and planned and that management will make it happen," he says. "Frank had become the master."

There was a coda to Stronach's ownership of Glorious Song, as it turned out, that suggested that he may have sold her too soon. Four years after his first investment in Glorious Song, Hunt resold the horse for $8 million to John Sikura, for whom she became a valuable broodmare. Sikura got half his investment back almost immediately in 1984 when he sold one of Glorious Song's foals for $4 million.

TROUBLE IN HORSELAND

If it galled Stronach that he missed out on the bonuses, he never let on. But that Glorious Song had wound up at Sikura's farm was a remarkable coincidence. Stronach and Sikura shared a background as successful immigrant businessmen and knew each other as horsemen as well as neighbours. Sikura, as a sixteen-year-old refugee from Czechoslovakia in 1950, turned his first job as a dishwasher at the Park Plaza Hotel in Toronto into the unlikely launching pad for a career in real estate, the stock market, and horse breeding as the owner of Hill 'n' Dale Farm, located not far from Stronach's spread. His career was not without its flair and controversy. Reportedly a friend of the likes of Donald Trump and Frank Sinatra, he was involved with a junior mining company whose chief executive was charged with fraud, and in a syndicate that made an unsuccessful bid to buy the Ontario Jockey Club, owner of several racetracks in the province.

In 1994, Stronach's and Sikura's paths would cross again when Sikura died in a mysterious and unsolved car fire in front of his mansion. Bryan Cousineau, the future chief of York Region police who investigated the incident and declared the explosion an accident, a conclusion later confirmed by the coroner, would later be sacked from the force for, among other transgressions, taking $125,000 from Magna well in advance of beginning a job as the company's head of security when he retired. There were other links, as well. Sikura's wife Sharon Dunn, estranged at the time of his death, later became a newspaper society columnist in Toronto and the girlfriend of Ontario premier Mike Harris, whom Stronach appointed to Magna's board on his retirement. To be sure, all the connections were never seen as anything but coincidental. But if nothing else, they served as a measure of how tightly knit the political, business, and racing elite were – and are – in Ontario.

Glorious Song wasn't the only broodmare that Stronach lost. Untimely accidents also claimed others. Sintrillium, a reliable horse that had won 14 times in 45 career outings to earn $743,602 and a Sovereign Award as Canada's top older horse, had seemed destined to continue earning as a broodmare until she broke her ankle and had to be destroyed. Sunny Galore, an unbeaten horse favoured to win the 1984 Queen's Plate, was scratched just prior to the race due to a fracture. Overall, in 1984, Stronach's horses started 79 times in Ontario, winning only 11 times while finishing second or third five times each, for total winnings of just $290,166. That year, when Stronach told shareholders he'd sold some Magna stock to cover his racing expenses, he may have been only half joking.

BREEDING PROFITS

On the positive side, rising horse prices, fuelled by new interest in racing in the Middle East, benefited the breeding side of Stronach's equine business, a surer income source than racing. The average price of horses auctioned at Woodbine in 1983 jumped 146 per cent from the previous year, to $61,922. In Keeneland, Kentucky, the average was about $500,000. But horses of exceptional pedigree commanded much more. An oil sheikh confirmed the sport's reputation as the sport of kings when he paid $10.2 million for a son of the famous Northern Dancer.

Stronach's racing success and Beechwood's growing prominence as a breeding stable made it difficult for the racing community to ignore him, especially after Glorious Song won the Eclipse, a much-coveted award that had eluded many who had spent a lifetime in the sport. Belanger depicts Stronach as having become something of a country squire, hosting Sunday brunches at his home, Beechwood Farm, to which he invited a coterie of like-minded horse aficionados, the big red pedigree books spread out on the kitchen table often playing a role in settling arguments or launching what-if breeding scenarios. Stronach's wife, Elfriede, who preferred her role as mother of his children to that of socialite, rarely shared a public spotlight with him, but she shared his love of horses. Although unable to interest her daughter, Belinda, in horses, Elfriede encouraged her son Andy's interest in breeding, which had begun fascinating him even while he was a teen.

Frank Stronach, of course, was already in the thrall of horses and racing. But he was increasingly irritated by the sport's diminishing popularity. He blamed the decline on an old guard of grandees that had dominated racing for decades but failed to apply the business principle of free enterprise to it. Convinced that his impressive results at Magna were a manifestation of his business genius, Stronach's achievement as a horseman added to his conviction that he was just as right about the business of horse racing. But it would be more than a decade before he would take on racing's establishment in an effort to revolutionize the sport. And the result would be far from the success he anticipated.

5

THRIVING IN A RECESSION

Everyone should be able to see a recession coming. With the clarity of hindsight, the early warning signals such as rising interest rates and unemployment seem painfully obvious. Yet recessions tend to creep up on every business. In 1979, for instance, Magna had just experienced its usual record sales and profits. But by January 1980, high energy and raw-material costs were raining on the steady parade of profits the company had celebrated. For Magna, the challenge became managing costs while divining the industry's future and the role in it of its biggest customers.

Accurate prediction was no mean feat. North American auto-makers' flirtation with smaller, more fuel-efficient cars had cooled as the 1973 energy crisis dissipated, and car companies happily re-focused on their full-sized, higher-margin products. Magna had adjusted with them, measuring its progress in penetrating the auto-motive market in terms of dollar-content per vehicle (CPV), about twenty dollars per car at the time. But while CPV measured Magna's contribution to vehicles made in North America, it ignored the impact of domestic car makers actually selling fewer cars. Yet that scenario, once unthinkable, was starting to play out as consumer habits shifted after 1973. Small, fuel-efficient cars from Japan, though initially found wanting in quality, had entered the car-buying public's consciousness as an alternative to Detroit's thirsty offerings. Having established a beachhead, the Japanese used it to launch an invasion.

THE JAPANESE REVOLUTION

How the Japanese had overcome the issue of quality was a story in itself. Following World War II, they'd sought the assistance of American statistician Dr. W. Edwards Deming to change the world's perception that Japanese goods were shoddy knock-offs. Deming's efforts were so spectacularly successful that he achieved god-like status in Japan. Invited to do the same for Japan's auto industry, Deming proved that his first result had been no fluke. Discarding conventional North American practices, he applied instead his fourteen-point statistical process control (SPC) approach, which emphasized analytical measurement as the basis for an entire manufacturing philosophy. SPC removed the need for any mass inspection of completed cars that rolled off the assembly line, for example; rigorous statistical monitoring employed at every phase of production from original design through final assembly, Deming reasoned, reduced waste, identified and remedied faults, and ensured the quality of the end result.

Deming preached the importance of management and allocation of resources, emphasizing that the objective was to meet the long-term needs of the company and its customers rather than short-term profitability, and he encouraged interdepartmental cooperation, communication up and down the lines, and training. Anticipating the practice of North American car makers, Deming also induced Japanese automakers to develop relationships and to sign longer-term contracts with fewer suppliers, ones that complied with the SPC practices.

North American car companies had been reluctant to embrace Deming's ideas, primarily on grounds that they allowed workers (largely unionized in North America) too much decision-making authority. But by the late 1970s it was apparent their reaction had been unwise, as his innovative approach to manufacturing had transformed the Japanese industry and its products. To make things worse, North American manufacturers unwittingly helped the Japanese export efforts by forbidding their dealers from owning a franchise of another North American company. General Motors went so far as to restrict a dealer for one of its brands from owning a "store" for another, so that, for example, a Chevy dealer couldn't also sell Pontiacs from another location. But they didn't impose the same restriction on selling foreign-made cars, so when the public began showing an interest in fuel-efficient cars that their own companies couldn't supply, many domestic dealers added a Japanese line, giving the Asian companies an early distribution network upon which to build.

Consumers who had become acquainted with the names Toyota, Honda, and Datsun during the first energy crunch in 1973 remembered them when the Iranian crisis of 1979 triggered the second one. Not only were the latest vehicles from Japan cheaper, they included features that Detroit was accustomed to tacking on as costly options. And concerns about quality were a thing of the past; Japan's products now met or exceeded that of North American cars.

The recession that began to take hold in 1980 compounded domestic companies' woes, and Chrysler's near-collapse in the same year crystallized them. Although a lineup of clunky models was probably the reason for Chrysler's travails, competition from the Japanese automakers was seen as the culprit. Bowing to pressure from auto unions and the manufacturers – rare bedfellows, to be sure – Ronald Reagan's government turned to protectionism and in 1981 negotiated a voluntary export restraint (VER) agreement with Japan, essentially a quota system designed to limit the flow of imports to North America.

DEMAND FOR HIGHER QUALITY SUITS MAGNA

Magna was decidedly impressed by the near-collapse of Chrysler; it was a $38-million customer that accounted for 17 per cent of Magna's output. The domestic auto industry, no less shocked by the growing flood of imports, saw outsourcing as one way to survive. Stealing a page from Dr. Deming's manual of efficient manufacturing, they pressured suppliers to share the costs involved in meeting closer tolerances, to participate more in the research and development of parts, and to meet "just-in-time" inventory control and replacement schedules modelled on the Japanese concept of *kanban*. Nor could suppliers expect that economies of scale that typically kick in later in contracts would fatten their margins; the automakers wanted a share of that, too. Over the term of a contract – typically six or seven years, the life-cycle of a car model – OEMs (car manufacturers) insisted suppliers build in an annual 5 per cent price reduction.

Not surprisingly, the car makers' tougher requirements destroyed many undercapitalized parts-makers. Their policy of laying off on suppliers more of the cost of new-model retooling was especially hard on lots of smaller operators. The Automotive Parts Manufacturers' Association (APMA) of Canada reported in 1983 that many of its member companies were either buying tooling outside, or turning their attention to other industrial sectors for work because they couldn't meet (or afford) the OEMs' tooling requirements. By contrast, this was ideal for Magna. It had always done most of its own tooling and Stronach's tool-and-die makers were among the best in the industry. Indeed, he took the opportunity to bolster Magna's position by picking up skilled toolmakers from the less fortunate companies.

Intuitively, in fact, Frank Stronach had already incorporated into Magna's operating procedures and structures many of Deming's principles. As a result, very few auto-parts manufacturers were better positioned than Magna to compete in the new world that was emerging in the industry. Research and development, paramount in Deming's formula for manufacturing perfection, had been inviolate from the outset at Magna. Anticipating the needs of customers, Stronach believed, gave Magna a head start in fulfilling them, and it wasn't unusual for the company to present innovative solutions for problems the OEMs hadn't yet identified, or new products they hadn't thought of. By the time the second energy scare in 1979 rekindled North American car makers' interest in fuel efficiency, for example, Magna was using reaction injection moulding (RIM) technology to develop interior and exterior parts out of polyurethane that were both lighter than metal and more corrosion-resistant. It had also developed ways to use higher-strength steel and electronic substitutes for heavier mechanical systems to cut vehicle weight and improve mileage and performance.

Stronach's congenital attraction to new ideas had manifested itself in a readiness to spend on research. But even when the recession pounded vehicle production down to 8.3 million units in 1982 (from 1979's high of 14.3 million) and Magna's profit in the same year drooped by $1.7 million to $5.3 million, its lowest level in five years, Stronach resisted the urge to slam the brakes on research to conserve cash. Instead he feathered the gas pedal, to slow spending to $1.1 million on R&D in the bumpy economy of 1982 (up from $903,000 in 1978), accelerating again as the road became smoother. Between 1983 and 1985, Magna spent a total of $12.8 million on R&D.

The seed money produced a harvest of new products ranging from brake- and clutch-pedal assemblies and door hinges to moulded plastic parts and sophisticated seat-adjustment mechanisms. By 1985, Magna's R&D had actually become a profit centre: engineering, design, and production-equipment manufacturing proficiency had reached the point that two new divisions generated income by selling products and services both to Magna's own production divisions and to third parties.

THE ASSAULT OF THE JAPANESE TRANSPLANTS

Meanwhile, on the wider scene, the voluntary export restraints reduced the number of Japanese imports to North America as expected. But manipulating markets and softening competition had a predictable result in this wicked world of international trade: the domestic manufacturers hiked prices and fattened their profits. A fundamental flaw of the VERs was that they were based on unit sales rather than dollar volume. So the Japanese began exporting bigger, better-equipped, pricier models that hit a sweet spot with consumers. For good measure, they added entire new badges – Acura (Honda), Lexus (Toyota), and Infiniti (Nissan) – to market new lines of upscale models. In short, they complied with the VER agreement by exporting fewer cars to North America, but dramatically increased their revenues and profits because the cars they sold, though smaller in number, were more expensive. And even at higher prices, they were penetrating the domestic market. By 1983, foreign (primarily Japanese) cars accounted for 25 per cent of the Canadian market and 26 per cent of that in the U.S.

Another questionable aspect of the VERs was that they exempted vehicles built in North America. The Asians viewed this loophole as an on-ramp to the market. By the early 1980s, most of the Japanese companies were assembling cars, either alone or in joint ventures with North American companies, in "transplants," which were fed by components mostly shipped in from outside North America. This did not bode well for struggling North American parts manufacturers. A further problem for them lay in the fact that Deming's quality standards, responsible at least in part for Japanese cars' popularity, were exported to operations at the transplants as well. Auto-parts suppliers who sought contracts from the Japanese soon realized how far ahead Japanese quality had surged. Toyota, for example, insisted that no more than 15 parts per million received could be defective; the North American industry had previously regarded 250 to 500 parts per million as acceptable.

STRONACH BETS ON TECHNOLOGY

Magna, however, had no qualms about meeting and even exceeding the rigorous standard. Stronach had always been a perfection maven; the standards set by the Japanese were already being achieved in his plants. To further improve productivity, Magna had invested in computer-aided design and manufacturing (CAD/CAM) processes, robotics, and computer numerically controlled (CNC) machines that were governed by software that reduced operator error. Typically, Stronach even went the extra mile in the name of quality: in 1983 Magna was one of the first North American manufacturers to adopt Deming's SPC system into its operations.

Fred Jaekel had been president of three different divisions of Magna and one of its star production executives before Stronach fired him in 2001 after nineteen years with the company. As an insider, he believes that Stronach made a number of bad calls in the 1980s. But overspending on state-of-the-industry equipment wasn't one of them, Jaekel insists. "It wasn't a mistake," Jaekel says of the capital spending on technology. "It was exactly the right thing to do, as was proven later on. Putting all those CNC machines in place cost a lot, but it made Magna the most modern company in the business."

Quality wasn't the only hurdle that domestic parts suppliers had to clear. Just as their domestic-car OEM customers were competing against Japanese and Korean vehicle manufacturers, parts suppliers discovered they had new competition as well – the Japanese companies' traditional suppliers, many of whom set up factories in North America. Not only were they just as aggressive as North America's suppliers in getting, serving, and keeping their Japanese customers, but in some cases, they were partially owned by a Japanese OEM. And they were casting their eyes on North American OEMs – Magna's core business – as potential new customers.

FRONTIER DAYS AT MAGNA

The operating principles and methods at Magna were not identical to the W. Edwards Deming rules so revered by Japanese manufacturers. But they engendered a similar ethos, albeit flavoured more by the macho culture of the North American car business than by tea ceremonies. Japanese companies eliminated employees' fear of questioning or criticizing policy or management and encouraged openness and co-operation. Translated into North American terms, and juiced at Magna by performance-based financial incentives, it became a high-energy culture.

Fred Jaekel characterizes the 1980s as Magna's frontier-manufacturing period. The hands-on managers, most in their thirties (as he was), tended to be highly skilled machinists who'd worked their way up. They'd been told to run their plant as though it were their own, so they did, often getting rich from their slice of the plant's profits, and becoming part-owners of Magna through share purchases. They were so emboldened by years of independence – and confident of their value to competitors should they be fired – that fear wasn't in their lexicon. "Those days were what some of us called the wild west," Jaekel says a little wistfully. "Everybody told everybody else to fuck off if they didn't like what the other guy was saying. Nobody meant it, or caused problems, but that was the way it was there in those days. There was a true camaraderie, and nobody worried about anybody firing them."

As North American car makers rationalized operations to become efficient enough to match their new competitors, the ever-flexible Magna accommodated them. If a new plant was needed to provide better service (or win a contract) Magna could throw one up faster than anyone in the industry. In 1983, Fred Gingl, Magna's president at the time, boasted that a plant to fulfill a $50-million contract dependent on an eight-week startup had actually been up and running a week early. Seven weeks from bulldozers starting to scrape the bare earth . . .

STREAMLINING MANAGEMENT

To stay in the vanguard of suppliers, Magna began streamlining its operating structure, re-emphasizing the automotive division, which was responsible for 85 per cent of the company's sales in 1981. Stronach packaged its aerospace and defence operations – mainly

three manufacturing plants that made aircraft landing-gear parts –
with Hermes Electronics, the Dartmouth, N.S., sono-buoy company
that the federal and provincial governments had practically given
Magna in 1977. He bundled the assets into a Magna group called
Devtek Corp. and then sold Devtek for $23 million to a manage-
ment group led by Magna president Helmut Hofmann, its CFO
Murray Kingsburgh, and Jim Renner, an operations vice-president.
In addition to clearing out some of the peripheral companies in
Magna's portfolio, Stronach also saw the Devtek deal as a means of
reducing the number of outstanding Class B shares. Although he controlled 59 per cent of the super-voting shares, he kept an eye on who
controlled the rest of the stock. Hofmann, Kingsburgh, and Renner
sold their B's back to Magna as part payment for Devtek. As part of the
deal, Magna also held on to a 20 per cent interest in Devtek.

Stronach also saw the departure of the three men as an opportunity to revitalize management by lowering the average age in the
executive suite. He appointed Fred Gingl, a loyal thirty-two-year-old
protegé, as president to replace Hofmann in 1982. Next Stronach
lured Michael Hottinger, thirty, a rising star at General Motors, to be
vice-president, and then quickly promoted him to executive vice-
president. Two years later, he hired CFO Jim McAlpine, a thirty-eight-
year-old Clarkson and Gordon accountant who had impressed
Stronach with his wizardry in structuring complex financial deals.
The three comprised the executive team of young guns that Stronach
designated to take Magna to the next level.

The former Magna executives who went to Devtek weren't the
only long-time Magna employees to leave the company payroll. Tony
Czapka, whose role as an employee had been largely handling real-
estate acquisitions and disposals on behalf of Magna, relinquished
his vice-presidency in 1981. Yet he carried on doing exactly the same
thing, mingling his own real-estate deals with Magna's, a practice not
unfamiliar to Stronach himself and to other Magna executives. The
only difference for Czapka was that he was now a "consultant"

working for a fee rather than a salary. That he carried on working from the same office across from Stronach's that he'd always had at Magna's Markham headquarters proved convenient when the two controlling shareholders of Magna wanted to chat about a real-estate deal. But that proximity would also lead to one of Magna's most embarrassing experiences.

THE GOOD TIMES ROLL AGAIN

Magna's effort to survive the recession turned into growth as the economy recovered. It had tenaciously held onto existing contracts, and aggressively pursued new ones, making a commitment to its core automotive business and shedding businesses that weren't related to it. It had spent on technology that improved its operations and added new product lines that positioned it to compete when the industry recovered. In 1983, it opened five new plants; in 1984, it added thirteen more and also acquired businesses that diversified it into sunroof mechanisms and new seat-making technology through the purchase of a West German firm. On its own and in joint ventures it moved upstream with the opening of an engineering and design division. With a partner, it explored battery technology, as increasing fuel prices raised the general awareness of the concept of electric cars as an alternative to those powered by fossil fuels.

Not much came of a project called GSM Design, partly funded by grants from the province of Quebec and the federal government, whose mandate was to develop a plastic-bodied taxi. But the project demonstrated Magna's evolving diversity and capability in a broadening range of automotive-related technologies. When automakers moved toward "single-sourcing" – signing longer-term contracts with fewer Tier 1 suppliers (companies selling direct to automakers) – Magna had moved high up on the short list. Instead of buying bits and pieces of, say, a seat frame that their expensive, unionized labour would assemble and bolt into cars, the auto companies now wanted finished modules – seats put together by suppliers that arrived at the factory just in time to be installed as cars moved along the assembly line. By controlling and refining the assembly process in purpose-built facilities, and by doing so for less with its non-union labour, Magna added value to the components it sold as completed units.

Suppliers like Magna, whose focus was on a module rather than on individual parts, were constantly on the lookout for new materials and methods they could introduce to improve their product, cut costs, and increase margins. When Fred Gingl read about a foamed-in-place manufacturing technique for car seats in Germany, Magna checked it out and eventually bought the German company, Grammer Seating Systems.

THE MINI-MAGNA CONCEPT

Magna continued to boast that the agility of its small plants, each under the general management of an entrepreneur, was a prime reason for its responsiveness to customers. But in the expanding market for suppliers, maintaining the target of one hundred or so workers meant increasing the number of factories. It was a challenge to reconcile the need to give the maximum decision-making autonomy to plant managers (primarily technical people, whose skills lay in production rather than marketing and finance) with Magna's growing need for sophistication in co-ordinating the sprawling federation, particularly as customer demand for modules called for more inter-plant co-operation.

Magna responded by clumping the plants into five groups. At first they were named more or less according to geographical location, but by 1984 the group names were more reflective of technology or their products: Creative Mechanical Technology (hinges, clutch and brake pedals), Decorative Products (interior and exterior trim), MACI (electric motors), Magna Manufacturing (heavy stamping, forming and welding of chassis components), and Maple (pulley manufacturing and self-tensioning accessory–drive belt systems).

Each group consisted of a number of plants, many of which had names that gave little indication they were a Magna company.

Stronach had mused for years about spinning off one or more of Magna's groups as separate public companies, propagating mini-Magnas in which the parent company would retain a controlling interest to ensure that Magna's genetic makeup and guiding principles were kept intact and to guarantee successful offspring. It was a lofty goal for any parent, but in 1982 shareholders had approved the idea in principle. The group structure that evolved in the first half of the 1980s was a step in that direction. Under the aegis of a Magna vice-president who had hands-on plant experience, groups had their own offices and management teams responsible for activities such as resource allocation, accounting, and monitoring the performance of their plants. Their sales departments could go after contracts for factories within the group but they could also work co-operatively to take on contracts that called for the technology and skill of more than one group.

Group managers reported to the executive level that set overall strategy and was custodian of Magna's "unique entrepreneurial culture." The executive group, which reported to the board of directors (and which, in fact, included some directors), represented and supported the organization as a whole. It could use Magna's buying power to negotiate lower prices for equipment and raw materials, passing the economies on to the groups and individual plants.

STRONACH ENSHRINES A CONSTITUTION

Operating structure wasn't the only aspect of Magna that was becoming more formal. Over the years, Stronach had missed few opportunities to praise the management concept he'd encapsulated under the rubric Fair Enterprise as an alternative to socialism, capitalism, and totalitarianism. "The Fair Enterprise system," he pronounced, "checks greed and the distribution of capital in a more constructive

way than the present economic system." He believed it balanced the
rights of investors, employees, the community, and customers.
Convinced that Fair Enterprise would enshrine him among industrial history's socio-economic thinkers, he was all too aware that later
managements could possibly toss the whole idea, and his legacy
would be lost.

In 1984, he took steps to prevent that distasteful eventuality.
First, he codified the principles of Fair Enterprise into a corporate
constitution. The loose wording left application of the document
open to interpretation in spots. It promised a majority of outside
directors, for example, but didn't address the fact that their appointment was purely at the pleasure of Stronach, who held indisputable
voting control of Magna as majority owner of the super-voting Class B
shares. And the clause that stipulated that 6 per cent of the company's
before-tax profit would be distributed to "senior management" did
not make it crystal clear that, in the mid 1980s, this fortunate group
was actually only the top five or so officers of the company.

Even so, the constitution boldly went where few corporations
dared, in that it committed management to allocate percentages of
Magna's profits to specific purposes. Certain clauses in the document
reflected how Magna had been operating for many years. For
example, Stronach had been committing 7 per cent of the company's
before-tax profit to R&D and 20 per cent of its *after*-tax profit to shareholders in the form of dividends since at least 1975. Other articles
were based on practices that had evolved: the percentage of pre-tax
profit that was to be given to employees in the form of shares or cash
was unspecified from 1974 to 1978, was fixed at 7 per cent from
1979 to 1983, and then bumped to 10 per cent in 1984 to coincide
with the constitution's first publication in the annual report. Similarly, the amount that Magna would give to social causes (charitable, cultural, educational, or political), which had been 1 per cent of
pre-tax profit since 1979, was increased to 2 per cent the same year.

Figure 5.1. Magna's Corporate Constitution, 2006

MAGNA'S CORPORATE CONSTITUTION

EMPLOYEE EQUITY AND PROFIT PARTICIPATION
Ten percent of Magna's profit before tax will be allocated to employees.
These funds will be used for the purchase of Magna shares in trust for employees
and for cash distributions to employees, recognizing length of service.

SHAREHOLDER PROFIT PARTICIPATION
Magna will distribute, on average, not less than 20 percent of its annual net profit
after tax to shareholders.

MANAGEMENT PROFIT PARTICIPATION
To obtain long-term contractual commitment from senior management,
Magna provides a compensation arrangement which,
in addition to a base salary below industry standards, allows for the distribution
of up to six percent of its profit before tax.

RESEARCH AND DEVELOPMENT
Magna will allocate a minimum of seven percent of its profit before tax
for research and development to ensure its long-term viability.

SOCIAL RESPONSIBILITY
Magna will allocate a maximum of two percent of its profit before tax for charitable,
cultural, educational and political purposes to support the basic fabric of society.

MINIMUM PROFIT PERFORMANCE
Management has an obligation to produce a profit.
If Magna does not generate a minimum after-tax return of four percent
on share capital for two consecutive years, Magna's Class A shareholders, voting as a class,
will have the right to elect additional directors.

UNRELATED INVESTMENTS
Magna Class A and Class B shareholders, with each class voting separately,
will have the right to approve any investment in an unrelated business in the event
such investment together with all other investments in unrelated businesses
exceeds 20 percent of Magna's equity.

BOARD OF DIRECTORS
Magna believes that outside directors provide independent counsel and discipline.
A majority of the members of Magna's Board of Directors will be outsiders.

CONSTITUTIONAL AMENDMENTS
Any change to Magna's Corporate Constitution will require the approval
of its Class A and Class B shareholders, with each class voting separately.

The new charter also gave shareholders more privileges (Figure 5.1). These included the right of the Class A shareholders to elect "additional directors" (without specifying how many) if the company did not generate an after-tax return of at least 4 per cent on share capital for two consecutive years. And in a clause designed to protect shareholders from management taking flyers on businesses outside its expertise – but one that would drive Stronach crazy in the coming years – the Magna charter stipulated that only 20 per cent of the company's equity could be invested in businesses unrelated to the auto-parts industry, unless the shareholders approved otherwise.

Magna's constitution as written in 1984 was a milestone in the company's history. Small changes in the wording would creep in over the years, but the basic tenets of the manifesto have held. Back in the mid 1980s, however, Stronach could not be sure that future management wouldn't trash the constitution, laying waste to the principles he believed would be his legacy to the world of business. So he took measures to ensure that Magna's executives would forever be bound to adhere to the constitution, and furthermore, that that adherence would be self-perpetuating. The B shares that he didn't control were owned primarily by senior management. First he established a Voting Trust Agreement that gave him alone voting control over all of their Class B shares. Then, to prevent their falling into the hands of outsiders, he required the executives to offer the B's to the other executives or their management successors before selling them to anyone else.

BUCKING THE ODDS TO SUCCEED

In 1986, as Frank Stronach and his executive team looked back on the first half of the decade, they could be justified in feeling proud and satisfied. What had been a disastrous five years for many other companies both inside and outside the auto-supply industry had proved to be a time of enormous growth for Magna. His company's tenacity, flexibility, and foresight had paid off. In the six years from 1980 to 1985, sales grew from $184 million to $690 million, a leap of 275 per cent. Profit dipped in the early 1980s to pre-1978 levels but then had steadily increased, pouring $43 million into Magna's treasury in 1985, an increase of over 670 per cent since 1980.

Magna also managed its money shrewdly. Though debt was to be a problem a few years down the road, it seemed well under control in the mid 1980s. With a long-term debt to equity ratio of just 0.38:1 in 1985, the company was well under an acceptable 1:1 ratio. Other measures of Magna's success were equally impressive. Earnings per share increased from $1.06 in 1980 to $2.00 in 1985. Its stock, whose high in 1980 was $15, was pushing $25 in 1985 and producing dividends of 48 cents, up from 36 cents in 1981. Furthermore, Magna's perennial measure of improved productivity, dollar content per vehicle, had doubled from $24.60 in 1982 to $49 in 1985.

Physically, Magna had matured as well. It had grown from a two-division company in 1980, one of which was non-automotive, to five auto-supply divisions that used thirty-three different processes in almost one hundred product applications. In 1980, it had employed 2,500 workers at twenty-eight locations near Toronto and two in Iowa; by 1985, the company had three times as many employees at over seventy facilities in North America and one, the seating plant, in West Germany. The workers also could be pleased that the company was doing as well as it was: during 1985, Magna allocated $8.3 million to its Employee Equity and Profit Sharing plan. Of that, $1.9-million, an average of about $250 for each of the 7500 employees, was distributed in cash. The balance, $6.4 million, was used to purchase shares; the market value of the Magna shares held in trust for employees was $31.8 million in 1985, about $4,240 per employee.

In good years (and even in some bad ones) there was also plenty left over that got kicked up to the corporate level. In 1985 the top

five officers shared $4.8 million; another fourteen senior managers
shared $5.5 million – an average of nearly $393,000 each.

Not surprisingly, as Magna's chairman and chief executive,
Stronach annually garnered the biggest share of the 6 per cent pre-
tax profit that went to the top five executives. In 1986, a $2-million
cash bonus augmented his relatively modest $200,000 base pay. The
pay packet was big enough by corporate standards of the time to
prompt the first query from an aggrieved shareholder – and the first
airing of what would become his stock response when questioned on
his compensation. "I'm glad you asked," Stronach sunnily responded
when a shareholder questioned his pay package. "I'm hoping to
increase it." Fair enterprise didn't mean equality, Stronach explained
to the *Globe and Mail's* John Partridge, but rather an equal opportunity to make a living and grow capital. In the same year, Stronach also
earned approximately $335,000 in dividends on his Class A and B
shares. While his total annual compensation during the mid 1980s
didn't yet put him at the top of the list of Canada's corporate money-
earners, he was moving up rapidly through the field.

STRONACH ON TOP OF THE WORLD

Magna's emergence as a multinational, industrial powerhouse in a
cutthroat business steadily added to the celebrity of Frank Stronach.
There were few, if any, public companies that had been established
and become so prominent and yet remained so completely under the
sway of a single person. Stronach's already healthy ego bulged with
the acclaim. The better Magna did, the more Stronach appeared to
believe some higher power had anointed him to achieve. The Magna
constitution seemed, in Stronach's mind, a modern Ten Command-
ments of business that would chart the company's course forever and
ensure the principles of Fair Enterprise, which he modestly declared
would distribute capital "to individual people on a much wider basis
than any other system known to man." The self-perpetuating aspect
was yet another example of his peerless judgment and foresight.

But as big as Magna had become, it was too small a canvas to contain the grandeur of Stronach's thinking. In the second half of the decade, his self-confidence caused him to increasingly detach himself from the reality of Magna in order to impart his ideas and prove his genius to a wider world.

6

THE SINC STEVENS AFFAIR

In May 1986, after intense pressure from the Liberal opposition, Prime Minister Brian Mulroney ordered an inquiry into the alleged conflict of interest of Sinclair Stevens, who at the time was the minister in charge of Canada's industrial development. He was also a close friend of Frank Stronach. From July 1986 to February 1987, the "Parker Commission," under Chief Justice William Parker, delved into the charges, calling ninety-three witnesses, including Stronach. It was the Canadian story of the year, capturing front-page headlines on a regular basis. Stevens was forced to quit his cabinet post and was found to have been in a conflict of interest in several respects. Although absolved in 2005 on what some observers considered a technicality (that Judge Parker's definition of conflict of interest exceeded the one in the guidelines that governed ministers in the cabinet at the time), the inquiry left Stevens's reputation in tatters. For nearly twenty years, his name remained synonymous with egregious conflict of interest by a government minister.

At the centre of the allegations, and therefore at the heart of the inquiry, were Magna International, Frank Stronach, and Stronach's long-time friend and business associate Tony Czapka.

The events that prompted the inquiry began with a visit by Sinclair Stevens's wife to Frank Stronach at Magna's head office in April 1985. Stronach introduced Noreen Stevens to Tony Czapka, whose office was across the hall. By the end of April, Mrs. Stevens and Czapka had reached an agreement whereby Czapka would lend $2.6 million to her and her husband's company, York Centre, to solve its dire cash-flow problems. However, when Czapka wrote the cheque a month later, he used an account that Magna had funded. Meanwhile, Mr. Stevens, throughout this same time period, as the minister, had very actively been negotiating and approving government grants, worth many millions, to Magna. In effect, Magna International, recipient of government aid through Sinclair Stevens's portfolio, had backed a $2.6 million loan that bailed out Stevens's private business.

The inquiry had the expected result of censuring Stevens on this and several other allegations related to his conduct as a government minister. But though it wasn't the commission's purpose to investigate Magna, the "Parker" inquiry shed significant light on how Magna, and its chairman, operated.

THE FREE ENTERPRISE COMPANY THAT LOVED HANDOUTS

For all its boss's trumpeting of free enterprise and entrepreneurialism, Magna wasn't averse to sucking up government grants to assist in its growth. Between 1972 and 1984, under Pierre Trudeau's Liberal governments, it had picked up just under $30 million in aid. Typically the grants were 50 per cent "non-repayable," with the other half to be repaid interest-free over five years. No one could deny that there was a mutual benefit. For example, in 1979, Magna had only about $32 million in equity and wanted to invest $25 million in new plastics technology. Initially, it would be used to make bumper-fascias out of polyurethane, lighter than the chrome and steel they replaced. Encouraged by Magna's promise that its Polyrim plant would create 450 new jobs, Ottawa chipped in $6 million in grants and $13 million in interest-free loans in development funding. Magna more than rewarded the government. Within five years, its plastics division employed 1,500.

Eager to attract voters through job creation, Ottawa saw the seemingly unstoppable Magna as an ideal vehicle. When Trudeau stepped down in 1984, John Turner, his successor as leader of the Liberals and prime minister, appointed former Trudeau cabinet minister Ed Lumley as minister responsible for the Department of Regional Industrial Expansion (DRIE). Lumley lost the job (and his seat) in that same year, when Brian Mulroney's Progressive Conservatives trounced the Liberals in a federal election. In one of his last acts in the portfolio before returning to Bay Street, Lumley signed a memorandum of understanding (MOU) that made available to Magna up to $50-million worth of interest-free loans and development grants. The agreement included a commitment by Magna to make capital expenditures of $500 million over the next five years. But the Liberal loss threatened to scupper the grants, none of which Magna had yet taken up.

SINC STEVENS – A GOOD FRIEND IN GOVERNMENT

Stronach caught a huge break, however, when Mulroney appointed Sinclair Stevens as minister of DRIE. Stevens had been a Member of Parliament since 1972, representing a riding in York Region. He was also a businessman and gentleman farmer, and a neighbour, friend, and acolyte of Stronach. Notwithstanding Stronach's outspoken aversion to free trade – despite the fact that Magna had taken off following the introduction of the Auto Pact in 1965, essentially a free-trade agreement – Stevens wasn't about to alienate a potential party patron, especially a proven job-creator in the automotive sector, which the government had earmarked as central to its industrial strategy. Only a few days after Stevens's appointment, he asked mandarins in his office to recommend ways in which Stronach could be recognized nationally. The DRIE staff suggested the Order of Canada or the Canadian Awards for Excellence.

Stevens also reportedly pushed the government to consider Stronach's Fair Enterprise theory as a national model for economic growth. Most important, Stevens also proved as eager as the Liberals had been to send mountains of money to Magna. Stevens readily approved the MOU that Lumley had signed and, under it, approved grants and loans totalling $21.5 million between January 1985 and April 1986, for eight Magna projects. Among them was almost $1 million in aid to Multimatic, the original Magna unit then run by Tony Czapka's son Peter. Another was $10 million to build a stamping plant in Milton, Ontario, to make body panels.

RAMMING THROUGH THE CAPE BRETON DEAL

Yet those disbursements were small potatoes compared to the "Magna Cape Breton" deal. In June 1985, Stevens signed another MOU that led to Magna being granted approximately $64 million in aid for the establishment of two plants and a training centre in the remote region of Cape Breton on Canada's east coast. The Mulroney government had placed "a high policy-priority" on encouraging "economic growth using the private sector in areas such as Atlantic Canada," in particular in Cape Breton, the most economically depressed area in the country.

Almost all of Magna's factories – seventy, by 1985 – were in the southern Ontario corridor from Toronto to Windsor, close to Detroit, the North American hub of auto-building activity. Indeed, Stronach's preference since the early 1980s had been to cluster factories in industrial campuses close to customers to facilitate intra-company co-operation and swift shipping. (The first such campus, in Newmarket, had turned out very nicely for Stronach himself. Magna built it on ninety acres of farmland that it bought for $705,000 from Stronach in 1983. He'd paid about $360,000 for it three years earlier.) Consequently Cape Breton didn't leap to mind as a logical place for more

Magna expansion. Stronach's managers objected on grounds of location, pointing out Cape Breton's distance from Magna's suppliers and buyers. Nor did Magna's management and board, assessing the investment purely as a business venture, share Stronach's enthusiasm. But Stronach had begun to appreciate the special dispensations from politicians that were available to anyone who promised jobs in Cape Breton.

He was also apparently attracted by Cape Breton's prospects as a sort of socio-economic laboratory in which to test Fair Enterprise. Charles Steadman, director of the department's automotive branch, would later observe during the Parker Commission that Stronach seemed motivated "to achieve a societal benefit in a controlled environment where Cape Breton is the beneficiary." Once Magna's application of Fair Enterprise reversed Cape Breton's economic torpor, as Stronach was sure it would, the concept would naturally be adopted as the panacea for the entire Canadian economy.

The civil servants in Ottawa were uneasy about this plan. But to Sinc Stevens, more politically aware than his staff, the friendship with Stronach was worth cultivating. Magna was a successful job-spinner, worthy of government assistance to benefit the nation. It doubtless crossed Stevens's mind that helping Magna help Canada would raise his own profile, not to mention help fulfill his campaign promises to Eastern Canada. So Stevens really wanted the Cape Breton project to happen, and he spent over a year making sure it did. Though Stronach wanted the deal, too, it was clear that his own senior management was against the development. "There was a 'dichotomy' at Magna," James Dancey, a manager at DRIE, wrote in a memo in October 1985, "between Stronach's 'visionary extrapolations' and the views of the more pragmatic executives who wanted nothing to do with Cape Breton." Meanwhile, Stevens's staff at DRIE repeatedly rejected proposals and counter-proposals because the terms seemed too generous to Magna.

Nonetheless, on April 7, 1986, after fifteen months of back and forth negotiations, Stronach and Stevens hammered out an agreement, ultimately ignoring much of the opposition from their respective staffs. Magna did not get most of the money up front as it had insisted, but Stevens cut the company a deal that it couldn't refuse: almost $64 million in grants, interest-free loans, tax credits, and other assistance to build two auto-parts plants and a training facility on Cape Breton island. Furthermore, though Stronach at one point had indicated that Magna would contribute $64 million of its own money to the development, the pact came with no obligation on Magna's part to invest in the project other than a mere $4 million in each of the two plants.

The Cape Breton deal was announced on April 11, 1986. Stronach spun it as Magna's creative and altruistic salvation of Cape Breton. "We believe in the people of Cape Breton," he said in announcing the project. "Some senior civil servants, after working on our proposal for nearly a year, came to the conclusion and expressed themselves that it was the most innovative and constructive proposal they have ever received."

Two-and-a-half weeks later, the *Globe and Mail* broke the story that revealed that a Magna line of credit had been used to back a $2.6-million loan made to a company controlled by Stevens.

A BLIND TRUST

"Sinc" Stevens was no business rookie. A lawyer turned entrepreneur, he had carried on his business activities after being elected to represent the Progressive Conservative party in the York Simcoe (later renamed York Peel) riding in 1972. When he won his seat in 1984 in the Brian Mulroney landslide and became part of the government, he and his wife, Noreen, a lawyer, controlled a holding company called York Centre that had interests in a construction firm, commercial real estate, and some oil and gas investments. When Mulroney appointed him to the cabinet, Stevens put York Centre in a blind trust to comply with conflict-of-interest guidelines.

Blind trusts are supposed to be managed at the discretion of trustees without any consultation with the owner. That two of the trustees were Stevens's former campaign manager, Ted Rowe, and his wife, Noreen, a business partner, seemed to violate the spirit, if not the letter, of the somewhat loose guidelines. It was – how to put this – highly unlikely that neither would ever have a conversation with Stevens about the state of his business. Indeed, Judge Parker would pointedly reject the testimony of Noreen and Sinclair Stevens, given during the inquiry, that they did not discuss the business affairs of their company while it was in the blind trust. It would also later seem more than coincidental that when York Centre was struggling from a lack of liquidity, Noreen Stevens turned for help to Stronach, recipient of so many huge grants awarded by Stevens's ministry. In September 1984, Stronach had declined to buy a building from York Centre that Noreen Stevens hoped to sell to raise cash. But he nonetheless became even more entwined with Sinc Stevens when, only a month later, he accepted Stevens's offer of a seat on the board of the Canada Development Investment Corporation (CDIC).

STRONACH AND THE CDIC BOARD

The Liberal government had created the CDIC in 1982 to manage the sprawl of Crown assets held by the Canada Development Corporation in which the CDIC held a 48 per cent interest. But while the Liberals had *planned* to divest some of the government holdings, selling them off at an appropriate price to private interests, the Mulroney government made the acceleration of the process its mandate and charged Stevens with the task. As a newly minted director, Stronach became part of the divestiture program.

It was odd that, despite his being a proven industrialist, no arm's length, non-governmental Canadian companies looking for experienced directors had secured Stronach's services. The fact that he accepted Stevens's invitation to join the board of the CDIC suggests that he was willing to serve, if asked. At the time, he was a trustee of York University in Toronto (in the same time period when his daughter, Belinda, was accepted in York's commerce program). He was also chairman of the York Region United Way and a director for Big Brothers of Canada. But his only other corporate responsibilities outside of Magna were as a director of the National Bank of Detroit and of Devtek, the company run by former Magna executives and in which Magna had a 20 per cent interest.

Stronach claimed that serving without remuneration on the CDIC board was an act of public service, but it also conferred on him prestige by association; among its directors were up-and-comers such as Lucien Bouchard, a future premier of Quebec, Trevor Eyton, a Brascan executive who was one of Canada's most powerful businessmen and a future senator, and Paul Martin Jr., a shipping company magnate who would go on to become finance minister and then prime minister of Canada.

At fifty-two, successful at horse racing and business, Stronach was already firmly ensconced near the top of both the Canadian corporate and sporting worlds. Now his old pal Sinc's fortuitous rise to the level of cabinet minister appeared to be opening to him the corridors of government as well. What began as a promising connection for Stronach and Magna, however, by 1986 would drag them through the most embarrassing affair either had yet encountered.

MRS. STEVENS GETS A LOAN

The business affairs that Sinc Stevens placed in the blind trust were a shambles when he took over DRIE in the fall of 1984. York Centre was close to bankruptcy. After Frank Stronach rebuffed Noreen Stevens in September 1984 when she tried to persuade him to buy a property to raise some cash, she and York Centre's president, Ted Rowe, pounded doors on Bay Street and elsewhere seeking capital with which to refinance the company. They even tried Magna again in February 1985, this time reaching out to its real-estate arm, MI Realty. But that approach and all others turned up nothing.

In April 1985, frustrated by her inability to find a financial angel for York Centre and facing new demands from bank creditors, Noreen Stevens paid another visit to Stronach at Magna's head office – "as a friend," she later claimed – seeking a loan, collateralized by commercial real estate that York Centre controlled. Stronach, despite having orchestrated many complex property deals, would testify in 1986 that because he wasn't an expert in real estate, he steered her across the executive suite to the office of Tony Czapka.

Czapka unquestionably understood real estate. Since retiring from Magna in 1981 to become a consultant for the company, he had mainly bought and sold properties to fit Magna's business needs. Wealthy in his own right – in 1985, he sold his nearly 14 per cent stake in Magna's Class B shares, and in 1986 he had a net worth of about $15 million – he not only worked for Magna but did real-estate deals on his own account.

TONY CZAPKA'S "GENEROUS FRAME OF MIND"

Like Stronach, whose partner he had been for twenty-five years, Czapka often profited from personal business that he carried out on Magna's behalf. In fact, he was in the midst of one such deal when Noreen Stevens turned up in his office in April 1985. That same month, he was negotiating a deal in which he would sell to Magna three properties that he owned on which Magna had factories, and Magna would sell to him two properties – a total of 115 acres – of undeveloped Magna-owned land. The arrangement was essentially a swap, inasmuch as Magna was to pay Czapka $3.2 million for his three properties and Czapka was to pay Magna $3 million for its two plots of land. When the closing of the deal became delayed, however, Czapka complained to Magna that his partners in the real estate wanted to be paid. But rather than follow through on a threat to find another buyer for the properties, he proposed that he buy out his partners and put the real estate in a numbered company. Then when Magna got around to closing, it would only have to deal with him.

Magna agreed to this proposal. Czapka, however, didn't see why he should have to use up part of *his* line of credit at the bank when he was buying out his partners and putting his properties into the numbered company as a convenience to Magna. So, in May, Jim McAlpine, Magna's CFO, duly advised the Bank of Nova Scotia that Czapka should be able to access up to $3 million of Magna's line of credit. "In order to facilitate Mr. Czapka's endeavours on our behalf," McAlpine wrote, "it is necessary for him to have credit with your bank that does not hamper his ability to finance his personal activities." McAlpine also comforted the bank that in light of Czapka's relationship with Magna, the company would cover any financial difficulties that he might encounter. This letter would prove embarrassing when Magna later tried to claim that Czapka had an arm's-length relationship with the company.

As he was putting together the deal with Magna, Czapka was also looking for a way to solve Noreen Stevens's money requirements. For all the dotting of i's and crossing of t's in dealing with Magna, with whom he'd worked for decades, Czapka was uncharacteristically sloppy in his dealings with Mrs. Stevens. He testified before the Parker Commission that Stronach had introduced her as a friend and given him no clue that she was Sinc Stevens's wife, or even that she was an executive of the company seeking help with a real-estate deal. Noreen Stevens hadn't been much more forthcoming, according to Czapka. "She told me she was a lawyer representing clients who had properties for sale," he later testified.

If that beggared belief, so did Czapka's admission that he hadn't bothered to do a credit check on her or York Centre. Nor did he do a thorough inspection of the properties, only giving their exteriors the once-over in the course of one day. Instead, being in "a generous frame of mind," as described by Judge Parker in his final report after the inquiry, Czapka cut an "unusually beneficial" deal with Mrs. Stevens. He agreed to lend her $2.6 million, taking back a five-year mortgage on the commercial properties that was interest-free for the first year and bore interest at 12 per cent for the rest of the term. If York Centre sold any of the property, Czapka was to get any proceeds up to $3.1 million and would evenly split anything over that with the owner. The deal provided immediate relief to York Centre, which was under no obligation to repay a cent of the principal or interest for two years. On top of that, Czapka incurred substantial financing costs and assumed extraordinary risk by advancing an amount equal to York Centre's equity in the properties. Despite that, Czapka claimed he was pleased. "I was just as anxious as Mrs. Stevens to do the deal," Czapka testified at the judicial inquiry, "because as it turned out, it was a beautiful deal for me."

THE LETTER OF THE LAW

To that point, the Parker Commission heard, the deal was between Czapka and Noreen Stevens, both friends of Stronach's whom he had introduced to each other. The detail that enmeshed Magna in the arrangement was the letter that McAlpine had sent the bank giving Czapka access to Magna's line of credit through the numbered company he created to buy out his partners in the unrelated Magna transaction. The idea had been that Magna would then only have to deal with the numbered company to purchase the real estate. But while Czapka formed the numbered company as planned, he never put the properties into it. That left the numbered company with $3-million worth of Magna-borrowing power that it hadn't drawn against. Rather than waste it, or dip into his own line of credit, the canny Czapka used it to borrow the $2.6 million that he advanced to Noreen Stevens. In effect, Magna had financed a $2.6-million loan that saved Stevens's private business from bankruptcy.

Meanwhile, Stevens – who later claimed to be completely unaware of these transactions involving his wife and his business – was approving millions of dollars in government assistance to his buddy Stronach's firm.

TURNING UP THE HEAT IN OTTAWA

The confluence of events – the Czapka-Magna property "swap," the loan to York Centre that used a Magna line of credit, and Sinclair Stevens's approval of aid to Magna – occurred in the spring of 1985 and became public a year later in April 1986 when the *Globe and Mail* implied that Stevens was doling out favours to Magna. The Liberal opposition in the House of Commons, led by a group of aggressive young Liberals known as "The Rat Pack" (which consisted of Sheila Copps, Don Boudria, John Nunziata, and Brian Tobin), seized the moment to begin baying for Stevens's head. Frustrated by the Mulroney government's stonewalling to protect its minister against conflict-of-interest charges, the Rat Pack pushed the issue into national prominence through its persistent harassment of Stevens. Sheila Copps, a future deputy prime minister, put the affair on front pages when cameras caught her climbing on a chair to pursue Stevens, who was slinking out the door to avoid further questioning. All the while, Copps was demanding his resignation, and not quietly.

Stevens eventually did resign in May 1986 – according to him, in an attempt to take the issue off the front pages and the judicial inquiry under Judge Parker, established by Prime Minister Brian Mulroney, began in June 1986. Meanwhile, Frank Stronach, who wasn't scheduled to give evidence until late September, took the time to give the world his own version of events. In an apparent rehearsal for his coming testimony, he tried it out in an interview with the *Toronto Star*.

STRONACH'S *STAR* STORY

In May 1986, Stronach had originally said he sent Noreen Stevens to Czapka because he himself didn't know enough about real estate. But in the *Star* interview, in mid September, he had a much more elaborate explanation, claiming he directed her to Czapka to placate his friend, who was upset that Magna was dragging its feet in buying his properties. It wasn't Czapka's partners who wanted things to speed up, he said; it was Czapka himself who was cheesed off at Stronach. The source of the dispute, Stronach told the *Star*, was that years earlier, Stronach had given him right of first refusal to buy his Class B shares – the super-voting shares through which Stronach controlled Magna – if Stronach died or changed their ownership for estate-planning purposes. Czapka still had the document. In his view, Stronach's recently announced plan to give Magna executives the right to vote his shares amounted to changing who controlled Magna, and therefore qualified as estate planning. In other words, Stronach said, Czapka believed that Stronach was violating the contract he had with him.

Stronach said that he attempted to defuse the situation. Czapka had wanted to retire from Magna, Stronach explained, but before doing so he wanted to make sure his son Peter was looked after. Accordingly, Stronach had accommodated Czapka's wishes in May 1985 by selling to Tony and Peter Czapka half of Multimatic Inc., a division of Magna. As part of the accommodation, Stronach agreed to buy, on behalf of Magna, the three properties Magna was leasing from Tony Czapka.

Here, Stronach's story starts to align with that of other witnesses at the inquiry. It was the delay in closing the purchases, Stronach said, that upset Czapka and his partners. Stronach had assigned to Jim McAlpine the task of valuing the land and plants, as required for public-company reporting purposes. But McAlpine hadn't had time to do so, Stronach claimed, which led to Czapka's complaint that his partners were getting antsy waiting for their money and that he wanted a letter of comfort sent to the bank so his credit rating wouldn't be impaired. Stronach directed McAlpine to send it, but said the letter was never intended for purposes other than to cover the costs of the land that Magna was in the process of buying from Czapka. Stronach concluded his interview with the *Toronto Star* by claiming he was looking forward to testifying, and that he would

"make Billy Graham and Martin Luther King look like choir boys."
Which was, when you come to think about it, an interesting turn
of phrase.

STRONACH TAKES THE STAND

So much for the warm-up. Frank Stronach's testimony promised to
be one of the more dramatic moments of the Parker inquiry, which
had over the summer titillated the public with its glimpse behind the
wizard's curtain at Magna.

Inquiry watchers who looked forward to Stronach's time on the
stand weren't disappointed. Before grilling him, Parker Commission
counsel David Scott, like virtually anyone who meets Stronach for
the first time, had to endure the "Full Frank" – an explanation of Fair
Enterprise, the socio-economic credo he believes has established his
credentials as an economic thinker ranking alongside such luminar-
ies as Karl Marx, John Maynard Keynes, and Adam Smith. Or maybe
just above them, given that Magna proved his theory. In Stronach's
view, the three existing economic systems, socialism, totalitarianism,
and capitalism, are all flawed. He informed the packed inquiry room
that Fair Enterprise – embodied in Magna – was a fourth model. All
that remained was to persuade more people of the concept's efficacy,
and its wide-scale acceptance would solve the world's economic
woes. Stronach's enthusiasm bordered on the evangelical when
explaining Fair Enterprise to anyone he could trap into listening.
Reporters granted an audience with the chairman typically spent half
their allotted time receiving Stronach's lecture. He habitually refused
to allow exemptions, even forcing visitors who'd heard it all before
to suffer the routine again.

True to form, Stronach began his testimony at the Parker inquiry
by going through his act, using felt-tip markers to illustrate the elements of Fair Enterprise on the flip chart he'd brought to the court-
room for the purpose. In a final flourish, as was his practice, he
offered to autograph the Daliesque result for Scott.

The lighter moment didn't remove the weight of Magna's involvement with Stevens. For all his bravado prior to and during the Parker
inquiry, Stronach had become more and more resentful that his and
Magna's reputations were being besmirched. He'd grown used to
being cut a fair amount of slack by the press, mainly out of respect
for what he'd created at Magna – and the fact that he was a refresh-
ing change from the usual corporate leader, right down to sporting
curly blond hair in a style that would later be known as a mullet.

But as the inquiry laboured through the summer and fall before
concluding in February 1987, the same reporters who'd kept a
straight face at some of his pronouncements became gradually less
deferential as inconsistencies cropped up between his pre-testimony
interviews and his testimony itself.

Stronach's promise – that he would clearly establish Magna's
innocence at the hearing – proved difficult to keep. Indeed, right off
the bat, he tripped himself up by contradicting earlier statements
he'd made about Noreen Stevens's April 1985 visit. In a May 1986
interview, he told broadcast media that Noreen Stevens had told
him in April 1985, "'We have a cash flow problem, we don't want
to make a fire sale, would you know of anybody who is interested
in real estate,' and I said, 'Yes.'" In newspaper interviews, he'd said
that she had come to him then as a personal friend regarding personal real estate. But in his testimony at the inquiry, he was "fairly
sure" that she had not revealed that she was seeking money to keep
Sinc Stevens's company afloat. He blamed the discrepancy between
earlier and later versions of the story on the fact that he'd been
reconstructing in the spring of 1986 an incident that had taken place
about a year earlier. In other words, he couldn't accurately remember that far back.

There was also considerable discussion about whether Stronach
had provided Noreen Stevens's name and her relationship to Sinclair
Stevens in his introduction of her to Czapka. The question was
important because if Czapka knew who he was dealing with, it lent

support to the charge that Magna, a recipient of government grants, had been directly involved in the loan to the minister's company. Stronach claimed he hadn't mentioned her name, precisely because he had not wanted Czapka to feel any pressure to help her because of her relationship to the minister. But Judge Parker didn't buy that. In fact, he concluded that Stronach's purpose was the exact opposite, that by introducing her as a friend but leaving them to discover their respective names themselves, he wanted "to ensure that help would be forthcoming from Mr. Czapka, since appearances would not permit it to come from him [Stronach]."

Stronach was also not able to repair the damage done when Czapka tried to extricate himself from the inquiry by portraying himself as having severed almost all of his dealings with Magna. The commission's counsel clearly established that Czapka was "ensconced in the executive suite of Magna at its Head Office," in an office adjacent to Stronach's. He was therefore in direct communication with senior officers at the company. Far from being uninformed of the relationship and dealings between Magna and DRIE, he had been directly involved in four applications to DRIE, including one for Multimatic. Czapka's claim that he had no knowledge of Noreen Stevens's relationship to Sinclair Stevens, the minister responsible for DRIE, was found to be disingenuous, to say the least.

THE CONSPIRACY THEORY

Nor was Stronach able to deflect questions raised by the "conspiracy theory" put forward by the commission's counsel. David Scott alleged that both the May 1985 agreement between Czapka and Magna and the letter of comfort that McAlpine sent to the bank had been "concocted." The land deal between Magna and Czapka, as originally structured, involved the exchange of cash and mortgages. But by the time the deal was actually executed in December 1985, it had become a straight swap, with no money changing hands and no assumption of the mortgages by Magna. The way Scott saw it, the entire complicated deal was trumped up to disguise Magna's involvement in funding the loan by Czapka to York Centre. He argued that the fact the dollar amounts for the loan to Noreen Stevens, the value of the land put up as collateral on the loan, the line of credit advanced by Magna to Czapka, and the value of the properties that Czapka and Magna were swapping were *all* about $3 million was proof. While Judge Parker rejected the allegation for lack of evidence, he also stated in his final report that "in view of the close relationship between Mr. Czapka and Magna, the need for such a cumbersome arrangement is not readily apparent, and its existence does raise some suspicion."

Finally, the inquiry, intended to probe Stevens's alleged conflicts of interest, questioned whether Stronach himself had used his position as a director on the CDIC inappropriately. At one hearing session, he acknowledged that Magna had been interested in bidding for Canadair, an aircraft-maker that was one of the candidates for privatization by the Canada Development Investment Corp. In January 1986, Stronach had directly approached Stevens (rather than submit offers through the CDIC, as was protocol) to propose selling Canadair to a syndicate of Canadian companies, in which Magna was willing to take a 30 per cent stake, in order to keep the company in Canadian hands. Stronach bristled at the insinuation that he had used his directorship of CDIC and his access to Stevens to cherry-pick assets being sold off, and found nothing irregular in the fact that the deal would have put him on the boards of both seller and buyer. He argued that his interest had been keeping the company in Canadian hands and, in any case, he'd recused himself from discussions surrounding the Canadair sale.

Judge Parker found Sinc Stevens in breach of conflict-of-interest guidelines in respect of the January 1986 meeting with Stronach to discuss his Canadair proposal. But Stronach, who resigned from the CDIC board after the Magna-Stevens-Czapka story broke in April, didn't attract the same censure. Parker absolved him of any real conflict of interest with respect to Canadair.

In fact, though the Parker inquiry ended disastrously for Sinclair Stevens, Magna and Stronach got off lightly. But Stronach was furious that the commission had impugned his and his company's reputations. He was livid at the incumbent government (Sinclair Stevens's Progressive Conservatives), at the opposition Liberals under John Turner, and at the media for, in his terms, deliberately sensationalizing the story.

Still, no one expected that Stronach's bitter complaints against the media and politicians would see him decide to take up with both groups rather than battle against them – or that the disastrous results when he did would make the Parker inquiry look like a celebration.

7

RIDING OFF IN ALL DIRECTIONS

Given Stronach's performance before and during the Parker inquiry, he hardly seemed entitled to the high dudgeon he expressed after the nearly eight months of hearings. When the commission was announced in May 1986, his strategy had appeared to be to remain as much as possible above the fray, and to keep Magna out of it as well. His tactic had been to pronounce the perfection of his business philosophy, and hence Magna's perfection as its expression. The way Stronach explained the situation, the Czapka loan had nothing to do with Magna, and so far as the CDIC was concerned, why, he had answered the call of his friend Sinclair Stevens to assist in implementing the government's industrial policy out of a sense of public service. But instead of garnering the praise he felt he and Magna deserved, they had been spattered with political mud from the probe into Stevens's conflicts of interest.

Stronach's attempt to brush away the specks of mud smeared it into an even bigger smudge. When the media pointed out that his testimony at the inquiry conflicted with earlier statements, he claimed the press was deliberately denigrating him and Magna in order to sell more papers. The press, eager to defend its position, then focused more closely on Czapka's deal with Noreen Stevens as a rare glimpse into Magna's operating style, and shone a spotlight on its considerable real-estate activities, few of which had made it into reports to shareholders.

THE LANGSTAFF FARM FIASCO

Stronach's claim that he introduced Noreen Stevens to Tony Czapka in April 1985 because he was "not an expert in real estate" was, let's say, very surprising, given that he and Magna had bought and sold all kinds of properties since the 1970s. Moreover, his claimed lack of confidence in his aptitude in such things didn't stop him from being personally involved in Magna's land assembly in Waterloo, west of Toronto, near Kitchener, in 1985 where the company intended to build ten to twenty factories. Nor did he refrain from helping Magna speculate on land during the property boom in York Region in the middle to late 1980s, frequently turning a nice profit. Magna's standard ploy was to finagle concessions from local government using jobs as currency. But in 1986, Stronach's attempt to use the practised strategy to make Magna's biggest-ever real-estate purchase came a cropper.

The land Stronach was angling for was a 541-acre plot known as the Langstaff Jail Farm on Highway 7 between Yonge Street and Bayview Avenue on the southern border of the town of Richmond Hill in York Region. The city of Toronto had owned the land since 1911. It had originally been a self-sustaining jail farm, then a mental institution, and had been vacant since 1958. When the city announced in 1985 that it was selling the property, Magna joined local developers, who'd all been drooling at its potential, in preparing a bid.

First, knowing the competition for the Langstaff farm would be stiff, Magna laid the groundwork for its tender when it approached the Toronto Harbour Commission with a seemingly unrelated proposal to build a 400-acre corporate campus, including offices, residential units, parks and factories, in the industrially zoned (and largely contaminated) land on Toronto's waterfront. Stronach expected that the 4,000 jobs promised by the company's "port land" scheme would leave Toronto politicians slavering. But, as usual, Magna attached conditions to its project. One was that the city would rezone the land to permit the housing units that were essential to financing the plant and park aspects of the campus. The biggest condition, though, made the proposal look more like a Trojan horse than a benefit to Toronto: Magna wanted the city to give it the inside track in bidding for the Langstaff farm, one of the most valuable pieces of undeveloped land in the entire York Region.

In early 1986, when Stronach put together Magna's offer on the farm land, his partners included Alfredo deGasperis, Marco Muzzo, and Jack Rose. Muzzo and deGasperis, along with their frequent business associate Rudy Bratty, were among York's biggest developers. Magna's story was that it was interested in the land (and willing to put up the purchase money) because it wanted to build its head office and a number of car-part plants on the site, while its partners would develop the rest of the land. But as part of the deal, Magna promised Richmond Hill's mayor, Al Duffy, that it would designate about ninety acres of the farm land for development of "sports and cultural facilities." It also pledged $10 million to kick-start construction of an academy that would select and train promising youths to Olympic calibre.

Duffy loved the deal. He figured the Magna group's bid would give the town of Richmond Hill about $25-million worth of benefits, and he had no trouble getting his council's approval. He agreed to front the low-ball bid of about $45 million – the market value of the land was estimated at around $70 million – using Magna's money. Usually governments that intend to sell surplus land offer first rights to the municipality in which it is located, before asking for competitive bids. Thus Stronach believed that because the farm was in Richmond Hill, Duffy had a shot at convincing Toronto to sell the land at the discount price in the spirit of public interest.

But having the Richmond Hill mayor as a partner, may have had the opposite effect: Duffy was a controversial little guy, and in the past had violated inter-government courtesy when Richmond Hill had bought land at a good price from the province and then quickly flipped it for a $2-million profit. Toronto Mayor Art Eggleton wasn't much impressed, either, by Magna's waterfront plan as a quid pro quo for giving the Richmond Hill–led Magna group a leg up in the competition. For one thing, Magna hadn't bothered to flesh out its plans for the port lands beyond public relations releases. For another, he didn't see why Toronto, in light of Duffy's previous indiscretion, should give Richmond Hill a deal at its expense.

The city refused to give special consideration to the Duffy/Magna bid and forced Duffy to bid Magna's money, dollar for dollar, against those of the other developers. Duffy, mindful that Magna's offer to Toronto was several million lower than the other developers', could see that the $25-million windfall to Richmond Hill was going down the tubes, so he attempted to obtain the same benefit from Lou Charles, the highest bidder at the time, by threatening to hold up development approvals unless $25 million or its equivalent in land and facilities was forthcoming. Charles, alarmed by Duffy's wrench in the works, retracted his offer.

Meanwhile, deGasperis and Muzzo defected from the Magna-led bid to support the consortium of developers that ultimately won the land, as did Duffy. Incensed by what he saw as a betrayal, Stronach adopted the pose of the simple, hard-working industrialist who'd been screwed by land developers. "This country gets raped over all the time for development," he griped. Unused to losing or being out-manoeuvred, he painted the outcome as crass commercialism trampling Magna's public-spirited beneficence toward the community. Duffy, though, found Stronach's self-portrayal as a rube wronged by slick developers excessive. "He buys and sells more land than any developer does and hides behind Magna," he observed. Indeed, in the same month, May 1986, that Magna lost its bid for the Langstaff farm, Magna and Tony Czapka were working out the details of the three-for-two land swap, and Magna was arranging the line of credit that Czapka would use to lend money to Noreen Stevens.

REAL ESTATE SURPRISES

Oddly, corporate profitability didn't always appear to be Magna's primary motive in its real-estate transactions. The company occasionally lost money on a deal that benefited the other party – sometimes a friend of Stronach's or a company insider.

The land swap between Tony Czapka and Magna that was at the centre of the Sinclair Stevens conflict-of-interest inquiry was a case in point. Czapka, who continued to draw an annual $1-million consulting fee from the company, hit pay dirt on the deal. The vacant land he got for the factories in the trade with Magna was valued at about $750,000 at the time; four months later he sold it for $4 million for a $3.25-million gain. Also in 1985, he bought a scrap yard that he peddled six weeks later to Magna for an $850,000 profit.

Another curiosity that wasn't fully explored in the Parker commission was Czapka's intimation that his partners' clamouring for a closing on the land deal with Magna was the reason he demanded the letter of comfort from McAlpine that eventually connected Magna to Noreen and Sinc Stevens. Had the inquiry looked more closely at who Czapka's fiercely clamouring partners were, it might have wondered at the legitimacy of some of his explanations. His partner in Roban Holdings Inc., owner of one of the buildings, was Robin Sloan, the Magna director and executive vice-president who ran MI Realty, Magna's real-estate division. His partner in the other two was former Magna president Helmut Hofmann, who had become majority shareholder and CEO of Devtek, of which 20 per cent was owned by Magna. It was improbable, in short, that either Sloan or Hofmann would be bitching overmuch about delays in closing a deal with Magna, as Czapka claimed they were.

That nobody thought to delve into details of insider deals at Magna was mostly due to the inquiry's focus on Sinclair Stevens. Magna's parsimony with insider information didn't help. In the fine-print "interrelated parties" notes to its financial statements, Magna prefers to use terms such as "certain officers and directors" rather than to burden shareholders with details such as exact names. In Magna's 1987 annual report, for instance, no mention is made of the fact that Robin Sloan also was the buyer of Magna's structural steel business, an operation he'd previously run in the 1970s under the name Unimade and in which Stronach had been a key investor. Sloan could afford the $3.6 million he paid; he only had to put 25 per cent up in cash, and as part of his retirement package Magna had bought his 65,000 Class B shares for just over $2 million.

The disrespect that Stronach claimed Magna suffered at the hands of the Canadian government's Parker commission came in handy to explain company decisions that might otherwise have attracted bad public relations, at least in Canada. As a means of expressing his antipathy for the Mulroney government's free trade agenda, Stronach began announcing that any new Magna plants would be built in the U.S. where there was no shortage of states ready to lay out a welcome mat. "In order to safeguard ourselves, we are going to go where the environment is better," he said. "We've tried to be good corporate citizens in Canada and we have got a lot of abuse. We'll just do less here and do more where we're welcome."

Another motive for his stance may have been concern that growing protectionism in the U.S. would make it more difficult for Magna to sell Canadian-made parts in the U.S. In any case, in a move that served to emphasize his concerns, in September 1987 he pulled the plug on the industrial campus in Waterloo, where Magna had been assembling land. But in the sell-off of the now-surplus real estate, Stronach yet again found a way to reward a Magna consultant. Instead of auctioning off one 24-acre plot to the highest bidder, Magna sold it for $800,000 to Heribert Polzl (a childhood friend of the Magna chairman, and also from Weiz), who'd been buying land for Magna. Polzl, who clearly knew the property, promptly resold it within a few months for $4 million.

Of course, not all of Magna's real-estate deals were questionable. Far from it. As it grew, the company had sensibly banked land, buying at a good price where it thought it might be required for new factories. In the five-year period leading up to 1987, it had spent about $300 million on land and buildings to accommodate growth. As land values rose, its real-estate assets became a hedge against a downturn in its automotive business. In 1987, CFO Jim McAlpine told shareholders that debt shouldn't be a concern; Magna could raise cash by selling real estate and by spinning its groups off as public companies. It could and it would.

A TASTE FOR RESTAURANTS

Stronach, who regarded money as the scorecard of success, had come to see his growing wealth as evidence that his entrepreneurial genius was universally applicable. Whether or not it was true in the case of his thoroughbred stables was difficult to determine. But in the belief that he had strengthened Magna's management to the point that it was self-sustaining, he now seemed to see his role as primarily that of a watchdog, ensuring that it followed the corporate constitution. Accordingly, he had more time to indulge in interests that were more glamorous than auto parts.

It may be hard to believe now, but in the early 1980s, owning a restaurant had become a status symbol among movers and shakers. For example, the multi-millionaire developer Alfredo deGasperis, with whom Stronach teamed up in the bid for the Langstaff farm, owned a couple of Le Parc restaurants in York Region. Stronach, apparently attracted by the idea of a permanent reservation, and eager to enjoy his growing celebrity, bought the tony Le Connaisseur in uptown Toronto and opened Rooney's, a disco, in the same build-ing. There is no indication that he was concerned that Rooney's was reputed to be favoured by recreational substance abusers, and by Hamilton mobster Johnny Papalia, when he was in town. According to the *Globe and Mail*'s Margot Gibb-Clark, Stronach himself was a good customer of both the restaurant and disco, dining in the company of attractive women whom he then escorted onto the dance floor.

Though he paid for those ventures with his own money, he thought that Magna should foot the bill for Belinda's, a restaurant on Steeles Avenue, the border between Toronto and York Region. He named it for his twenty-one-year-old daughter, who had recently dropped out of her first year in university to work for Magna. He justified the investment on the grounds that it was the model for a chain that he envisioned becoming a suitable diversification for Magna. The fact that not even a second outlet was built, however, suggests that the first was a less than resounding success. In any case, Magna never thought it necessary to reveal to shareholders how much Belinda's cost them.

IN SEARCH OF GOOD PRESS

For most of Stronach's career, the press had portrayed him as a prodigy – a quirky and mercurial one, to be sure, who seemed an adherent of the Gordon Gekkoesque belief that greed is good – but who was nonetheless colourful and very successful. So, generally speaking, he got good press. But when the press turned on him during and after the Parker inquiry, Stronach revealed that he understood even less about the media than he did about the restaurant business. Displaying either a disregard for advice from his communications and public relations staff, or a talent for hiring and listening to dumb advisers, he announced he would henceforth grant interviews only to reporters who signed an agreement permitting him to edit stories prior to publication. Only after Magna vice-president Dennis Mills persuaded him that no reputable media outlet would comply with such a preposterous request did Stronach agree to modify it.

But his fall-back was almost as outrageous: he decided he only needed to *review* stories prior to publication, not edit them. Showing that he still didn't get it, he insisted on equal time in the same issue that a story appeared, to rebut anything he found negative. Naturally, the press dumped on him for that policy, too, viewing it as further confirmation that Canada's best-paid executive (according to *The Financial Times of Canada*) was also its loopiest. Stronach eventually took Mills's advice and grumpily dropped his demands. But in an attempt to save some face, he insisted on the right to tape all interviews to ensure he wasn't misquoted. His surprise that reporters didn't mind *that* request at all only confirmed that Stronach hadn't yet grasped that the media wasn't going to automatically accept and compliantly repeat without comment anything he wanted to say.

In 1986, he came up with a plan to change all this: Magna, he decided, would establish its own radio, television, and print outlets. In effect, Magna and Stronach would *become* the media.

Although many of Stronach's ideas fail to make it past the concept level, he was never hesitant about nourishing even the stranger ones with cash. Lots of cash. In fact, it was frequently Magna's money rather than his personal capital, but so long as spending on non-automotive investments didn't exceed 20 per cent of Magna's equity, a limit imposed by the constitution, he didn't have to ask shareholders for permission to invest in – wait for it – media assets.

FRANK BECOMES THE COVER STORY

The 20 per cent limit wasn't especially restrictive. Shareholder equity in 1986 totalled $346 million, which meant Magna could invest up to about $70 million in non-automotive ventures. Stronach got started on his media empire in late 1986, with the launch of *Focus on York*, a lifestyle magazine distributed free to 50,000 readers in York Region, where some 8,000 Magna employees lived. Never a piker in the pursuit of quality, Stronach signalled his commitment to the publication by poaching experienced editorial staff from Toronto magazines that couldn't compete with Magna's cash. But journalists' delight at having a new free-spender in the industry gradually faded. The concept of editorial content being free from the owner's influence continued to elude him. As good as *Focus on York* looked, the lifestyle it portrayed tended more toward Stronach's view of what an ideal lifestyle *should* be than toward reality.

The magazine's staff bit their tongues, says editor Camilla Cornell, when the boss asked them to find something for his daughter Belinda to do, despite her lack of related experience of any kind.

But Stronach's insistence that the magazine publish a cover story on him, the owner, ultimately proved too much for Cornell and Lynn Cunningham, a well-regarded magazine editor who was working for the magazine as a consultant. Both quit. "You don't write about your owner except under unusual or extraordinary circumstances," noted Cunningham, who moved to *Toronto Life*, one of Canada's most profitable publications, as executive editor.

Undeterred, in February 1987, Stronach hired Michael Vaughan, a talented business journalist for *Venture*, a Canadian Broadcasting Corporation television show that extols entrepreneurialism. By spring, Magna had also bought 45 per cent of CKAN, an AM radio station in Newmarket, a community a few kilometres north of Aurora. Vaughan, meanwhile, was given a $750,000 budget to put together a television-production facility called Tier One Communications, through which Stronach intended to communicate with Magna's workers in North America and Europe. To help cover some of its costs, it also intended to do contract work for third parties.

VISTA – FRANK'S VERY OWN MAGAZINE

Then, in June 1987, Stronach announced he was introducing *Vista*, a business publication that would celebrate and disseminate the principles of Fair Enterprise to a national audience. Unlike publications such as *The Economist* and *Business Week*, which he labelled "mediocre," his magazine was going to be positive. "The world is full of criticism," he told the *Globe and Mail*, another publication that made his list of mediocrity. *Vista*, he pronounced, would be "a form of education, a form of provocation, a form of information and a form of solutions."

Vista certainly provoked. When its newly appointed publisher John Dunlop, a veteran of the magazine business in Toronto, went looking for an editor in the spring of 1988, he discovered that journalists, recalling Stronach's earlier attempt to smother criticism by insisting on editing rights before granting interviews, were leery of working for Stronach. Eventually, Malcolm Parry, a Vancouver magazine editor, was signed to a reported three-year, $100,000-a-year contract to edit *Vista*, which billed itself as "Canada's alternative business magazine." While Parry was directing a young staff in putting together the inaugural issue, Dunlop was promising advertisers a circulation of 100,000, large by Canadian standards.

Even before the first issue hit the newsstands in November 1988, however, Parry had made waves in publishing circles when he allegedly made insulting remarks to female journalists he was interviewing for editorial positions with the magazine. Stronach may not have been particularly bothered by the accusations against his editor. He was used to operating in Magna's macho culture, which would come under fire years later for contributing to alleged sexual harassment, as would the chairman himself. He was upset, however, when the first issue of *Vista* was flayed by critics for its disjointed editorial focus and for pandering to advertisers. "The only thing in this first issue is a promise to advertisers that *Vista* will deliver an upscale, self-absorbed reader," observed David Hayes, host of a CBC television program that discussed media. When the second issue, featuring a model in lingerie on the cover and a story on an underwear designer, was similarly panned, Stronach began doubting Parry's qualification. Two issues later, Stronach replaced Parry with Rod McQueen, Magna's vice-president of communications.

McQueen had come to Stronach's attention with the fair treatment he afforded Magna and its chairman in *Blind Trust*, a 1987 book on the Parker inquiry. An experienced magazine writer with *Toronto Life*, *Canadian Business*, and *Fortune*, and a former financial editor and managing editor of *Maclean's*, McQueen brought some order out of the chaos Parry left behind. He also had the local contacts to raise *Vista's* editorial quality. Despite McQueen's impressive business-journalism background, however, in the eyes of publisher Dunlop and Stronach, his editing diverted *Vista's* focus from business and toward general interest. After only a few issues, he got the gate and was replaced in 1989 by former *Canadian Business* editor Joann Webb, who didn't last much longer.

Stronach's enthusiasm for the black-ink world of journalism was rapidly waning. The magazine never came close in editorial quality to the publications he'd earlier labelled as mediocre. It hadn't exactly led to cries for the immediate adoption of his Fair Enterprise ideology, either. On the other hand, the ink on *Vista's* income statements was all red. Stronach had budgeted $10 million to cover projected losses in the first five years of publication, far more than most Canadian magazines have to work with. By the time Webb took the job as editor in the summer of 1989, *Vista* had zipped through an estimated $6 to $8 million. It had taken about a year. Stronach, who distances himself from any failing activity for which he might be blamed, dispatched a team of Magna executives to *Vista's* lavish uptown Toronto offices, ostensibly to whip *Vista* into shape. But the turnaround team lacked any publishing background – it included his daughter, Belinda, and Don Amos, a Magna employee who'd mainly looked after Stronach's equine interests – which hinted at its real purpose. Within months, sure enough, Magna pulled the plug on the magazine, ending Stronach's publishing experiment.

DEBT – A WAVE RISING ON THE HORIZON

That *Vista* and *Focus on York* lasted as long as they did – after unsuccessful attempts to sell both, the former was shuttered in May 1990 and the latter four months later – spoke more to Stronach's ego than to financial prudence. Certainly Magna's 1987 performance provided justification for some cuts. Although sales rose to $1.2 billion from just over $1 billion a year earlier, profit slid to $40.3 million from $47.3 million in 1986.

Long-term debt cast a longer shadow on Stronach's plan to put management in the hands of his three-man executive team; it had more than doubled to $293 million in 1986, and in 1987 it hit $481 million. Magna was left with almost as much capital debt as shareholders' equity. Debt that is used to add capacity, expand business, or improve productivity can boost a company's return on investment (its ratio of net income relative to the amount invested). But in cyclical industries, it can dangerously tilt a balance sheet and accelerate a small slide into a precipitous skid, especially during an industry downturn.

And that was exactly what was on the horizon. Domestic automakers hadn't expected that their Japanese counterparts would acquiesce happily when forced to build cars in North America as a quid pro quo for selling there. In fact, they had embraced the idea, encouraged by governments eyeing increased employment. By 1987, Japanese automakers had already grabbed close to 26 per cent of the integrated domestic market in North America. Unlike American automakers, however, Japanese and Korean manufacturers that set up in Canada weren't bound by the Canadian-content provisions of the Auto Pact. Instead, they saw their Canadian operations as production centres for U.S.-bound vehicles.

Canadian *parts* manufacturers who'd hoped to get business from the Japanese car makers found them reluctant to abandon existing suppliers, many of whom they partially owned and who had followed them to North America. What was worse, these parts makers were huge, efficient, and well capitalized and had begun regarding domestic car makers as potential new customers. A University of Michigan study in 1986 had forecast that as many as 200 Japanese auto-parts companies would eventually set up in North America and capture up to 27 per cent of the domestic car-parts market. Given that scenario, Magna had little choice but to continue to spend on technology to maintain its competitive edge if it hoped to meet the Asians' quality standards. Its existing domestic customers, moreover, were not only raising their standards, but also seeking lower prices in order to compete with the Japanese and Korean car makers. Inevitably, the competitive environment squeezed margins.

To be sure, Stronach's high-profile diversions into a couple of restaurants, the Rooney's disco, and a budding media empire probably weren't a major financial contributor to Magna's ballooning debt (though an absence of information made it difficult for shareholders to determine the exact cost of Magna's new ventures). But along with revelations about his real-estate wheeling and dealing, and his preoccupation with his still-developing racing operation, there was a growing perception that Stronach was distracted from his duties as chief executive. And then there were the rumours about the potentially biggest distraction of all, his supposed ambition to win a seat in the federal cabinet – a possible stepping stone to the prime ministership of Canada.

By the time Magna's annual meeting took place in December 1987, investors had indicated their nervousness; Magna's stock price, which hit a high of $33 at one point in the year, had dipped to about $10. In what had become his trademark, a rambling address to shareholders, Stronach's stream-of-consciousness rant at the meeting included a reiteration of his objection to free trade. His primary concern seemed to be that subsidies available in Canada which put parts makers like Magna on the proverbial level playing field with U.S. competitors, would be illegal under free trade, and would lead to lower profits and a falling stock price as shareholders moved their money to U.S. companies.

The slide in value of Magna's shares had exposed a flaw in Magna's employee stock-ownership plan. It had been based on the

assumption that the value of the shares set aside for employees'
retirement would steadily increase year after year. But by December
1987, those due to retire and finally cash in were suddenly looking
at a kitty that was about one-third the size it had been at the beginning of the year. Stronach addressed the problem by guaranteeing to
pay about $20 each for the shares of employees with ten years' service
who would be retiring in the next five years. But the solution didn't
offer much consolation to those shareholders who weren't employees, and whose money would now be contributing to the bump-up
of retirement funds.

Nor were shareholders buoyed by Jim McAlpine's forecast that
1988 was shaping up to be even less profitable than 1987, and that
auto production was likely to be flat for five years. All the same, they
voted in favour of management's latest restructuring plan that
renamed its operating groups as Atoma, Tesma, Decoma, and Cosma,
supported by two new entities, Diversa and Ventures, both of which
incorporated businesses that didn't fit with core automotive groups.
Ultimately, Stronach said, Magna intended to spin off the operating
groups into separate, publicly traded companies in which Magna
would continue to hold a majority share. Cosma International, a
company created to consolidate Magna's body-panel stamping plants,
was to become the first stand-alone operation. Mike Hottinger, a
former member of the parent company's executive team who'd
moved to Cosma as vice-chairman, noted that Magna would realize
capital when it sold some of its Cosma shares en route to turning it
into a publicly traded company.

IN PRAISE OF MAGNA'S ACHIEVEMENTS

Notwithstanding the current travails, Magna was still an indisputable
phenomenon in Canada, and in North America, a company that had
fundamentally changed car-parts manufacturing. Its small-plant
structure gave it nimbleness. Its autonomous management, driven by
incentives, had been organized under more sophisticated management

teams heading groups that were slated themselves to become independent public companies, clones of their parent. Its readiness to bid contracts of all sizes, then deliver quality products largely made with tooling of its own design and manufacture, had made Magna the most diversified company in the industry. Competitors such as Dana Corp., a Toledo, Ohio company, specialized in such things as chassis and axles, but by 1987 Magna manufactured thousands of different car parts, ranging from hood and door latches, mufflers, dashboards, and bumpers, to body panels, drive-trains, and seats.

In fact, Magna president Fred Gingl believed that Magna's diverse product range gave it an edge in the future. His forecast in 1986 that the company would soon take on complete design, engineering, and assembly of entire vehicles on behalf of its giant customers didn't seem all that outlandish. Magna's non-union cost structure would permit it to put a profitable, relatively low-volume niche model in showrooms without disrupting customers' economical, high-volume assembly lines. It didn't hurt, either, that Magna was based in Canada. Its costs were incurred in Canadian dollars that in 1987 were worth about 25 per cent less than the U.S. dollars it received in payment for its products, most of which flowed south of the border under the Canada–U.S. car pact. Indeed, exchange rates made Stronach's threats of moving to the U.S. ring a little hollow; doing so would have been disadvantageous. But it also made Stronach's tirades against the bogeyman of free trade hard to understand; the Auto Pact, after all, amounted to free trade in the auto sector, and it hadn't damaged Magna's competitiveness.

On the other hand, free trade made a good platform upon which to run for office.

POLITICS AND MAGNA

Unquestionably, Stronach recognized the role politics could play in Magna's fortunes. An unspecified portion of the 2 per cent of pre-tax profit that Magna's constitution dictates the company will spend on "social responsibility" each year goes to political parties as well as to cultural, charitable, and educational causes. From the mid 1980s it appeared to be unwritten policy that Magna and its subsidiaries should have at least one former elected official on their boards. William "Bill" Davis joined Magna's board in 1985, shortly after retiring as Ontario's Progressive Conservative premier. When he left the position in 2001, Stronach filled it with Mike Harris, who was also a former Ontario premier, and also with the PC party. But, loath to take sides politically, Stronach would seek pols of any stripe. The Liberal party was represented on Magna boards by two other former premiers, David Peterson, who was Ontario premier from 1985 to 1990, and Brian Tobin, who led Newfoundland from 1996 to 2000. Even the lefty New Democratic Party was briefly represented; the NDP's Bob Rae, who succeeded Peterson at the helm of Ontario's government in the early 1990s (and who would become a federal Liberal leadership candidate in 2006), held a position on a Magna company board for a short time. Federal politicians whom Stronach thought could help Magna included Ed Lumley, the former Liberal industry minister who had originally involved Magna in the Cape Breton project, Doug Young, a cabinet minister in the Liberal governments during the 1990s, and former Magna executive Dennis Mills, who had left to be a Member of Parliament in the 1990s, returning to Magna after his 2004 defeat. In 2005, Stronach would also entice, with a salary of more than $700,000 (U.S.), Paul Cellucci, former U.S. Ambassador to Canada, to join the board of his racetrack company, MEC.

For all Stronach's claimed non-partisanship and proud identification with the working classes, most observers assumed that his sympathies generally lay with the right-leaning, business-friendly Progressive Conservative party. But if that was so at the time that Sinclair Stevens was first elected, he was less enthusiastic about the Tories after Stevens resigned. Furious at having been enmeshed in the conflict-of-interest charges that ended Stevens's political career, Stronach was also annoyed that his own perception of the value of his wisdom and guidance wasn't shared by the country's leadership. Prime Minister Brian Mulroney, attempting to put some space between himself and Sinc Stevens, wasn't about to listen to Stronach's treatise against free trade, a major plank in Mulroney's political platform. It was perhaps a measure of Stronach's growing self-importance that he was offended by the prime minister's refusal to take his calls. "I find it incomprehensible that the PM never granted me an audience," he snorted to the *Globe and Mail*.

FRANK STRONACH, LIBERAL

If the Conservatives weren't interested in Stronach's contribution, his long-time friend, Dennis Mills, a Magna vice-president of communications and a former aide to Pierre Trudeau, most certainly was. He had long seen Stronach as a potential asset to the Liberal party and had worked to make sure he met the right people. In 1983, he'd managed to get Stronach a seat at Trudeau's so-called "last supper" attended by friends and supporters. By 1988, Stronach had decided that Canada needed him and Fair Enterprise. Mills, who was preparing for his own Liberal candidacy in a Toronto area riding, urged him to approach John Turner, leader of the party, about seeking the nomination for the federal riding in which Stronach lived.

Stronach had to swallow hard to do so. He'd shown little fondness for Turner, whom he'd accused of turning the Liberal Rat Pack on him during the Sinc Stevens affair. But Turner, as Mills suspected, needed a few star candidates. So he welcomed the high-profile, and, more importantly, perhaps, extremely well-funded, Frank Stronach. Doing his best not to appear presumptuous, Stronach insisted that he hadn't made his candidacy contingent on any assurance of a cabinet position in a Turner government. But he then admitted to presumption. "I have more influence now as head of Magna than I would as a backbencher," he told journalist Stevie Cameron in a 1988 interview. "I think I could bring some sanity and some discipline to government, as well as a framework to help the economy."

Perhaps mindful of the fact that his already full plate of interests might become a topic of discussion with respect to Magna's results, he held off disclosing to shareholders that he'd added a seat in Parliament and a cabinet post to his aspirations. But in early 1988, when he announced that he was putting his voting control of Magna in the hands of management, few doubted the reason. Stronach could seem to be erratic while bouncing his latest ideas around, but there were some predictable patterns to his behaviour. Disliking the media coverage he and Magna had been getting, he went into the media business to do it his way. Now, having failed to interest the Mulroney government in adopting his socio-economic theories, he decided he would become part of government and do that himself, too.

So on April 18, 1988, Stronach handed the job of CEO to Fred Gingl in order to seek the Liberal nomination in York Peel, a new suburban constituency that had been created in a rejigging of federal ridings. York Peel, as it happened, encompassed much of the York Simcoe riding that was held by Sinclair Stevens.

THE CANDIDATE FROM MAGNA

Stronach's inclination to throw resources (preferably Magna's) at projects wasn't an option when running for Parliament, thanks to election-spending restrictions designed to discourage plutocrats from buying their way into office. The limits, however, didn't apply at the earlier stage of seeking the party nomination to run. Backed by a campaign machine that included political consultants and full-time staff (some of whom were paid as Magna employees), Stronach hoped that by slathering cash around the riding to gain the nomination, any name recognition bounce he got would resonate until the actual election campaign.

The bid for the local Liberal nomination by Canada's wealthiest wannabe politician became an exercise in wretched excess. After being introduced at a beauty pageant at a Portuguese community centre, he donated $15,000 to the centre in the name of Magna's many Portuguese workers. He provided buses to transport retirement home residents to a park for the day. And full-page campaign ads proved a boon to local newspapers (one of which Magna partly owned), who recognized Magna as the employer of many of their readers.

He used his position at Magna just as effectively, initiating factory "information meetings" that he maintained were to educate employees about the impact of free trade. Occasionally, his enthusiasm got the better of him. Magna at one point offered to pay $10 per employee ($25 per family) to underwrite membership in the local Liberal party so employees could vote on the candidate of their choice. Stronach hastily ditched the plan when its illegality was pointed out to him, blaming the scheme on overzealous campaign workers. On the nomination day, though, he made sure that employees got time off or had shifts changed so they could attend a free barbecue with live music that he threw.

Burton Pabst, his one-time partner, had left the Magna board, but was still a consultant for the company and recalls Stronach's campaign as something of an internal joke because of its overkill. "He'd truck in whole busloads of employees to yell and stuff," chuckles Pabst. "It was kind of fixed." Few of the newly enfranchised Liberals – 1,000 of the party's 3,000 new members were Magna employees or family members – failed to take the opportunity to exercise their voting right. In the end, Stronach spent $20,000 to $30,000 on his nomination campaign and breezed to a win over Tom Taylor, a long-time Liberal riding worker, whose total nomination budget was $9,500.

INTO THE ELECTION: "LET'S BE FRANK"
Turner may well have had some moments of trepidation at the prospect of Stronach winning the election, slated for November 1988. Toeing the party line, any party line, had not historically been

Stronach's long suit. If anything, he was more inclined toward contrariness with respect to tradition and ideals that he hadn't initiated. But before the campaigning was under way, Brian Mulroney's Conservatives had some issues to settle as well. Chief among them was whether the party should endorse Sinclair Stevens, badly tainted by the Parker inquiry. As the Conservative candidate, he'd be running against Stronach. In the end, Mulroney robbed Canadians of the prospect of the former friends facing off; he refused to authorize Stevens's nomination in the riding.

Once the election campaign began in the fall, Stronach again put his money to work, festooning virtually every vertical structure in the riding with his catchy "Let's be Frank" and "Bring FRANKness to Ottawa" posters and signs. He also did his best to appear a Liberal team-player by taking on the co-ordination of the party's annual Confederation Dinner, a major fund-raiser. His arm-twisting methods, though, raised some hackles. Leaning on friends to buy $3,000-a-table tickets was standard procedure in the position. But the *Globe and Mail's* Stevie Cameron reported that Stronach instructed Magna's head office staff and many of its plant managers to push the tables on their business associates and suppliers to pry ticket money out of some who might otherwise have avoided the event. Some clients received numerous letters and follow-up phone calls, which they found annoying enough. But a few were even more displeased by the distinct impression that their future contracts with Magna could be considered firmer if they attended the political function – and perhaps less firm if they didn't. Although Stronach failed to see even a smattering of coercion in the message, he backed off when the complaints threatened to attract negative publicity. Ever the Teflon tycoon, he implied that the letters had been his managers' idea. "My managers are non-political, but this worry about free trade is the reason they are so supportive of the Confederation Dinner," he said. He seemed genuinely mystified, however, that any supplier would take umbrage at the political demands of a customer. "If Roger Smith [chairman of GM] calls me for something," he observed, "I'm not going to argue with him."

It wasn't long before Magna's corporate announcements were apparently being skewed to his political purpose. Vehma International Inc. was a new Magna division created to co-ordinate the design and engineering of a prototypical car-model. Fred Gingl had earlier indicated that Magna hoped to produce, under contract, 8,000 to 10,000 vehicles catering to a niche market for Chrysler. Stronach saw the project as an opportunity to push his anti-free-trade agenda. To emphasize his threat that the assembly plant – and its jobs – might go to the U.S. if the Conservatives were successful in negotiating a free-trade agreement, Stronach arranged to make the announcement about the new venture in Detroit, rather than Canada.

Throughout the campaign Stronach continued to attract controversy related to his non-political affairs. The "Frank Stronach" cover story in *Focus on York*, appearing in the July/August 1988 issue just as he began campaigning, became an embarrassment when its editors departed in protest against what they regarded as shameless self-promotion. Before it published its first issue, *Vista* magazine, a pulpit from which he'd hoped to evangelize with his Fair Enterprise sermon, became embroiled in a dispute with Adrian duPlessis, the writer of a major feature critical of the wild and woolly Vancouver Stock Exchange. DuPlessis claimed his story had been edited beyond recognition and sought to enjoin *Vista* from publishing it.

FRANK CHALKS UP A FAILURE

Still, as a political candidate, Stronach presented a formidable challenge for John Cole, his Conservative opponent in York Peel. A Newmarket optometrist and town councillor, Cole delayed announcing his intentions until Mulroney denied Sinc Stevens the party endorsement, just two weeks before the campaigning period began. Reminded by the Stronach posters plastered all over the riding that their candidate couldn't compete with the auto-parts mogul financially or in name recognition, his campaign strategists turned to substance rather than image.

It had been duly noted by Cole's advisers that "Let's be Frank," memorable though it was, didn't actually mean anything. They were also aware that Stronach's platform was based on Fair Enterprise, to which he attributed Magna's success and which he posited could do the same for Canada. Some bright person on Cole's campaign team, having apparently been subjected to Stronach's magic-marker-enhanced depiction of Fair Enterprise, recognized it as interminably boring, and also saw that Stronach was obsessive about presenting it at every opportunity. Cole's strategy, recalled in *One Hundred Monkeys* (Robert Mason Lee's 1989 book on Canadian politics), was to make sure there was a blackboard and chalk on stage at every all-candidates' meeting, and to have a shill in the audience innocently invite Stronach to elaborate on how government should operate. "Stronach always rose to the bait and started in with his lecture," a Conservative strategist told Lee. "There was absolutely no doubt: the more we could expose him, and keep him talking, the more votes we had." The strategy worked to perfection. Cole whipped the free-spending Stronach by an embarrassing 6,700 votes, as the pro-free-trade Mulroney Conservatives steamrollered the Liberals and the NDP, who split the anti vote, across the country.

The election was notable for a couple of related events. Magna's Dennis Mills, like Stronach a self-promoter and free-trade opponent, won his Toronto seat as a Liberal. So did Stronach's former fellow-CDIC director Paul Martin Jr., launching a political career that would see him become Canada's most influential finance minister and, eventually, prime minister – the sort of future Stronach had envisioned, but had now seen dashed.

8

MAGNA ON THE BRINK

"**N**aturally I'm disappointed," Stronach told his supporters after losing the election. "I know I could have served the country quite well." But the chairman's failure to gain a seat in Canada's federal government in November 1988 may have been the best result for all concerned. Accustomed to operating in a high-octane environment that *he* controlled, Stronach would not likely have represented his constituents effectively, working at the glacial speed of Parliament. And had he been elected as a Liberal in the Tory sweep, his cabinet ambitions denied, he'd have been reduced to sniping at the governing party from the opposition benches with little hope of promoting his own ideas. Stronach's loss, on the other hand, spared parliamentarians his incessant lectures on Fair Enterprise. Even Stronach himself, after expressing initial regret, almost seemed relieved in defeat. At first he displayed the characteristics of a politician in accepting no personal blame and attributing the loss to kismet, or at least astrology. "It's written in the stars, and life goes on," he said. But in refusing further comment, he dropped the pose of a people's-choice politician and reverted to corporate chief.

The group probably most anxious following Stronach's election loss was Magna's management. When he'd left to run for Parliament in April 1988, Stronach had handed the CEO's job to Fred Gingl. But the executive team of Gingl, Jim McAlpine, and Mike Hottinger had not arrested the profit slippage that had begun early in 1987 and continued after Stronach left. Despite a 25 per cent lift in sales ($1.5 billion versus $1.2 billion), profit for the 1988 fiscal year (ended July 31) plunged by more than 50 per cent, to $19 million from $40 million in 1987. Worse, 48 of the 70 cents in earnings per share in 1988 came from asset sales, mainly real estate. Gingl and his team could have certainly pointed out that Stronach, CEO for all but four months of fiscal 1988, bore some responsibility for the lousy results. But it was just as certain there would be no attempt to pin the loss on the boss.

The question became whose imprint would be on the *next* fiscal year's results. Would Stronach leap back into the breach or would he let Gingl and his team continue? Throughout the early and mid 1980s, as chairman he had okayed massive capital expenditures and expansion that resulted in an unprecedented level of debt for the company. When the industry began to slump in 1987, Magna was left with over-equipped, under-utilized plants – albeit thoroughly modern ones. The downturn, deeper and longer than expected, then strangled earnings, which made debt service problematic. In fact, the spending on plants and equipment had made sense. It would pay off once auto production levels recovered to soak up excess capacity, and the new technology boosted productivity.

In the meantime, though, the situation presented a quandary for Stronach. While seeking a seat in the government, he'd been able to disassociate himself from Magna's slide in fortunes. Now, if he immediately resumed control of the company, and Magna's financial situation continued to go downhill, he knew that he, rather than his lieutenants, would draw the flak. Furthermore, if he snatched the CEO's job back, it would be an admission that his protegé, Gingl, wasn't up to the job, and that he'd erred in selecting him.

STRONACH, THE BACK-SEAT DRIVER

Stronach decided to stand off. Reaffirming his faith in management, he indicated he would continue on as chairman but would remain disengaged from Magna's day-to-day automotive business while tending to personal interests and Magna's non-automotive ventures. But according to Fred Jaekel, president of Magna's Atoma division at the time, the likelihood that Stronach would keep his hands off the wheel quickly became something of an internal joke among Magna's managers. "He never left," says Jaekel, who in those days considered Stronach a mentor and friend. "He said later, 'I'm coming back,' but he never left. He just used that."

Stronach, who turned fifty-six in 1988, had no shortage of interests and activities – and concerns – outside of Magna's core business in which he could immerse himself, to give the impression that he was easing away from the core automotive business. His involvement in horse racing had metamorphosed from a hobby into an obsession and a huge personal enterprise, but one in which prestige was perhaps greater than profitability. The retirement of his headline horses from the early 1980s had been followed by a dry period in which he made few winner's circle appearances. And although he boasted in 1985 that his horses had won $700,000 in purses at North American tracks and that his breeding operation had $500,000 in sales in the same year, some horsemen suspected his return on investment was low. Stronach had fed the perception in 1984 when he sold 400,000 Magna Class A shares to raise about $7.5 million. When a shareholder at the annual meeting in December wondered what kind of signal it sent when the CEO began selling shares, he'd joked, "If you question me further, I might have to say some of my horses didn't run fast enough."

Nevertheless, in August 1989 he significantly added to his breeding operations with the purchase of Adena Springs, a magnificent 640-acre farm near Lexington, in Kentucky's fabled bluegrass country. The same year, his luck seemed to turn for the better when all three horses he paid $3.5 million for were thought to be good enough to race in the seven-race Breeders' Cup series, considered the world championship of racing, that was being run in November at Gulfstream Park in Florida. However, only one of them, Mi Selecto, ran, and it placed last.

Few doubted that Magna's Challenger jet would take Stronach to Florida for the race. Clearly, Stronach regarded the jet as a perk that was untouchable. Though he made it available on occasion to worthy causes, in keeping with Magna's constitution, he appeared to be the main arbiter of what was worthy. It helped if the cause had public relations value or appealed to him personally. In 1986, for instance, Marilyn Darte, the pretty skip of a glamorous, world-champion Canadian women's curling team, injected a touch of sex appeal into that sober sport with what passed for daring dress at the time. Stronach had hitherto showed no interest in curling. But when he offered to fly the Darte team to a bonspiel in Magna's jet at company expense, the team suspected that Stronach's motivation was something other than a sudden enthusiasm for curling.

TURNING HOBBIES INTO BUSINESS

Stronach, ever the entrepreneur, seemed incapable of looking at or participating in any activity without extrapolating its potential as a revenue stream. If something fascinated him, he seemed to believe, it only needed the right promotion to similarly capture the interest of a much broader audience and become the basis of a business. Furthermore, given his view that he and Magna were one and the same, he didn't find it untoward that Magna should fund some of his schemes. From his horse racing activities in the early 1980s, for example, he'd perceived a need for durable stabling. Using Magna's metal-handling capability, he created StallMaster, a company that manufactured steel stable stalls. He put his sister Elisabeth's son, Werner Czernohorsky, in charge of the venture. Gerry Belanger, his on-again,

off-again trainer who had seen his share of stalls, says the idea was ter-
rific and the "model suite" Stronach donated to Woodbine Racetrack
in Toronto is still in use. But few horse owners actually proved willing
to pony up, as it were, to buy the stalls, and Stronach shut it down
and moved Czernohorsky to another position within Magna.

Because Stronach was an avid tennis player, he thought Magna's
shareholders would be pleased to capitalize a business around that
enthusiasm as well. In January 1989, he put up $500,000 of Magna's
money to create Sports Products International Inc. (SPI). Although
the intent was to market clothing and an exclusive line of tennis
racquets made in his native Austria, Stronach was at least as interested in the company as an athletic hothouse. Athletic ability in his
beloved horses was to some extent innate, born and bred, but not so
in humans. Talent could be nurtured, he appeared to believe, by
selecting those who showed promise and underwriting their training. He'd first floated the idea in 1986, when he proposed developing world-class Olympians in an academy on the Langstaff farm in
Richmond Hill. The SPI program awarded seven promising American
and Canadian teenagers on "Team SPI" between $12,000 and $15,000
each to use SPI equipment in tournaments. The idea was that equipment sales, boosted by the athletes' tournament success, would fund
the program on a self-sustaining basis.

Tennis pro Don Steele, a sometime tennis partner of Stronach's
and former executive director of Tennis Canada whom Stronach
hired to run SPI, wasn't surprised when SPI shut down within a year.
Although he'd admired Stronach's tenacity as a tennis player, he
found him less focused off the court. "I found him initially easy to
deal with and good at dealing with problems, but he lost interest and
it became quite frustrating," says Steele. "I'd go into meetings and he
was all keen, and then suddenly there was no communication. He
had trouble focusing . . . He just shut it down."

Stronach was also an avid skier. He maintained a lodge in Beaver
Creek, Colorado, to which he flew whenever he had a chance.

Believing there were enough others of similar means ready to emulate his lifestyle, he bought property near his massive chalet and had his friend Aurora architect Steve McCasey design the $55 million (U.S.) Vista Resorts. In 1989, the foundations were poured and Stronach assigned Edward Parent, who had once headed up MI Realty, Magna's real-estate division, to manage the project, whose fifty units, built around a main lodge, were priced at about $2 million (U.S.) each.

Other ventures in which he had invested Magna's money weren't exactly roaring along. *Vista*, the alternative business magazine, had seemed in the throes of self-destruction almost from its inaugural issue in November 1988. Meanwhile, *Globe and Mail* reporters were embarrassing Stronach by suggesting that Magna sold land for less than market value in return for a personal favour. In a letter to the *Globe*, Stronach angrily denied the charge, and further denied that he or Magna were involved in land speculation. But in reiterating his usual claim that he and Magna were paragons of transparency, he overlooked the fact that Magna's shareholders only learned through newspaper reports just prior to the annual meeting in December 1989 that their company was in the ski-resort business.

MAGNA'S FIRST LAYOFFS

While Stronach was ostensibly dealing with his extracurricular ventures in 1989 and keeping out of running the company, Magna continued to stagger. Results for the third quarter of 1989, issued in April, showed no improvement in profit. He'd hoped to distance himself from Magna's deteriorating financial situation, but had not been as hands-off as he'd promised when he turned the day-to-day operations over to Gingl, McAlpine, and Hottinger. A letter above the signatures of Gingl and McAlpine that stunned employees in May 1989 had Stronach's fingerprints on it: it announced head-office layoffs and an end to company-subsidized car phones, and warned that existing vehicle leases paid for by Magna wouldn't be renewed when they ran out. The layoffs at headquarters, unprecedented at

Magna, were shocking enough. Magna employees didn't regard leased cars and phones as perks so much as benefits that offset salaries below industry levels. Conditions that Magna placed on the layoffs, moreover, flew in the face of the fuzzy, family feeling Magna liked to believe it had incubated: the company told the fired employees that if they refused to sign a non-disclosure agreement regarding conditions of their severance, or if they contested their dismissal, they would be ineligible for more than the minimum two weeks' salary.

The hapless Gingl, left to explain the layoffs, bungled the task. He refused to reveal how many employees got the chop or lost leases and car phones, and tried to downplay the situation as a shifting around of jobs. Swiping a tactic from Stronach's PR handbook, he adopted a policy of responding only to written questions. "I'd like to see nice precise stories written, which are of genuine interest," he said.

FRANK KILLS THE TORRERO

There were more clear signs that Stronach's return to the executive office was inevitable. Early in 1989, Gingl had introduced a specialty vehicle that Magna had spent $8 million and a couple of years developing. Gingl presented the vehicle – dubbed the Torrero, and featuring four-wheel-drive, a 535-horsepower engine, space-age materials, and a buffalo-hide interior – as a demonstration of Magna's ability to design, engineer, and co-ordinate the assembly of low-volume vehicles on a contract basis. An exotic-car enthusiast, Gingl was justly proud of the prototype. In terms of the yet-to-occur boom in SUVs, some of which are nearly as monstrous in size as the Torrero, the souped-up "concept vehicle" wasn't as weirdly excessive as it seemed when he introduced it. But with car sales slipping, prospective production-partners weren't lining up to launch a new model, especially one like the Torrero that had a selling price of about $200,000.

Disappointed that Chrysler had abandoned the project (to the extent that Chrysler didn't even want it known that it had been the initiator of the project), Gingl still hoped to attract a partner willing to underwrite production of a more modest version of the vehicle, built by Magna under contract. In the event that no manufacturer came forward, he suggested that Magna could take on the project itself. Had this happened, Magna would have launched the first SUV. Stronach, however, instantly put paid to that idea. The last thing he wanted was to give Magna's automaker customers the impression that Magna intended to compete with them by building cars. Leaving little question as to who was calling the shots, he was crystal-clear in contradicting his CEO. "We are not going ahead," he announced definitively in June 1989. "We never intended to. Never."

In some respects, the Torrero decision was a watershed in the affairs of Magna. When he'd left in early 1988 to run for office, Stronach had felt that Magna was pretty much on cruise control. He'd believed the reorganization of the 120 plants into "automotive systems groups," a first step in his spinoff strategy, would require only a light touch on the wheel from the young executives he'd left in charge. If they temporarily lost their way, he was available – at least when he wasn't attending to another of his growing interests. Now, while making no immediate move to oust Gingl, Stronach's readiness to countermand and embarrass his CEO in public served notice that he was not pleased. His experiment in creating a self-perpetuating management was not going as planned. Instead of thriving, Magna was disintegrating.

THE EAGLE PREMIER FAILS TO TAKE WING

In a sense, Magna had become a victim of its own strategy. Its policy had been to accommodate customers, primarily the Big Three North American automakers – in any way it could to get and keep contracts. But expansion, the engine of Magna's spectacular growth, turned out to have a hidden hazard: whenever Magna built a plant to fulfill a contract for parts in a new vehicle, it amounted to a bet that the car would be a success. American Motors Corp.'s new Premier model exemplified what could happen when the company bet wrong.

The Premier had initially seemed like a good deal for Magna. The car was projected to have a production run of about 150,000 units annually. In 1986 Magna's Cosma subsidiary had signed a contract to supply body panels for it that would have seen Magna's content per Premier reach $1,400, compared to Magna's average CPV of $132 in 1989. Assisted by a $10 million grant from the federal government and another of equal value from the Ontario government, Magna had expanded its Karmax metal-stamping plant in Milton, Ontario, to handle the contract. The Premier failed to attract buyers, however, which helped to precipitate the sale of AMC to Chrysler in 1987. After rebadging the Premier as the Eagle Premier, Chrysler couldn't sell many either, and pulled the plug on the model in 1992. The move left Magna's $187 million plant operating well below the capacity level at which it was profitable.

Nor was Magna's effort to get more business from Asian car makers proving overly successful. By the late 1980s, the Japanese already had a quarter of the car market in North America and all indications were that their market share would grow. But the Magna content in Japanese vehicles was valued at only about $50 compared to at least $150 in cars made by the Big Three. As the Japanese share of car sales increased at the expense of the North American car makers, Magna stood to lose ground. Even when it lowballed bids to get a foot in the Asian producers' door, it lost. In one instance, it bid so aggressively to get a job that it had to go hat in hand to the manufacturer for price increases, never an impressive tactic. "Every part we shipped cost us a few dollars," Stronach lamented to the *Report on Business* magazine.

MAGNA STRUGGLES WITH INDUSTRY CHANGE

The 1988 Free Trade Agreement with the U.S. that Stronach had campaigned against proved to have little impact on the Auto Pact or on Magna's operations. While competition from the Japanese and a bad bet on the Eagle Premier had hurt Magna, it was Magna's missteps in its response to structural changes in the North American auto sector that led it into trouble. Carrying on a trend begun in the mid 1980s, domestic OEMs accelerated the outsourcing of production to fewer suppliers, whom they involved more in the design and engineering of subsystems. These so-called Tier 1 suppliers sold directly to car makers on longer contracts, doing subassembly work using components they manufactured themselves or that they purchased from Tier 2 or Tier 3 suppliers.

For Magna the change seemed to be an opportunity to add more value to its products and increase profits. It had become an article of faith that spending in the short term on plant capacity and technology would improve productivity. Since it already did much of its tooling and equipment-manufacturing in-house, buying parts from itself seemed a logical progression. Through vertical integration, the argument went, Magna would be able to control quality and delivery better.

To accommodate its elevation to Tier 1 status, in 1988 Magna reorganized its operations into what it called Automotive Systems Corporations (ASCs) based on four core groups, Atoma, Cosma, Decoma, and Tesma, each of which provided modularized systems directly to the OEMs. Vehma International, a design-oriented group added in 1988, and Symatec, an engineering-support group created in 1989, brought the number of ASCs to six. A central objective of the ASC structure was that each group would establish its own identity in dealing directly with OEMs, and once mature enough, would be spun off from Magna as a public company. Each ASC had its own management to whom operating units reported directly. The rationale was that the ASC group structure would add more focused, professional management heft, with the financial, legal, and marketing skills to establish a foundation for even greater growth. In theory, management would be more closely attuned and responsive to their plants' interests, leaving Magna's head office free to develop overarching corporate strategy and handle financing under the Magna umbrella.

The structure was successful in that the growth mandate of the systems groups attracted aggressive young managers, whose bonuses depended on pre-tax profits. They went after all the business they could find, sometimes competing with other Magna groups for contracts. The unfortunate effect was to depress prices, narrowing margins. Meanwhile, Magna was footing the bill for their expansion to take on the new business. When it was needed, Magna would finance a new plant. And when Magna was asked to, it would buy the latest technology and equipment to go in it.

All of this expansion, however, had a startling effect on Magna's balance sheet. Magna, the parent, had financed the growth of the ASCs with debt. In 1988, Magna's long-term debt had stood at $631 million. By the end of fiscal 1989 (July 31), it was up to $702 million. That wasn't immediately alarming because, since at least 1982, Stronach's plan had been to spin off the "groups" as public companies. The concept hadn't made much progress, but now the grit of the growing debt gave it some traction. The plan was to start with Cosma and Decoma, and to use the proceeds from the initial public offering of shares (IPO) to pay down some of the money owing. In the summer of 1989, McAlpine was putting the finishing touches on a share offering that was expected to raise $114 million.

Cosma, with $704 million in sales, had grown into Magna's biggest division, accounting for about 37 per cent of the parent company's total. Decoma, whose sales of $510 million made up 27 per cent, wasn't far behind. Together, they contributed $83 million to Magna's net income. The Bank of Nova Scotia, in particular, was eager to see Cosma spun off, since it held $245 million in Cosma-related debt. The $52 million that Magna hoped to raise through the

Cosma IPO was to be given to the bank to relieve that pressure. Magna also planned to peddle 25 per cent of the equity in Decoma, the division that manufactured trim parts and wheels and plastic components, to raise another $62 million.

STRONACH GRABS THE WHEEL

But before McAlpine could finalize the prospectus, Stronach, who had been giving directions from the back seat, leaned forward to wrench the wheel. In September 1989, on the eve of the scheduled share issue, he astonished Magna-watchers and shareholders by suddenly cancelling it. That grab at the wheel sent Magna into a near-fatal skid that would last almost two years.

Magna's abrupt change of direction reminded many industry watchers of when Stronach, the chairman, and Gingl, the CEO, had seemed to be on different pages with respect to the Torrero's future. The sudden departure in October of McAlpine, a key member of the three-man executive and Magna's CFO, now suggested that the chairman had issues with him as well. Unaccountably, the normally ebullient McAlpine was incommunicado. Since Stronach wasn't commenting either, analysts – and shareholders, with whom Magna had always claimed to be completely open – were left to speculate on what had changed the company's mind.

One theory was that Stronach realized the two subsidiaries would have been a tough sell, given forecasts of a slump by U.S. car makers, who were customers for about 82 per cent of the two groups' output. The release of dismal financial statements in October 1989 supported the view. Magna reported fiscal 1989 sales of $1.9 billion and a profit of $34 million. But the profit had been propped up with $64 million from the sale of real estate and another $8.7 million from the sale of an earlier private placement of Cosma and Decoma shares. When the non-operating items were stripped out, Magna had actually lost $38.7 million.

This was new. This was a crisis.

COST-CUTTING OUT OF THE CRISIS

In light of the dire state of Magna's finances, Stronach had begun to doubt that spinning out the groups was a good idea. Even though Magna would still control Cosma and Decoma, the presence of more shareholders would complicate his hope of regaining control of what he viewed as runaway costs. Now, in 1989, Stronach emphasized his return to Magna's driver's seat by making sure the cost-cutting message reverberated through the entire company. Though hardly material to Magna's results, the subsidized cafeteria was shut down. Magna employees were still reeling when Stronach offered his own explanation for the dramatic changes: on a tour of the six automotive systems corporations, he'd been shocked and alarmed by what he claimed were opulent offices, bloated management, and excessive executive salaries.

Stronach began to address the problem by slimming down and otherwise dismantling the ASC group structure put in place only a year earlier. In his view, the structure, intended to add efficiency, had swollen into a layer of bureaucracy. The worst of it was that the ASCs had earned the enmity of the factory managers, the very people who had been the cornerstone of Magna's success. They now felt they had been dictated to by the ASC management, which was siphoning off too much of the profit. What bothered Stronach most was that the bill for the overspending by the six ASCs was sitting on Magna's books in the form of debt that threatened to sink the company.

Stronach and Gingl began hacking away at the bureaucracy. The reorganization effort, which focused on shaking up the management of Magna's operating groups – Cosma, Decoma, Tesma, Atoma, Symatec, and Vehma – wasn't an unqualified success. It terminated some executives, as intended, but some that they hadn't wished to cut left of their own accord, thinning out Magna's management bench strength. One who departed was Jim Nicol, a lawyer who had headed Decoma and was considered one of Magna's brightest lights. Mike Hottinger, who'd moved to Cosma as vice-chairman in anticipation of its going public, returned to Magna, and was trying to arrange the purchase of some of Cosma's stamping operations. Instead, he was fired, and, like many who suffered the same fate, sued Magna, charging that it hadn't lived up to the terms of his employment contract.

BRINGING IN FAMILY

To beef up the restructuring team, Stronach conscripted two family members. One was Don Walker, an ambitious young engineer hired away by Stronach from General Motors in 1986. Walker had proved a manufacturing adept who moved quickly up the ranks to vice-president of corporate development. From there, Walker had caught the attention of another Stronach – Belinda, Frank's daughter, whose ascent at Magna proved, depending on your point of view, that education was entirely unnecessary to succeed at Magna, or that having the right name was essential to it. Since dropping out of university in 1985, she'd showed such promise in her work in everything from clerical level jobs to personal assistant to the chairman, that in 1988 Frank Stronach had invited her, at twenty-two, to join Magna's board. She and Walker married in 1990.

The second family member on Magna's weight-reduction team was Werner Czernohorsky, Stronach's nephew. Stronach insisted that Czernohorsky, whom he proudly claimed had worked his way up from the shop floor to a management job in Magna's real-estate division, was a worthy choice as a Magna vice-president. Fred Jaekel ventures that Czernohorsky's willingness to act as an executioner for Stronach made him even more worthy. While Walker's role on the restructuring team was primarily evaluating businesses, Czernohorsky's was to be the axe-wielder who announced layoffs and cutbacks.

1989 – A DIFFICULT ANNUAL MEETING

Magna's fiscal 1989 numbers provided ample potential for volatility at the annual meeting of shareholders in December. Stronach promised that his new team would restructure Magna to staunch the outflow and boost profitability. But the cost was great. Restructuring costs of $30.3 million, which included such things as severance payments and retirement allowances in connection with layoffs, had helped drag down net income. Magna's habit of dramatically overpaying departing executives, in exchange for their silence through extensive non-disclosure agreements (still integral to the secretive Magna culture), proved expensive. McAlpine, who had earned $466,000 in fiscal 1989, and who knew where all the skeletons were, received a "retirement allowance" of $700,000, a $3-million consulting contract, and an insurance policy whose $103,000 premium Magna was paying. Despite claiming a severe case of the shorts, moreover, Magna scraped together $1.7 million to lend – at zero interest – to Czernohorsky, so that he could buy Magna stock.

But it was Magna's swelling, long-term debt that grabbed the most attention at the meeting. The cancellation of the Cosma and Decoma share offerings that McAlpine had been working on had had repercussions. The $114 million in expected proceeds had been earmarked to pay down some of Magna's obligation. While many analysts doubted it would have made too big a dent, without the $114 million as a brake, Magna's snowballing debt picked up momentum and became an uncontrollable avalanche, approaching a horrendous $1 billion by the end of 1989. Magna's debt-to-equity ratio of 1.48:1 meant it owed $1.48 for every $1 of equity shareholders owned in the company. This was not good.

Shareholders had already expressed their concern about a stock price that had spiralled down to the $9 range from its fifty-two-week high of about $16. When Magna slashed its 12-cent quarterly dividend in half, they had even more reason to be testy. Magna called the move a cash conservation measure, but at the same time it had found enough to boost Chairman Stronach's annual stipend to $1.2 million from the $935,000 he'd taken in 1988. Shareholders weren't inspired, either, by the news that Stronach had been dallying in

Colorado condos with Magna's money, or that the company had posted a $9.9 million loss for the first quarter of 1990.

Sashaying back and forth across the stage of Toronto's Roy Thomson Hall, Stronach did his best to deflect responsibility for the company's straits onto Magna's executives as he outlined restructuring changes he'd already begun. "When I walked away, I left too much on the plate for our management team," he told the audience. Overlooking the fact that he hadn't resigned as chairman of the board that had approved all management's projects, he suggested that rising debt and sinking profits in his absence had come as something of a surprise, but that he would in any event be addressing them, "and to do that I am going to call the shots and direct the traffic flow."

In a style that was part philosopher-king and part Catskills stand-up raconteur, Stronach tried to make light of some issues brought up by shareholders. He thanked the *Globe and Mail* for free publicity in revealing the existence of the Colorado ski chalet development, which he insisted was a great opportunity. But he castigated *Toronto Star* reporter Jim Daw for being "inflammatory." Daw's crime, in Stronach's eyes? He'd revealed that Stronach had received a $240,000 pay raise. He blamed the substitution of coffee and sandwiches for the usual beer, wine, and buffet at the annual meeting on cost cutting. "Word gets around," he joked, noting the lower than usual attendance. Magna employees, he added, would share stockholders' pain. "I have also closed the corporate dining room and now they telephone out for pizzas and fried chicken," he said.

Gingl, who had seen his Torrero plans countermanded by Stronach and now faced the return of the former CEO, perhaps had reason to resent Stronach's self-portrayal as what one analyst called an improbable "caped crusader of cost-cutting," setting out to correct the wrongs from Gingl's eighteen-month watch. Instead, he remained the faithful factotum. Responding to a shareholder who asked about Stronach's participation in a federal trade mission to Russia during

Magna's hour of need, Gingl observed, "If our chairman of the board is a national treasure, I guess we have to share him."

MAGNA HEADS TOWARD JUNK STATUS

Despite promises made by Stronach and Gingl at the meeting, not much improved. All the cuts to spending didn't address the $1-billion lump of accumulated debt. The Dominion Bond Rating Service (DBRS), a Canadian credit-rating agency, figured that was far more than the $300 million it considered appropriate for an auto-parts company of Magna's size to carry. It also felt that Magna's intended $200-million capital expenditure plan exceeded what would be reasonable for a company losing money. Although Stronach had scoffed at the notion that the mighty Magna would fail to meet its obligations to lenders, DBRS thought otherwise. In February 1990, it downgraded Magna's commercial paper (short-term debt, often in the form of unsecured bonds that mature within a year and that companies frequently use for such things as operating capital) to junk status. The move meant that lenders who bought the paper in the future would expect to be paid a considerably higher interest rate to account for the greater risk of default. The higher interest rate, in turn, raised Magna's operating costs. Furthermore, institutional buyers are prevented from buying debt classified below "investment grade," so a major market for Magna's commercial paper disappeared.

The credit downgrade slammed the door on expansion. Undaunted, Stronach saw opportunities in Europe that he thought would broaden Magna's customer base. In his native Austria, where Magna had a couple of minor operations, he invested in a joint venture with the state-controlled steel company Voest-Alpine Stahl AG, creating Automobiltechnik AG, which sold welded steel subassemblies and parts to European automakers.

In North America, though, things were getting bleaker. In March he had to negotiate a standstill agreement with lenders that would permit him to pare costs, divest unprofitable operations, and put together a debt-restructuring plan.

The cost-cutting team found plenty of flab in operations as well. Peripheral businesses that couldn't be sold were summarily chopped. By the spring of 1990, Belinda's, the one-restaurant chain that Stronach had started, the Newmarket radio station CKAN, the Tier One multimedia operation that had helped prepare his political campaign material, the publications groups that put out *Vista* and *Focus on York*, and the Colorado ski-resort development had all been sold or shut down. In the unkindest cut, Magna announced that its Challenger jet, Stronach's ultimate symbol of corporate power, was up for sale.

In streamlining Magna's groups, Stronach's goal was to return to the model of smaller units run by plant managers that had been so successful in building the company. He also sought to raise $50 million by selling 25 per cent of Atoma, which made seats and wheels. When no Canadian buyer emerged, he sold the stake to Mitsubishi Corp., a Japanese company.

Not everything went on the block. Vehma International, the design and engineering group that had worked on Gingl's Torrero, escaped the crusher. In fact, it got a new lease on life when the city of Los Angeles awarded it a $300-million contract to design, engineer, and assemble electric vehicles based on GM vans. Stronach, who liked to see himself on the cutting edge of technology and social trends, saw the move into so-called green-power ventures as an expression of Magna's forward thinking. Using its own battery technology and components from its plants, Magna expected to build 1,500 units by 1991, with more production dependent on future orders.

But not many of the other groups escaped the scythe. All told, the reorganization team proposed selling twenty plants, turning two into joint ventures with partners, and eliminating another sixteen through closures or mergers. The scale of the downsizing, however, created yet another problem. Since it was permanent rather than an operating adjustment, Magna's auditors insisted that the company take a writedown.

SHARES SINK, ALONG WITH EMPLOYEE PENSIONS

Not surprisingly, investors had long been acquainted with Magna's plight. By the time Stronach reluctantly requested a halt in trading in March 1990, pending his announcement of a $153-million writedown of assets, Magna shares were trading at $6.75 each on the Toronto Stock Exchange. The writedown triage – essentially a declaration that Magna was walking away from the investments and applying the loss against earnings – lopped another 26 per cent off the stock, deflating it to $5.

No one was more aware of the decline than Stronach. At $5 a share, the value of his Magna holdings had plummeted to about $4 million, only marginally more than he'd spent for three horses a year or so earlier. More tellingly, the plunge savaged the retirement fund for employees, the alternative to a pension plan that was an integral part of Stronach's Fair Enterprise system. In 1986, when Magna had 10,300 employees, shares in the fund had had a value of $55.6 million, an average of $5,400 per employee. When the CAW warned at the time that the deferred share-ownership plan was risky compared to a conventional pension such as, for example, its union members enjoyed, Stronach had dismissed the suggestion as a union-organizing ploy. But in 1990, the union felt vindicated: the value of the fund had collapsed to only $8 million, an average holding of less than $500 for each of Magna's now 16,000 employees.

In 1987 when a dropping share price had imperilled the employee fund, Magna had offered to pay a premium to purchase shares of employees who were retiring, ensuring that they wouldn't lose money. But even if non-employee shareholders were willing to go along with such a plan now – doubtful, considering their own losses – it was no longer an option that Magna could afford to offer. It had no cash to spare.

Naturally enough, employees' sympathy for Stronach and for Magna management in general, began to disappear. From 1986 to 1990, they'd seen their retirement funds wither; during the same period, a handful of top executives had taken home over $12 million in compensation and the chairman had been tootling around in a company jet. Now ownership of the shares in the company, which Stronach claimed to be an incentive to work harder and which was a cornerstone of his Fair Enterprise thesis, was turned on its head vis-à-vis employee productivity. If their shares' increasing value was an incentive to work harder, why wouldn't the *devaluation* of the shares lead to declining productivity? "When you're going through a cash crunch, there are lots of problems with morale," admitted Stephen Akerfeldt, McAlpine's replacement as Magna's CFO. "People have to make adjustments to how they operate."

Certainly Magna did. Many of Magna's loans had covenants requiring it to maintain certain levels of financial performance. The $153-million writedown the auditors had demanded had put Magna in default of those obligations, raising the spectre of creditors seizing assets as security, petitioning it into bankruptcy, or taking control of the company.

THE BANKS SEND IN HIRED GUNS

None of the creditors was prepared to go quite that far. Yet. But, after the writedown was announced, the Bank of Nova Scotia, believing Stronach had been dawdling on the restructuring, forced him to bring in forensic accountant David Richardson of Ernst & Young to monitor its and other banks' interests. Stronach reportedly wasn't pleased at the optics of Richardson's forced appointment. The accountant had recently been in the spotlight while handling the bankruptcy of Osler Inc., whose principals were jailed for their part in what was at the time the biggest stock brokerage collapse in Canadian history. His presence raised concern that he'd taint Magna with an undeserved whiff of fraud. In fact, that never happened, and Richardson chaired a debt-restructuring team that consisted of himself, Stephen Akerfeldt, and Magna general counsel Jory Kesten. But Stronach still regarded Richardson, hired by the banks to protect their interest, as an unwelcome mole within Magna, someone who had the right to challenge him.

Stronach, who doesn't do humility well, was forced to swallow hard in dealing with debt-holders in order to save the company that had been his life's work. At fifty-eight, he'd irritated enough people through his career with his pious hectoring on the benefits of his Fair Enterprise credo that his and Magna's predicament now generated more *schadenfreude* than it did sympathy. Magna, it seemed, had been led by an autocratic, would-be emperor who was now unclothed.

Both the federal and provincial governments had a more visceral concern than the comeuppance the investing public might feel Stronach was due. Auto-parts and assembly operations accounted for nearly 33 per cent of Canada's exports. That the biggest auto-parts concern in the country was hobbled by debt raised the exposure level of the entire economy. Notwithstanding his crafty historical facility for snaring government grants he felt were Magna's due, Stronach's pride, which, depending on your point of view, either bordered on arrogance or defined it, prevented him from grovelling publicly for handouts.

But he was aware of Magna's integral role in the Canadian and Ontario industrial strategy. Magna was a major employer, a point with which he'd seldom missed a chance to impress governments. Magna was also one of the largest buyers of raw materials such as petrochemicals, and it was a customer of Stelco and Dofasco, Ontario's two biggest steel companies. If the government became worried enough about Magna's collapse to offer financial help, Stronach had ready precedent to justify accepting. Only a few years earlier, Lee Iaccoca, chairman of Chrysler, had sought U.S. government help; it had resuscitated Magna's biggest customer.

In the absence of assistance from the government, Stronach put the arm on his customers, knowing that they also relied on Magna.

When starved for cash to keep daily operations going, Stronach dispatched Gingl to swing by the offices of the Big Three automakers to request an acceleration of payment of Magna's receivables. Gingl returned to Markham with $60 million in his pocket, enough for Magna to continue battling.

MISSTEPS IN A DIFFICULT TIME

Whether he was waiting for a buyer to come forward or simply trying to separate what to keep from what was disposable to raise cash, by the summer of 1990, Stronach's failure to make a major cut had exasperated creditors. So far as they were concerned, getting rid of the high-profile but relatively low-value media companies, and closing a few plants, was just window dressing. He still hadn't pruned anything approaching a major trunk from the complex Magna family tree.

Moreover, Stronach's botching of some transactions hadn't boosted the confidence of his creditors. For example, in late 1989, Stronach sold 25 per cent of Atoma to Mitsubishi to raise $50 million to help Magna. Tony Czapka and his son, Peter, had been 50 per cent partners with Magna in Multimatic. Earlier, without informing the Czapkas, Stronach had sold Magna's half of Multimatic, along with some debt, to Atoma for $5.2 million. This had violated an arrangement that gave the Czapkas right of first refusal to buy the Multimatic shares. So when Stronach did the Atoma–Mitsubishi deal, the Czapkas contended they were due a share of the $50 million. While the two parties eventually settled, it was messy.

A lawsuit launched by Mike Hottinger claiming he was owed $840 thousand in severance and wages was also settled out of court in August 1990, but the fact that it was launched at all suggested another case of carelessness as Magna struggled to recover.

RE-ENTER JIM NICOL

Finally, in July 1990, recognizing that the major debt-holders were nearing the end of their patience, Stronach made one of his best-ever decisions; he persuaded Jim Nicol to rejoin Magna to oversee the restructuring. Nicol, former head of Decoma, had departed when Stronach returned in 1989 to begin meddling with the management of Magna's groups. A lawyer and graduate of the London School of Economics, he had the ideal qualifications to work on Magna's restructuring. Furthermore, he had credibility with Magna's creditors; in his pre-Decoma days, he had worked on the restructuring of Dome Petroleum and Massey-Ferguson.

Nicol also held the respect of the banks (and Richardson, their emissary within Magna), and Magna clearly had to work with them if it was going to reach some accord with creditors. Led by the Bank of Nova Scotia, they were threatening to emasculate Stronach by forcing him to put his voting shares in a trust that they would control. The banks had reason to force the issue. At 1990 fiscal year end (July 31), debt sat at about $1.1 billion and Magna's plants were operating at an unprofitable 50 per cent capacity. Although layoffs had hit 900 (180 of them permanent cuts), and Stronach was promising to raise $400 million, the banks thought there was still some culling to be done.

MAGNA HITS BOTTOM

At the December 1990 annual meeting, a chastened Frank Stronach confessed to shareholders that the company wasn't yet out of the woods. Few needed to be reminded. Dividends, which had been cut in half the previous December, had been eliminated altogether in June of 1990. Their stock, which had traded at more than $16 within the previous year, had cratered to $2. Stronach described how he and Nicol had already pared debt to $846 million in the five months since the 1990 year end. But Magna's success in restructuring the rest of its major loans, he admitted, would depend on the willingness of debenture holders to defer repayment of the $75 million they were owed by the end of the year.

The proposal, instead of placating creditors, infuriated them. Magna wanted the debenture holders (mainly insurance companies) to accept payment spread over the first half of 1991, with a higher interest rate as compensation. In the meantime, it proposed, Magna would pay off the banks. The debenture holders, apoplectic at being put behind the banks, threatened to let Magna default on December 31, and then force it into bankruptcy.

Recoiling at the response they got, Nicol, Akerfeldt, and Richardson retreated to come up with a Plan B. To soothe debenture holders, they persuaded Magna's lenders to provide bridge financing so they could repay them. To make the loan more digestible, they got Stronach to make a personal contribution. At the same time, they asked Magna's board to form a committee of independent directors, led by former Ontario premier Bill Davis, to ride herd on the situation. The testy debenture holders bought the arrangement, giving Nicol and his team the six weeks they needed to put together a plan for the rest of the debt.

With time, Nicol and Richardson came up with an elegant solution. Part of the problem from the outset had been that much of the debt had been taken on by Magna, the parent, to fund the operating groups' expansion. Cosma, Decoma, et al., had indeed grown, but the debt remained parked on Magna's books. It seemed logical to Nicol, Akerfeldt, and Richardson to shunt about $560 million of Magna's debt off onto the groups and to take some cash back in return.

First, to the four groups with plants, they sold the land and buildings they were using. To get the money to buy the assets, the groups had access to the bridge financing that Magna's bank lenders (and Stronach) had agreed to provide. The banks were more comfortable having Magna's operating groups owe them money than they were with having Magna's debt on their books. Unlike the parent company, the operating groups at least had secured assets – real estate, equipment, buildings, receivables, and the like – that, in a pinch, could be seized and sold.

There was still the matter of $286 million in debt left at Magna. The amount seemed manageable, but $160 million of it was due by

May 31, 1991. Since the groups had used up the bridge financing, the company could only cobble together $100 million. Recognizing that nobody in Canada was likely to pony up the difference, Stronach figured U.S. investors, not as familiar as Canadians with Magna's woes, would respond to an issue of convertible debentures. His hunch proved correct when he raised $110 million in the U.S. with a debt issue that closed a few weeks before the May 31 deadline.

That Stronach put up his own money to make up the difference was noteworthy, though he never revealed the amount of his contribution to the bridge loan, or whether the bankers insisted that he have some skin in the game. Stronach later related to Martin O'Malley, one of his ghost-writers, his satisfaction at having thwarted what he perceived as an attempt by creditors to strip him of control of Magna. "He'd managed to outflank the accountants," says O'Malley. "He was quite proud of that."

TURNAROUND TIME

By September 1991, it was clear that the restructuring had been a stunning success. Sales in fiscal 1991 increased 5 per cent to $2 billion from $1.9 billion a year earlier. Profit rose to $16.5 million compared to a $224-million loss the year before. The fact that Magna had turned itself around despite a 12 per cent decline in vehicle sales was even more impressive. Total company debt was still about $700 million, but the banks, happy with their security, were now onside. There was no one pushing to fold Magna or dump Stronach, as had been suggested during Magna's darkest days. Although it was difficult to identify how much of the spectacular turnaround could fairly be credited to Stronach, he had clearly helped spearhead it after returning to active duty at Magna in 1989.

Magna continued to have an overhang of debt, but even a mild recovery in the auto business, combined with a lid on capital expenditures, would enable Magna to pick away at it. Stronach was feeling so confident that he bandied about the notion of buying back the minority position in Cosma held by Bank of Nova Scotia, as well as the shares in Tesma, Magna's drive-train group, that the Canadian Imperial Bank of Commerce owned. Styling himself as a poster boy for debt reduction, he took to proclaiming in interviews that debt is evil. He also vowed to amend Magna's corporate constitution so that future managements would be forbidden from permitting debt to exceed 50 cents for every dollar of equity. But he never did.

An atmosphere of bonhomie prevailed at the annual meeting in December 1991. Shareholders were delighted at the recovery of their stock. It had bottomed out at $2 when Magna was teetering on the abyss, but was now trading at $19, an 850 per cent boost. Stronach, blessedly forgoing his customary sermon, basked in deserved accolades for overseeing the greatest recovery in Canadian business history. While it would be overstatement to describe his performance as humble, he did acknowledge the role of Jim Nicol in Magna's rescue. Wooing Nicol back to Magna to oversee the financial restructuring team had been an inspired move. Determined not to lose him again, he appointed Nicol as Magna's vice-president of corporate development.

Stronach had already done some management "restructuring" to deal with Magna's recovery, as well. Doubtless glad to see the back of Richardson, who returned to his practice at Ernst & Young, he felt Akerfeldt and Kesten, the Magna employees who'd worked with Richardson, were too expensive at $225,000 each. He also may have regarded them as allies of Richardson. In any case, both left the company.

To carry on with the corporate rejigging, Stronach, now fifty-nine, announced that he and his CEO Gingl were stepping down from the day-to-day operations, yielding management to a five-man executive made up of vice-presidents, a group of loyalists that included two family members. In addition to Nicol, the group included Werner Czernohorsky, in charge of administration; his now son-in-law Don Walker, heading operations; CFO David Copeland; and veteran Magna executive and lawyer Brian Colburn, looking after human resources. Gingl, an imaginative tinkerer, happiest when trolling for new ideas that he could translate into a new product or way of doing things, was assigned the role of product and technology development.

Stronach was not really leaving, of course. In the new scheme of things, he planned to devote his energy to "strategic initiatives." The immediate goal, he told shareholders, was to build on what Magna already had – a thoroughly modern auto-parts manufacturing operation, as a result of the free-spending expansion in the late 1980s – to create an industry powerhouse. Three years earlier, such a vow might justifiably have been dismissed as merely another instance of Stronach's hubris. But few who'd watched Magna's narrow escape from near-death could deny that there was something special about the dimpled toolmaker from Weiz and the company he'd created. And as he would prove over the next decade, as he entered his sixties, he was just getting started.

9

A KINDER, GENTLER - AND RICHER - FRANK

If tension defined the mood at Magna during its battle to survive, cautious euphoria prevailed as it became clear that the patient had not only survived, but was gaining strength. Surgery on the debt had left Magna a leaner, more efficient company. Sales, closure, and consolidation of plants had reduced the number of them to 75 from 110 and cut the work force to 14,600 from the high of 17,500 in 1989. At the same time, the $1.5 billion spent on technology and new plants in the late 1980s had created one of the most modern auto-parts operations in the world. But the best news for shareholders came in March 1992, when it was announced that Magna would pay a dividend for the first time in two years.

Stronach himself emerged from the ordeal claiming to be a kinder, gentler Frank. Not known for teary contrition, or even for acknowledging any weakness, he admitted that the flop of his non-automotive projects, his rejection at the polls, and then the crisis at Magna, had rattled him. "Sometimes you wake up in the middle of the night and your wheels start turning," he said. "You know there is a flaw here and you got to fix this and you have a hard time falling back to sleep." He conceded that he may have deserved some of the negative press. "Over the years, it might have been that I sounded a bit abrasive or know-it-all," he allowed. "There was a perception that I was not disciplined, that I was all over the map." The born-again Frank, he added, would "have a little more of a low-key approach to everything."

One move Stronach had made during the financial restructuring doubtless left him sleeping a little easier. Insider trading reports show that in February 1991 his 697,929 B shares, the ones representing voting control of Magna, were now safely tucked away in a family trust controlled by his wife, his children, and him. As a trustee, he intended to continue voting the trust's shares, which represented a 61 per cent voting control of Magna, to impose his wishes on the company. But the move also put control of Magna further out of the reach of creditors. As an estate-planning item, too, it had been a good one. It amounted to an estate freeze that fixed the shares' value at their current low price for tax purposes; any dividends and future gain in the shares' value would be taxable in the hands of Stronach's heirs.

An equity issue that raised $95 million in late 1991 was a vote of confidence from the market and the proceeds were spent on debt reduction, a point on which Stronach had become evangelical. Magna did even better in 1992, posting a profit of $98 million on sales of $2.4 billion. As Stronach saw it, once auto production recovered, Magna's plants, which were still operating at less than full capacity, would capitalize on their new technology to increase productivity and profits. "We have fewer of them so now we can focus and fine tune and get more efficient," he observed.

SITTING PRETTY ON CAR SEATS

The sensational growth of Magna's seating-systems business was an example of the prospects that, ironically, some of the debt had made possible. In 1984 Fred Gingl had read about a new technology for making car seats called "foam-in-place." Developed by a German company, Grammer Seating Systems, the new process involved bonding pieces of pre-cut upholstery to the seat foam, instead of stitching them around the form. Though Magna had never before made any kind of seat, Gingl could see the potential. When Grammer, prompted by Chrysler, went looking for a North American partner, Gingl seized the opportunity; in 1984, Magna and Grammer entered into a joint venture. Over the course of the next few years, Magna refined the technology. The seat systems it developed – the seat itself plus the assorted sliders and hardware associated with it – were less costly to make, more durable, more comfortable, and lighter than those made using older methods.

Chrysler had already been a primary buyer of the seats in the late 1980s, but Magna hit a homer in 1990 when Chrysler's mini-vans, fitted with more seats than a normal car, became the hottest-selling vehicle in the auto market. By 1992, minivan components accounted for 20 per cent of Magna's total sales. The $200 million Atoma had spent to build and equip two plants to manufacture foam-in-place seats had contributed to its debt in 1989, but was paying off by 1991, when Magna was cranking out seats for Chrysler, Ford, and their minivan competitors. Helped by its seat contracts, which boosted Magna's minivan content to about $1,000 per unit, Magna's average content per vehicle reached a new high of $173 in 1991; by 1992, it was up to $190.

In 1992, Kenneth Kidd described in a *Globe and Mail* article the frenetic pace at which Magna worked in its seating plants to keep up with the orders:

> Magna has come a long way from its days as a mere metal-bender, and its seat business neatly sums up the more demanding environment in which it must now operate. As production starts at Chrysler's Windsor assembly plant, the paint shop sends Magna an electronic order for seats, spec-ifying not just the variety of colours, styles and fabrics, but the exact sequence needed to match the minivans scheduled

for assembly that day. Magna then has a mere four hours to line up and pack the required seats, in precise order, before a truck arrives to cart them off to Chrysler for immediate installation. There's little room for error: the Magna plant keeps an inventory of only 900 seat sets, about 10 per cent less than Windsor's daily production of minivans.

Magna's Karmax stamping plant in Milton, Ontario, which had almost gone bust after the Eagle/Premier failed, also typified the rise in capacity and the innovative use of technology at Magna in its recovery years. Instead of expanding the plant to handle higher volumes, the plant's manager and staff devised a way of moving metal blanks in two directions through the giant presses that stamped them into doors, trunk lids, roofs, and the like, adding 33 per cent to the plant's capacity. By altering the way dies used to produce parts were made, and incorporating them into automated production lines, the tonnage of blanks handled was increased from 1,400 to 4,400 kilograms an hour. By October 1994, the *Globe and Mail*'s Tim Pritchard reported, the Karmax plant was running "flat out, three shifts, six days a week, making steel fenders, doors, trunk lids and other body pieces." Employment had tripled and "every day, 154 trucks haul[ed] away parts" to plants in Canada, the U.S., Mexico, and even for shipment to Europe.

Magna's simpler plants benefited from technology as well. For example, Cam-Slide, a factory that made seat hardware, window mechanisms, and gear shifters, one of the first buildings on the property slated to become Magna's new corporate campus and world headquarters in Aurora, introduced computer-controlled pallets that could be directed along different assembly lines so that window components for different models could be produced simultaneously, avoiding changeover time.

Under Don Walker, vice-president of operations, Magna was happily accommodating the needs of the "new domestics" as well.

Believing that it had missed Asian business by not being involved in the early engineering stages of model planning that was done in Japan or Korea, Magna paid more attention to the expansion of European manufacturers who had begun looking at North American assembly operations. It was repaid with a contract from Volkswagen AG in Germany to supply bumpers to a Mexican plant from Magna's own new 100,000-square-foot factory in Mexico, and another to supply body parts for a new BMW sports car being built in South Carolina. Although the BMW Z3 was to be a low-production niche model, Magna's content per vehicle was about $1,300.

TOP DOLLARS

Magna's senior executives had suffered during the years when the company was struggling to survive. Their compensation, which included a relatively low base salary plus a bonus based on profit, had plummeted when the company was losing money in 1989 and 1990. For example, both Stronach and Gingl stumbled along on a paltry $200,000 each in 1990, compared to $1,175,000 and $588,000, respectively, the year before. As soon as the company's bottom line turned black, however, Stronach wasted no time in rewarding his executive team, and himself, for steering the company back from the brink. Total compensation for the top seven executives in 1991, the year of the turnaround, was $3.7 million. A year later it tripled to more than $12 million.

The five-man group that Stronach, in December 1991, had picked to run the company (Jim Nicol, David Copeland, Werner Czernohorsky, Don Walker, and Brian Colburn) sufficiently impressed investors that the stock price had risen from the mid-$20 range in late 1991 to $35 in mid 1992. To keep it moving in that direction, Magna granted 50,000 stock options to each of the team members. Stronach and Gingl got an even bigger incentive, options on 775,000 shares and 100,000 shares respectively. The options awarded Nicol and Copeland, however, were soon looking more like a reward for past performance than an inducement to work harder. In October 1992, they announced they were leaving Magna.

MAGNA'S CONSULTING GRAVY TRAIN

The market immediately put a value on the departing executives' talent. Magna's stock price dropped 10 per cent on the announcement. The reason that Nicol and Copeland offered for their sudden departure was that they'd come on board in the first place as a restructuring team and the company now needed more operational management. "The kind of sophisticated financial skills Dave [Copeland] and I have are really no longer required," said Nicol, in announcing his and Copeland's intention to pursue other restructuring projects.

Stronach, however, didn't appear to believe their services were no longer needed. Like Jim McAlpine before them, they got juicy consulting agreements from Magna, which proved more lucrative than the paycheques they'd received while working for the company as employees. McAlpine was still collecting on his $3 million, three-year consulting deal; Nicol and Copeland each got one-year contracts that paid $67,000 a month – $804,000 each for the year, a combined total of $1.6 million. The rest of their retirement arrangement made it look even more like a negotiated deal. Again, as he had when Jim McAlpine resigned, Stronach asked that Nicol and Copeland sign agreements not to compete with Magna for three years. And to keep quiet about any goings-on at Magna. In return, he awarded them $100,000 retirement allowances, and forgave the $100,000 housing loans each had received.

Werner Czernohorsky, Stronach's nephew, left Magna at the same time. That he claimed he was leaving Magna to pursue a career as an administrative consultant was greeted derisively in some quarters within the company. Like Stronach's other relatives at Magna, he'd risen quickly; he'd gone from odd jobs, such as handling a horse-transport business and running the StallMaster venture for Stronach, to eventually becoming his uncle's assistant, available for special assignments. Perhaps because Czernohorsky had the least to lose in terms of popularity, Stronach had made him the designated hit man, the one to deliver downsizing news throughout Magna during the staff and departmental cutbacks in 1989. Czernohorsky's tendency to leave wreckage in his wake had earned him the nickname Werner Chernobyl, according to Fred Jaekel, who describes Werner as a "bull in a china shop."

Jaekel, who set up Atoma, Magna's latch and seat hardware group in the mid 1980s, had first-hand experience dealing with Czernohorsky. Jaekel believed, and still believes, in the Magna ethos of profit-sharing and management incentives. He'd become one of Magna's highest-paid managers under the system and had done his best at Atoma to follow "the Magna Way" to develop employee loyalty and dedication within the operations he managed. He had solid evidence that the approach worked. Under Jaekel, Atoma's sales had gone from $79 million to $689 million, boosted by the growth of the seating systems line for Chrysler's hot-selling minivans. But Czernohorsky had showed up amid the cost-cutting campaign in early 1990 and demanded that Jaekel cut his staff like everyone else. No dice. Jaekel refused to dump loyal staff who'd performed well. "Those people had made sacrifices for Magna," Jaekel says. "What happened wasn't their fault."

Called on the carpet by Stronach after Czernohorsky reported his intransigence, Jaekel, who admits that being one of the highest paid of Magna's line managers made him a "burr on Frank's ass," told the chairman he wasn't going to violate the trust he'd built in employees who'd helped set up the two seating plants. Stronach fired him. A few months later Stronach recognized that in backing Czernohorsky, he'd lost one of his most valuable managers. In a rare admission of error, in the spring of 1990, he apologized before the board and rehired Jaekel, assigning him to the Tesma division that made engines, transmissions, and drive-train components. While

Jaekel continued to regard Stronach as a friend, it was not the last of the fiery exchanges between them.

As for Czernohorsky, he was hardly short-changed when he left Magna. In addition to giving him a $3-million "retiring allowance" similar to McAlpine's, Magna retained him on a five-year consulting contract at $20,833 per month ($250,000 a year or $1.25 million in total). If nothing else, the nearly $3 million in retainers guaranteed to Nicol, Copeland, and Czernohorsky must have comforted Stronach that he had enough consulting firepower on tap to handle any restructuring or administrative problems that might arise in the near future.

EXIT GINGL

Still to be cleared up was the future of Fred Gingl, Stronach's avowed loyalist, still nominally CEO. Gingl had decided it was time to move on. That, at least, was the public spin put on things. But with three of his five-man executive team already gone, and Gingl wanting out, Stronach desperately needed new blood. Don Walker, father of his first grandchild, Frank Jr., might have been a candidate for CEO. Stronach instead added the title of president to Walker's chief operating officer's responsibilities and declared that he was on the hunt for an outsider to become CEO.

This time the market seemed satisfied with the news. The share price, which had dropped when Nicol left a month earlier, had already recovered by November 1992, when Stronach made good on his promise with the hiring of John Doddridge, fifty-two, president of Dana Corp., a Toledo, Ohio-based parts company, as Magna's new CEO and vice-chairman.

To make room for Doddridge, Stronach offered Gingl a graceful exit strategy that appealed to his protegé's entrepreneurial bent and interest in technology. Stronach set him up as part owner and CEO of Aeon Automotive Inc. (later changed to Torrero International Corp. when it was discovered the Aeon name was taken), a 50 per cent joint venture with Magna. Magna bootstrapped the company by contributing to the partnership four plants that supplied engine and transmission components to automakers. The solution included yet another Magna executive insider getting a gigantic payoff. In addition to the 100,000 Magna options he'd already received, Gingl's retirement allowance came to $3.8 million. He also got a four-month consulting contract worth more than $133,000 a month for a total of $532,276. .

Gingl, who financed his share of the Aeon business with his retirement allowance and proceeds from the sale of some of his shares, did his best to spin the ownership of his own company as a "car fanatic's" dream come true. "Now I'm not just the president, I'm the owner," he said. Although he didn't see himself as having been pushed out of Magna, he had an odd way of expressing the future he might have had. "I could have stayed at Magna and kept moving up," he said – ignoring the fact that he'd already been president and CEO, about as high as it was possible to go without becoming chairman, an unlikely prospect while Stronach still drew breath.

In the event, it wasn't long before Gingl concluded that he'd cut a bad deal. For one thing, the plants that Stronach had put into the Aeon-Torrero venture were distinctly not the ones on which Magna had overspent to upgrade with technology, so he had no engineering base on which he could build. What's more, it turned out that being a fifty-fifty partner of Magna's didn't necessarily mean that you were an *equal* partner. In October 1993, he negotiated what amounted to a make-good when Magna put up 45 per cent of the cost of Blau KG, a company based in Gingl's Austrian hometown of Weiz that made fuel-handling equipment. As a majority shareholder, Gingl finally had control of his own company.

JOHN DODDRIDGE, THE CEO FROM OUTSIDE

Doddridge, who left a sound career at Dana, began his new job full of enthusiasm. Taking the job, he said, had been a matter of heeding the counsel he'd always given Dana managers, that calculated risks led to greater rewards. "Frank was twisting my arm, and I woke up one morning, looked in the mirror and said, 'Hey dummy, why don't you take your own advice? This is the kind of company you've always thought could really go somewhere and do something spectacular.'"

The plan was that Doddridge, who had a reputation of being a solid asset manager with impeccable industry contacts, would operate out of Detroit, as part of a triangular management, with Stronach and Don Walker at the other corners. Doddridge saw his role as strengthening relations between Magna and its bread-and-butter contracts with the Big Three automakers. It was also expected he would take a more structured approach to running a company that was huge and growing rapidly. Industry analyst Ted Larkin of Bunting Warburg Inc. in Toronto said, "Doddridge brings some of the management skills of a large organization that will help them with the transition to becoming a larger supplier. He's a good catch for them."

After Doddridge's arrival in the executive suite, Stronach announced that he was moving permanently to Switzerland, setting up a consulting company called Frank Stronach & Co., and embarking on a program of developing Magna's business prospects in Europe. Doddridge wholeheartedly agreed that Europe was the next big opportunity for parts makers as car makers rolled out global strategies. That Stronach would spend much of his time out of the country might also have had some appeal for the CEO.

It certainly appealed to analysts and investors, who rested a little easier when the chairman allowed his managers to manage. They viewed Doddridge as a capable manager with outside experience who would be a low-key, conservative foil to the mercurial Stronach. Within a month of his arrival, the market had clearly got the impression that Magna was at last maturing from an entrepreneurial, risk-taking company into a more professionally managed outfit, and Magna's share price hit $41. By mid 1993, it was trading at $52 on the Toronto Stock Exchange, and at $41 (U.S.) on the New York

Stock Exchange to which Magna had changed its listing from NASDAQ in 1992.

Doddridge, appreciative of the vote of confidence, candidly admitted that his experience at Dana, considered one of the industry's best-run companies with a promote-from-within approach, hadn't totally prepared him for the job at Magna. The recent shake-up, he noted, meant that most senior managers had only been at the company slightly longer than he had. He compared his new relationship with Magna to "getting married without dating."

Doddridge also confessed that acclimatizing himself hadn't been easy. Six months after joining Magna, in May 1993, he found that splitting his time between Detroit and Toronto was making it tough to settle into a leadership role as CEO. "It caused me to have to be in Toronto a lot," he said. "That's one aspect of this job I really have a question mark in my mind about." Somewhat ominously, he added that if he was unable to exert influence as CEO, he would be disappointed at the job he was doing. "If that doesn't occur, then I've made a bad marriage and I'll have to do something about it," he said.

Outwardly, Doddridge and Walker were doing fine revamping operations in Canada, still the location of most of Magna's plants. Doddridge, however, was finding his mandate to impose a more traditional structure on Magna difficult to execute. He recognized the merits of retaining the decentralized approach that devolved decision-making to operations managers driven by incentives, knowing that had been Magna's strength. But the free-form, entrepreneurial culture, with line managers used to more autonomy than at most companies, occasionally clashed with his more conservative approach.

Fred Jaekel recalls that Doddridge was lukewarm to his plan to invest in a new technology called hydroforming, which used water under high pressure to form metal. Jaekel believed the technology, initially employed to make plumbing materials, could be scaled up to manufacture vehicle chassis components. The parts would be cheaper and faster to make, as well as lighter and stronger than those made using conventional cutting and welding techniques. But he had difficulty convincing Doddridge that Magna should invest in it. "John opposed [hydroforming]," says Jaekel. "He said that they'd looked into it at Dana and rejected it."

Jaekel eventually persuaded Stronach and Don Walker that the technology was sound and Magna went on to develop it as the foundation of a new plant and some multi-million-dollar contracts. Notwithstanding Doddridge's cautious objections on that issue, Jaekel says he had the experience and savvy that gave him exactly the right qualifications for the CEO's job, as well as invaluable contacts in the industry and management savvy. "But Frank changed his mind [about Doddridge's role]," Jaekel says. "Frank began thinking of John as somebody whose job was having a lot of lunches with industry guys."

FRANK LOOKS TOWARD AUSTRIA

Stronach hadn't given any indication of retiring when he'd hired Doddridge and moved to Europe. But he'd left the impression that he would slow down a touch, ease out of mainstream management. It hadn't worked out quite that way. While Doddridge was having difficulty splitting his time between Detroit and the Markham office, Stronach seemed less troubled by hopscotching back and forth between Europe and North America to tend to both business and personal interests.

Far from slowing down, Stronach, impressed by the reception he'd received in Europe, especially in Austria, was more enthusiastic than ever about Europe's potential. Doddridge had agreed at the annual meeting in 1993 that the time was ripe to go after new business in Europe. But now it seemed, surprise, surprise, that Stronach was cooling to the CEO's attempt to impose a more conventional, buttoned-down culture on Magna's four North American operating groups. Indeed, Stronach made it clear he wanted to expand even more into Europe – without the rigour that Doddridge was trying to instill in the organization, but *with* some of the capital Magna was generating in North America.

Realizing, as have many other sadder-and-wiser senior executives, before and since, that Stronach would always call the shots at Magna, in October 1994, Doddridge filed for divorce two years into the unsteady marriage. Magna's newly appointed executive vice-president Graham Orr was left to explain the departure of Magna's second CEO in as many years: "John's sitting here . . . asking, 'What role am I playing? You have so many strong managers and I'm not the top decision-maker,'" Orr told journalists.

"A company can't have two CEOs," Doddridge agreed, in a separate interview accompanying the announcement of his resignation. "It wasn't working and I didn't want to be there as a figurehead."

MAGNA AFTER DODDRIDGE

Stronach quickly filled the gap. He promoted Don Walker to CEO. At most public companies, a management shake-up that saw a respected CEO replaced by the son-in-law of the chairman would be disturbing, to say the least. For that matter, it would also be disturbing to see a sixty-two-year-old chairman and controlling shareholder continuing to insist on doing things his way. Magna, though, was an unstoppable force that rolled over any obstacle it encountered. Investors who had seen Doddridge's departure coming and had been pushing Magna's stock price down for a couple of months, sold it off by another $2 when the news was finally announced. But a few days later it more than recovered to trade above $50 on the TSE.

Whether because of Stronach's presence, or in spite of it, Magna gave the impression of a company so efficient, so diverse in its products, so nimble in its response to market or management changes, that it almost ran itself. Though sparsely attended, the annual meeting at New York's Four Seasons Hotel in 1994, the second in a row held outside of Canada and Walker's first as CEO, only reinforced the impression. Thanks to a booming car market, Magna turned a profit in fiscal 1994 of $234 million on sales of $3.6 billion.

THE MAGNA RETIREMENT BENEFITS

That the meeting was sparsely attended may have been what Magna intended. The low turnout had the happy effect of minimizing attention given to the extravagant payouts that had accompanied the most recent management shuffle. The fat retirement allowances paid to Nicol, Copeland, Czernohorsky, and Gingl had already raised eyebrows in Canadian media. Doddridge, too, turned out to have negotiated a handsome alimony package, which might have encouraged more questions in Canada than in New York. Including a $935,000 "signing bonus" put toward Magna stock in his name when he joined the company, Doddridge had collected a total of $1.3 million in 1993, $4.6 million in 1994 (including $1.5 million gained by exercising stock options), and $10.8 million in fiscal 1995, when he collected $5.4 million from options and $3.3 million (U.S.) in retirement and severance. Altogether, his two-and-a-half-year stint had cost Magna's shareholders more than $17 million. It was small wonder that he told reporters he was "going with a smile on my face."

In the context of Stronach's own compensation for fiscal 1992 to 1995, though, Doddridge's pay looked like chump change. Stronach's 1992 salary was $200,000 but his incentive-based bonus was $3.9 million, based on 2.4 per cent of Magna's pre-tax income. In 1993 the bonus doubled to $7.7 million (3.5 per cent of pre-tax income). In 1994, it was off slightly, to $7.3 million, but Stronach got an additional $4.5 million (U.S.) in consulting fees paid to his Frank Stronach & Co. in Europe, and he exercised options for a gain of $27.2 million. Altogether, the chairman pocketed $40.7 million in 1994 in salary, bonus, fees, and options gains.

In 1995, he did even better. His consultancies collected fees of $10.8 million (U.S.), to which he added his regular salary of $200,000 and $32.2 million in gains on his options, for a total of $47 million. If nothing else, Stronach proved there was a significant difference at Magna between chairman and CEO, especially if the chairman also controlled most of the votes: in the same period that Doddridge collected just over $17 million as CEO and vice-chairman, Stronach rewarded himself to the tune of $100 million.

"It's not enough," Stronach responded to the chorus of complaints over his ever-increasing compensation. Maybe not. But nobody actually knew, since Magna never offered an itemized account of what it got in return for the massive fees that it annually paid his one-man, Swiss-based consulting company. Instead, it came up with a justification, subsequently refined into boilerplate, that it still repeats in filings to securities commissions (but not in the annual report): "Mr. F. Stronach's historical compensation reflects his special position as the Corporation's founder and architect of Magna's unique, entrepreneurial corporate culture."

THE FAIR ENTERPRISE INSTITUTE

When Magna was on the ropes financially, Stronach had been less inclined to deliver sermons on the Fair Enterprise model. Its weaknesses were more apparent, its strengths less obvious. But as the recovery picked up momentum, he once again shouted its merits with great enthusiasm. In 1993 he made an effort to entrench and legitimize the concept by creating the Fair Enterprise Institute, a think tank inspired by his growing disenchantment with the Canadian political system. The FEI began life as a "non-political and non-profit organization founded to improve Canadian living standards."

Stronach complained to journalist Diane Francis, "The flaw of Canada and of democracy is that the country is mismanaged because it is run by political reasoning rather than economic reasoning." And he saw Parliamentary reform as the answer. To effect it, he had developed a variation on the classical Greek democracy concept that permitted all citizens to vote on everything. In Stronach's version, a "jury" of citizens selected at random by computers would replace senators and become a court of public opinion. Sitting part-time for a one-year term, the chamber of citizen representatives would vote in secret on legislation. Since the citizens wouldn't be influenced by having to be re-elected – as Stronach believed politicians were – political motives for voting would be replaced by practical, economic reasons that more accurately represented the views of ordinary citizens.

As wacky as the idea sounded, Stronach had no trouble committing Magna shareholders' money to develop it. In his mind, it qualified for funding – Magna has never revealed exactly how much – from the 2 per cent of pre-tax profit that Magna sets aside for charitable, educational, political, and social causes, which Belinda Stronach administered. Despite the FEI's characterization as nonpolitical, Stronach hired Progressive Conservative backroom strategist and public-policy wonk Hugh Segal, a very political figure, to flesh out his government-by-jury idea. A twice-failed candidate for a seat in Parliament in the 1970s, a former aide to Ontario Premier Bill Davis, and at twenty-nine, the province's youngest deputy minister, Segal may well have been motivated to take the job more by economics, his own, than any genuine belief in a pressing need for Senate reform. The citizens' senate was still just an idea when he left FEI within a year or so. Ironically, in 2005, Segal accepted an appointment to the Senate.

There wasn't much evidence, either, that FEI was able to drum up interest in another of its goals, that of helping companies to qualify for certification as "Fair Enterprise corporations." By 1995, in fact, FEI had reinvented itself. Under executive director George Marsland, Segal's replacement and another Tory backroom organizer, it was sponsoring the national Magna For Canada Scholarship Fund, a contest dreamed up by Belinda Stronach, and one she was doubtless dead certain her father would approve. The program invited college and university students to submit essays on what they would do as prime minister "to improve the living standard and unify the country." Regional winners received $5,000 and a Magna internship as well as a chance to win another $5,000 (and $10,000 for their school) if selected as the national winner.

Perhaps to ensure the quality of submissions in the contest's early days, Magna also invited non-students, whom it characterized as "recognized Canadians" and to whom it awarded a $20,000 prize, to contribute essays on the same topic, which were assembled annually in a book, and published alongside the students' efforts. Prominent Canadians who contributed essays included: Ted Byfield, ultra-conservative founder of *The Western Report* newsmagazine; comedian Steve Smith, creator of television's madcap inventor Red Green; Canadian Auto Workers union executive Hemi Mitic; and former media tycoon Conrad Black, who renounced his Canadian citizenship to receive a British peerage, and, just a guess, probably didn't need the twenty grand.

Magna, through FEI, has continued to sponsor the "As Prime Minister" contest. Although the contest is no longer open to non-students, Magna has borrowed from reality television and now buys television air-time and presents a program featuring a panel of four former prime ministers, trying to be polite to one another, that judges contestants' essays to determine the winner of the now $50,000 prize.

DON WALKER – THE SON-IN-LAW ALSO RISES

Shareholders got full value from Don Walker as Magna's CEO. Now father of Stronach's three-year-old grandson Frank Jr. and fifteen-month-old granddaughter Nikki, Walker ran Magna's day-to-day business, meeting with Stronach when he was in Canada to discuss the chairman's longer-term strategy. Not surprisingly, Walker, thirty-eight, was simpatico with his father-in-law on the benefits of sharing technology and expertise between European and North American operations. He was also enthusiastic about hydroforming, the technology Jaekel had been developing, which was coming to symbolize

Magna's full recovery as an industry maverick that not only spent on innovation, but was capable of turning it into a profit producer.

Jaekel and others at Magna had first begun looking at the technology in 1992. In 1994 Magna acquired GSM, a German plumbing-component firm with hydroforming expertise, then scaled the technology up to make it applicable to auto parts. The process involves injecting highly pressurized water into special, sealed steel tubes that were developed in conjunction with Dofasco, Canada's biggest steel company. After the ends of the tubes are sealed by hydraulic cylinders, they're positioned in dies designed to mould the finished product. Under pressure from the water, the tube's metal "flows" into the required form.

Using hydroforming in the production of vehicle frames lowers cost, accelerates production of stronger, lighter components, and reduces scrap by 40 pounds per unit, compared to older cut-and-weld methods. But the technology took some time to refine. The first frames made using the technique had proved too strong: they didn't crumple under impact so didn't meet vehicle safety standards. Once the technical problems were solved, however, hydroforming presented Magna with a new line of business. Magna hadn't been in the vehicle-frame business before. But it was able to demonstrate enough benefits to GM that, in 1995, the company awarded Magna a $400-million contract to supply 1.2 million frames a year for its Silverado/Sierra pickup trucks, beginning in the 1998 model year. Magna also snared hydroforming contracts from Chrysler and Ford for engine carriages and radiator supports. The 1995 GM contract alone helped boost Magna's stock price and Walker saw hydroforming having the potential to add as much as $30 to Magna's average per-vehicle content in North America.

Early hydroforming presses were set up in a plant in Troy, Michigan, but the new Formet Industries plant in St. Thomas, Ontario, built by the Cosma group headed by Jaekel, became one of the world's biggest applications of the technology. Magna holds numerous patents related to hydroforming and is one of its foremost practitioners.

Almost more important than the production benefits that hydroforming offered was its symbolism. At a time when automakers were looking to hand off more design and engineering work to fewer suppliers in order to shorten their new-model development cycle, hydroforming redefined Magna as a technology-oriented, can-do culture. Customers no longer sent over blueprints and asked suppliers to make a component, Don Walker observed, but relayed their objectives and let suppliers come up with solutions. "Now all they'd say to us is, 'Here's the weight we're targeting, here's the cost and here's how it has to be bolted into the floor . . . you go off and build the prototype.'"

10

MR. STRONACH GOES TO VIENNA

The accolades that rained down on Stronach for his role in Magna's remarkable recovery appeared to restore his reputation. But they did little to improve his vision of Canada's future. In 1992, the recent candidate for Canada's Parliament had moved to Zug, on the outskirts of Zurich, and taken out Swiss residency, a process he'd found enlightening, and enriching. Switzerland's 30 per cent limit on personal taxes, he allowed, had been the main reason for his electing to set up a luxury apartment in Zurich. But he'd also been impressed by the flinty economic approach (as opposed to a political or social one) that he'd encountered with the Swiss. "Corporate taxes in Switzerland are negotiable," he marvelled in relating his experience. "The government sat down with me and said, 'You're our customer,' and that was its attitude."

As the trend toward global economies and companies grew, he opined, "Europe is the place to catch that fever." Or at least it would be at some point. The fact that Europe wasn't yet glowing with prosperity didn't bother him. "The current economic downturn in Europe provides Magna with a number of excellent opportunities to acquire automotive facilities cheaply," he said.

In announcing in 1994 that he would be spending more time in Europe, he took another swipe at Canada. Though it had provided the environment in which he'd been able to build Magna, the company that paid him more than $40 million that year, he foresaw Canada's $45-billion federal deficit as a harbinger of a bleak economic future and denounced its "user-unfriendly" attitude. "There's a sense that business success means you've taken advantage of somebody," he said.

But though Stronach tried to hide behind economic motives for heading to Europe, there were perhaps personal reasons as well: his embarrassment over the Stevens inquiry, voters' rejection of him, and evidently of his Fair Enterprise theories, at the polls, and accusations that his "visionary" diversions had been at least partly behind the near-collapse of Magna. Obliquely, he suggested that ingratitude for all he'd done for Canada, and the bureaucracy he'd had to overcome to do it, were elements of his business life he would be happy to leave behind.

Most recently, the town of Aurora's refusal to rubber-stamp his proposal to develop land from his farm into Magna's extravagant new corporate campus and international headquarters seemed to symbolize for him the obstacles to doing business expediently in Canada. Aurora, immediately north of Toronto, objected to Stronach's plans because they violated zoning regulations; Stronach didn't see why the regulations couldn't be waived in light of all the benefits the development would bring to the area. "If the company announced it would build its headquarters in the United States, kids would get the day off school [and] there would be a parade with banners," he groused to the *Globe and Mail*.

Ironically, Aurora's politicians agreed with Stronach that Canadians tended to equate business success with taking advantage of someone. They were among those suspicious of Stronach's intentions. At least part of the town's obstinacy was due to having seen other communities jump through hoops to rezone land to accommodate

Magna's head-office plans, only to be jilted when he changed his mind and flipped land at a profit. Stronach saw such a sale as a business success; the folks in Aurora saw it as taking advantage of the communities. They wanted guarantees to ensure that Aurora wouldn't become Magna's next victim. As Stronach expanded Magna's presence in Austria, a number of communities, including the city of Vienna, would come to wish they'd adopted a similar wariness. As it was, Stronach admitted that Europe wasn't totally free of red tape. "It's not that European countries are much better than Canada," he said. "It's that they're not getting worse as fast, and Europe has advantages that Canada can't match in the global economy."

If the Canada-bashing marked an end to the kinder, gentler posture he'd promised after almost losing his company, the move to Europe demonstrated that he'd lost little of his genius for reading the future of the automotive industry. He believed the next phase of global restructuring would create opportunities in Europe. And now that Magna had found its feet again he wanted to lead the charge. He saw his own European background, and the Euro-culture that many of Magna's managers brought to the company, as competitive advantages. He intended to be point man for a thrust into Europe.

EUROPE – THE NEW AUTO WORLD

Stronach believed that structural changes in the auto industry, already underway in North America, were bound to spread to Europe. Traditionally, profits in auto-making accrued from mass production that saw, say, 300,000 or 500,000 virtually identical vehicles put together on assembly lines. The fewer changes required, the greater was the potential for automation to reduce production costs. The thinking led to a wave of consolidation in the late 1980s and early 1990s and saw big companies buy smaller ones, hoping to achieve cost savings with longer production runs. GM, for example, absorbed Sweden's Saab and Korea's Daewoo, and entered joint ventures with Japan's Isuzu, Subaru, and Suzuki. Ford took over Volvo and Mazda. France's Peugeot annexed Citroën, and Renault invested in Japan's Nissan. Germany's Volkswagen acquired SEAT in Spain and Škoda in the Czech Republic. Even Magna's biggest customer was not immune; although it wouldn't take place until 1998, Chrysler would fall prey to Daimler-Benz.

That few brands disappeared, however, demonstrated a weakness in the consolidation strategy. The existence of so many brands in the first place had reflected the fragmentation of the global auto market. Different countries, and even regions, had varying preferences. As communications and technology such as the Internet shrank the world, greater choice became a consumer expectation. Automakers that bought a smaller car company, intending to eliminate the brand and replace it with another of their products in that market, found that they ran the risk of losing customer loyalty to the old brand. Maintaining the badges of acquired companies, on the other hand, turned car makers into brand managers who marketed vehicles bearing a variety of names, each appealing to a different buying public. Still, they had acquired an entrée to new expertise and technology – say, experience in building small cars, or a luxury brand. Unable to get economies of scale by producing one-size-fits-all models, they adopted a global strategy, winnowing the number of basic platforms – chassis, drive-train, whatever items could be shared – upon which a wide variety of their vehicles could be assembled.

Manufacturing so-called global platforms had a number of benefits. Sharing a single platform among a number of makes and models lowered design and engineering costs. Saab or Volvo didn't need to go to the expense of developing basic chassis for their cars; they could use one created for a Chevy or Ford model. Consistency also meant lower warranty and recall problems. And while the economies of mass-producing entire vehicles were lost, the platforms themselves could be made on long assembly lines, then shipped to different markets where assembly could be completed using locally made parts designed to meet local vehicle preference. A basic two-litre engine block was cheaper to make on one mass-production line and then tweak for different models in different markets, than it was to produce the blocks separately in each market.

It turned out that the economies and profits of high-volume, uninterrupted assembly lines set up to crank out 400,000 or more identical vehicles didn't disappear entirely. And shorter-run assembly lines based on global platforms, using components that fulfilled demand in local or niche markets, weren't as costly to interrupt as had been anticipated. In fact, they permitted "mass customization." Manufacturers discovered they could charge a premium for changes or margin-fattening options added late in the production cycle. The bigger profit offset losses caused by lower-volume inefficiency. The net effect was that rather than reducing the number of models, which had been the original idea, consolidation was creating a market more fragmented than ever.

The big automakers' outsourcing of components to be assembled on global platforms had already become a driver of Magna's growth in North America and was now about to take off in Europe. In executing their strategy of using basic structures adaptable for use across a number of models and in different local European, Asian, or North American markets, car makers sought suppliers with the wherewithal – capital, expertise, systems – to participate in the production of vehicles.

This presented Magna with an enormous opportunity. A proven Tier 1 supplier and already one of North America's most diverse sources of auto parts, it could similarly furnish original equipment manufacturers (OEMs) in Europe, or anywhere, with body parts, interiors, exterior trim – well, with just about anything they needed.

STRONACH ON A NEW STAGE IN AUSTRIA

Despite Stronach's Swiss residency, there was no question that Austria was to be the focus of his European ambitions. Familiar to him, and geographically central, Austria had a transportation infrastructure

and technically skilled work force that he believed would attract
more European business.

Stronach also saw that Austria was at an economic point in its
history that favoured his plan. Following World War II, the country
was divided into four zones, each ruled by one of the Allies until
1955. Partly to prevent the occupying powers from gaining control
of its economy following its return to independence, Austria's
postwar reconstruction had included the state takeover of many of
the bombed-out factories. The resulting economy became dominated
by public-sector ownership, particularly in industries such as steel,
salt-mining, and chemicals, as well as in banking. By the late 1970s,
government-related companies accounted for about a third of
Austria's employment and almost half its exports. But by the 1980s,
debt and inefficiency had diminished the structure's competitive
position in an increasingly privatized world economy. So the
Austrian government started to privatize its assets.

Stronach was familiar with the scenario. As a director of the
Canadian Development Investment Corporation under Sinc Stevens
in the 1980s, he'd been part of Canada's own privatization initiative
and had recognized opportunities for Magna among the assets the
government was hawking. He believed that Austria, a few years
behind Canada in its privatization phase, would also be putting
some worthy assets on the sales block. In 1990, despite a moratorium on new investments during Magna's debt crisis, he'd entered
into a joint venture with state-owned Voest-Alpine Stahl AG, an integrated steel maker, creating Magna Automobiltechnik AG (MATAG),
an operation that stamped vehicle body parts. Although Magna had
established a couple of small factories in Austria during the 1980s,
the Voest-Alpine investment was the real beginning of the company's
Austrianization.

To assuage Austrian nationalists' concerns about a foreign predator in their midst, Stronach emphasized his roots. His homilies on
business success ("Deliver the best product at the best price"), the

merits of Fair Enterprise ("Ownership motivates employees and management"), Magna's beneficence to the local economy ("Jobs are the most precious commodity in the world today"), and how government should operate ("Make decisions based on economics not politics") had been repeated so often in North America that they were now largely ignored there. But coming from someone who'd achieved success in North America, the slogans found a new life in Austria, and Stronach played to a new crowd in frequent television and press interviews. Austria, a nation of eight million, began to see Stronach in the same light as skier Franz Klammer and actor-politician Arnold Schwarzenegger, its most prominent international personalities.

Stronach found his image as a returning prodigal – a rich one, ready to invest in his native land and create jobs – useful in winning acceptance in social and business circles and in getting access to politicians. In Canada, he'd been miffed that Prime Minister Brian Mulroney wasn't interested in giving him an audience. In Austria, an audience with Chancellor Franz Vranitzky was easy to arrange. Indeed, Stronach and Vranitzky became chummy.

Stronach's penchant for the grand gesture amplified his presence. He assigned Robert Gruber, a former Austrian banker whom he hired as managing director of Magna Europe, with the task of finding a European headquarters. "He told me, 'Look for a nice property close to Vienna,'" Gruber recalled. "I know how modest Frank is, so I drove around looking at castles." Gruber thought Schloss Oberwaltersdorf, a 400-year-old castle on 247 acres near the village of Oberwaltersdorf, 25 kilometres south of Vienna, was just the ticket. Its developer-owner had built a subdivision and a couple of faux lakes on one part of the grounds but had been discouraged from continuing when plans for a golf course and community centre were stalled by local regulations. Stronach, though, was confident he'd be able to overcome those obstacles and bought the place in March 1994. Drafts being what they are in dank medieval castles, and Stronach's predilection for

luxury being what it is, he remodelled the *schloss* to make it habit-
able, adding personal living quarters, guest rooms, offices, and a
training centre.

What it all cost never turned up in Magna's financial reports. But
we do know that he proposed spending $200 million on the complex
which would include a golf course and clubhouse, tennis courts, and
a luxury subdivision on the castle grounds, mirroring the extravagant
design of the North American headquarters in Aurora. The scale of
the project raised the celebrity quotient of citizen Stronach, a $40-
million-a-year industrialist, in the Austrian public mind. As a businessman who actually promised to part with his company's money in
Austria, he also got the attention of local government. The sort of
zoning and environmental entanglements that were stalling the Aurora
development simply disappeared in Oberwaltersdorf. Contrary to the
experience of the previous owner, Magna's municipal approvals were
reportedly issued in record time.

MAGNA SHOPS IN EUROPE

In North America, Magna's efforts in the early and mid 1990s were
focused on improving capacity in existing factories. In Europe,
Stronach was on the acquisition trail. He followed up the 1990
Voest-Alpine joint venture with a bigger one in the fall of 1993, the
$41-million purchase of a 12.5 per cent interest in Kolbenschmidt
AG, an engine-parts manufacturer. He also paid $53 million for 60
per cent of one of Kolbenschmidt's subsidiaries, which made air bags
and steering wheels. Stronach considered the price of the two a
bargain. The companies came with combined sales of $1.5 billion.
And joint-venture was the way to go, he said: the total $94 million
it cost to invest in the partnership gave Magna Europe control of
research into air bags that he estimated would have cost $150 million
had Magna undertaken it on its own.

New relationships with European car makers brought in more
business. By 1995, Magna Europe had lined up contracts to support

$105-million worth of new plants (some acquired and some in joint ventures with existing companies), bringing the total number of European facilities to nineteen, including three in his hometown of Weiz. And he didn't restrict expansion to Austria. In 1996, Magna entered into about $215-million worth of acquisitions and joint ventures. Among them were the $110 million acquisition of Marley PLC, a U.K. supplier of instrument panels and interior and exterior trim, which came with about $200 million in sales contracts, and the U.K. purchase of Caradon Rollinx PLC, a company that manufactured bumpers, for $45 million. A further deal worth $29 million, with a German company, Pebra GmbH Paul Braun, involved contracts worth $250 million, which Stronach saw as giving Magna an introduction and opportunity to prove itself to customers such as Mercedes-Benz, Audi, BMW, Volvo, Rover, and Ford.

THE EUROSTAR WARS

Business practices honed by Stronach in North America travelled well. Playing off regional governments with the promise of jobs had been his primary method of inveigling assistance from government when expanding Magna, and it proved as effective in his native land as it had in Canada and the U.S. He'd also learned to compete with and outmanoeuvre local suppliers, much as the Japanese had done to Magna in North America. How he won a contract with Chrysler to supply its Eurostar plant was an example.

Magna had plans to build a new stamping plant in Austria and had been playing off two neighbouring Austrian provinces, Burgenland and Styria, for assistance in building the factory. In the battle between the two jurisdictions, Styria had sweetened its offer to Magna when the latter had agreed to take over Maschinenfabrik Liezen, a bankrupt company in the town of Liezen, a city in Styria province. (Stronach's friend Franz Vranitzky, chancellor of Austria until 1997, represented the Liezen plant on behalf of Bank Austria, the plant's biggest creditor.) Meanwhile, Chrysler, a major customer of Magna in North America, had been assembling Jeep and Voyager minivans for the European market in a plant called Eurostar, a joint venture with an Austrian government–controlled company called Steyr Fahrzeugtechnik (SFT). When Chrysler announced that it intended to boost output by sourcing components locally rather than shipping them in from the U.S., SFT, which had a parts factory near the Eurostar plant, looked like a lock to get the contract.

Stronach, however, swung into action. First, he abandoned pursuit of both the Burgenland and the Liezen plants. Instead, he proposed investing between 500 billion and 700 billion Austrian schillings in a new plant in Albersdorf (in Styria) near Chrysler's Eurostar plant. A contract to buy 60,000 tonnes of steel annually from the state-controlled Voest-Alpine steel company (with whom Magna was already in the MATAG joint venture) convinced the Austrian government that Magna would be a wonderful candidate to supply Eurostar. But the clincher was support from Chrysler. It regarded Magna as a premier supplier. Aware that Chrysler needed Magna as much as Magna needed Chrysler's business, Stronach persuaded the company to give it the nod as the Eurostar supplier. In the end, Magna not only beat out Chrysler's joint-venture partner, SFT, for the Eurostar contract, but also won a 100-million schilling construction subsidy from the province of Styria to expand the plant.

Stronach was elated. He saw Magna's new plant not only serving the Eurostar plant, but also assembly plants of Audi, Opel, and Suzuki in nearby Hungary. But the losers in the transaction – which included SFT's parts plant and the province of Burgenland – were not pleased with the result. Nor with Frank Stronach.

FLYING HIGH

During 1997, Stronach broadened the scope of Magna Europe's capabilities with several more acquisitions. He spent $49 million to buy 75 per cent of Georg Naher GmbH, a German interior specialist with contracts worth $185 million annually that supplied interior panels, trunk linings, carpets, and sound insulation to Daimler-Benz, Volkswagen, Opel, and BMW. He paid $71 million for seating specialist Tricom Group Holdings, a U.K. company with $100 million in sales. And under a systems-integration contract, Magna Europe put together the body and space-frame for the innovative SmartCar, made by Micro Compact Car AG, a consortium of Daimler-Benz and the Swiss watch-manufacturer Swatch. To handle the contract, Magna set up in the customer's plant in France. Through these and other purchases, Stronach positioned Magna to manufacture modules, such as entire interior systems, in anticipation of growing demand from European automakers for that service from its suppliers, as had been the case in North America. Systems integration – taking on design, engineering, parts production, and assembly – had become a Magna proficiency that had added value to its products.

Far from exhausting himself, Stronach seemed to revel in the activity, his energy and imagination expanding with each new challenge. In 1961, he'd trundled home a Pontiac Parisienne as an iconic symbol of his success. By the mid 1990s, a Dassault Falcon 50 jet was his power-symbol calling card. Although it was nominally a Magna company jet, few within the company thought of it as anything other than the chairman's personal ferry. One of three jets the company maintained and occasionally leased to other users when not required by Magna, the $14-million aircraft gleamed with custom leather, brass, and mahogany fittings. Its three engines gave it trans-Atlantic capability, and the ability to land in Buttonville (where Magna built its own hangar), a few minutes from both Stronach's home and Magna's head office. Twice a month he flew back to Markham to share his most recent inspirations with the board and management, or to tend to his horse breeding and racing operation.

His landings at either end of the trip weren't always the happiest moment for employees. A former Magna Europe employee says news of his arrival spread instantly through the Austrian office: "You knew when Frank had landed. It had people in the office buzzing like bees." Stronach's habit during his three weeks in Austria, the former executive says, was to set in motion projects without much definition or direction "that we [management at Magna Europe] tried to bring down to earth." The chairman would then fly to North America and come up with *different* ideas and ventures. "He would return to Austria three weeks later from Canada and meet with politicians and businessmen and tell them of all the new plans he developed there in the last three weeks and none of us knew what they were. For the next three weeks it was our business . . . to make things clear and bring *them* down to earth."

Not infrequently, he announced plans that caught his own executives off guard. In 1995, for instance, he told Austrian officials that his intention was to list Magna Holding AG, Magna Europe's holding company, on the Vienna stock exchange. To be eligible for a listing, the Austrian company had to be financially and managerially independent from its Canadian parent. Stronach said he thought that would occur within two years. This was news to Magna's management in Europe, not to mention to the surprised folks back in Canada.

The Buttonville end of his commutes could be chaotic as well. In his spell as CEO, John Doddridge had found Stronach's return trips from Europe too frequent and his interference too pervasive. Don Walker, whipped out of the wings to replace Doddridge in 1994, wasn't likely to complain about his father-in-law. But a growing concern was the need to make sense of the increasingly bizarre public pronouncements Stronach made from Europe – or perhaps from a racetrack somewhere to which he'd flown to watch his horses run, or from one of his training or breeding operations in Kentucky or Florida. Brian Colburn, Magna's corporate secretary, and Graham Orr, an executive vice-president, spent much of their time trying to explain or deny Stronach's latest "vision," activity, or statement, a role known as the "What's Frank said now?" detail.

"WHAT'S FRANK SAID NOW?"

It was no easy job. Colburn tried dismissing inquiries about the money-swallowing renovation of the castle at Magna Europe's headquarters by calling it more of "a manor house." But the challenges were many. Among the controversial Magna activities in Europe that Stronach initiated and Colburn or Orr had to explain to shareholders were a luxury airline business and a major theme park. He also slammed Canada and the U.S. while he was in Canada to watch one of his horses in the Queen's Plate in the summer of 1996. Europe, he said, had it all over North America in its ability to produce technically oriented managers who could run plants. "The system over here doesn't breed people who are involved in making things," he complained during his visit to Canada. "The system here breeds financial engineers."

Stronach didn't feel there was anything untoward in the fact that Magna had found jobs for current and former Austrian politicians and officials (or their spouses) at Magna Europe. The phenomenon, as he cheerfully described it, was a public service of Magna: the company wanted to expose more politicians to the ways of business to help create an environment of co-operation. Stronach also drew criticism for opposing the establishment of work councils, the equivalent of unions, at Magna's factories in Austria.

When a majority of employees at three plants voted against setting up councils at the Magna sites, no sanctions were imposed, but Magna's intransigence infuriated Österreichischer Gewerkschaftsbund (ÖGB), the national trade union group. It charged that Magna was importing from America ideas that undermined Austria's traditionally co-operative labour environment. Stronach's response was typical of the pronouncements that left staff smacking palms on their foreheads. He called an Austrian labour law that forced employers to take out compulsory membership in the Austrian Chamber of Commerce "like something out of the East Bloc," which was fighting talk in Austria. To make matters worse, he added the accusation

that the ÖGB was possibly corrupt. Until it made its financial statements public to disprove his charges, he advised workers that continuing to pay union dues amounted to "paying protection money
to the Mafia."

THE ROAD TO THE ALL-MAGNA CAR

By 1996, Stronach gave the impression of having made good – or at
least of having made a good start – on most of the objectives he'd
had for Europe when he moved there. Driven by its indefatigable
finance director, Robert Gruber, Magna Europe employed 6,800
workers in 27 plants that generated $1.3 billion in sales, about 22
per cent of Magna International's consolidated revenue. If there was
a blemish in the picture, it was the fact that much of the sales growth
had come through acquisitions. On the other side of the ledger, the
costs of building the head office, the pricey jet carrying Stronach
back and forth, and the $15 million (U.S.) in consulting fees paid to
Frank Stronach & Co. in 1996, all made the cost of sales high. The
$49-million operating profit Magna Europe made on $1.3 billion in
sales looked a little puny compared to the $513 million earned by
the North American operations on sales of $4.6 billion in the same
time period. Cosma alone, the division that was benefiting the most
from the hydroforming applications, had sales of $1.7 billion, greater
than those for all of Europe.

Gruber, whose credentials include a PhD in business and economics as well as an MBA, nonetheless believed that Magna Europe
was on the right course, and that once the existing automotive operations were rationalized, the European business's profits would grow.
He had precious little interest in the non-automotive businesses that
Stronach was dreaming up with alarming frequency. In fact, he didn't
seem to take the chairman's musings on a luxury airline, a casino-
racetrack, or a $787-million theme park seriously. As the man who
once went shopping for castles for Stronach, however, he should
have known better.

But though the European operations continued to lag behind the activity, and profitability, of the North American operations, Stronach's announcement in January 1998 of his biggest European acquisition yet was a major step in correcting the imbalance. That month he announced that he'd reached agreement in principle to buy 66.8 per cent of Steyr-Daimler-Puch (SDP) and 50 per cent of the related company, Steyr Fahrzeugtechnik (SFT). The two companies' combined sales of $1.5 billion more than doubled Magna's size in Europe.

The price of the package hadn't been revealed yet (it was rumoured to be about $400 million), but strategically the acquisition was brilliant. The prize was the 50 per cent of SFT that Stronach had long coveted. It had expertise in vehicle engineering, four-wheel drive systems, and car assembly. As well, one of SFT's assets was a 49 per cent interest in Eurostar, Chrysler's European assembly operation for which Magna had won the supply contract. All in all, it was a neat fit with Magna's global strategy, embodied in the new Symatec division created to integrate systems and technology from Magna's Cosma, Atoma, Decoma, and Tesma groups, co-ordinating the intercompany aspect of projects.

In essence, Magna was taking on total project responsibility in the building of a vehicle. SFT, which was already assembling niche vehicles and had about seven hundred engineers, would become the first manifestation of the strategy. It would function as a laboratory of sorts, a model for similar operations in North and South America – in fact, anywhere in the world Magna saw an opportunity to advance toward its goal, which was to become the first auto-parts supplier capable of turning a customer's design into a finished vehicle.

Stronach painted the purchase as a victory for Austria. He acknowledged that the profitable Steyr-Daimler-Puch was part of the nation's industrial heritage; it employed about 7,000 people around the country, making everything from tractors and military vehicles to munitions. Since he first arrived on the business scene in Austria, Stronach had emphasized his own Austrian-ness. The sale to Magna,

managed by Austrians and controlled by an Austrian, he said, kept
SDP in Austrian hands.

Unlike in Canada and the United States, Stronach was not obli-
gated, under Austrian law, to make a follow-up offer to buy the 33.2
per cent of SDP not included in the deal. But as a true industrial democrat, and out of respect for the mostly Austrian shareholders who
owned the shares, he promised to buy minority shares at the same
price he paid Creditanstalt, a division of Austria Bank, for the majority. Growing Magna's operations and creating new jobs, he claimed,
was his way of paying back his homeland. The training he'd received
there, he said, had become the base of his fortune. Cheers all round.

Within weeks of the January announcement, however, Austrians
were starting to wonder aloud about some of the unusual relationships that seemed to be entwined in the transaction. Worse, Stronach
became a victim of his habit of firing off in all directions, hoping to
hit one of the ill-defined targets that popped into his imagination.
This time, he shot himself in the foot, threatening the most important deal he had done in Europe.

11

THE AUSTRIAN MESSIAH

In the spring of 1998, in television talk-show appearances, and in newspaper and magazine interviews, Stronach appeared eager to depict himself to Austrians as a bred-in-the-bone patriot who had returned to rescue his homeland's economy. But he might have over-played his hand. Austrians couldn't deny the jobs he'd created in new plants, or those he'd preserved by consolidating fragmented operations across Europe under the Magna banner. But the size of the Steyr-Daimler-Puch/Steyr Fahrzeugtechnik (SDP/SFT) transaction, and the expectation that Magna would break up SDP and sell off the parts in which it had no interest, drew more than the usual public attention to Stronach's methods. As details of his deal trickled out, Austrians began wondering whether Stronach's business practice was in tune with the national temperament.

Stronach's tactic of insinuating his way into the good graces of politicians had arguably enjoyed greater success in Austria's more compact political structure than in Canada's. For instance, shortly after moving to Europe, he'd established a relationship with Chancellor Franz Vranitzky, for whom he became an "economic advisor." Help-fully, prior to going into politics, Vranitzky had been a director of Creditanstalt, the division of Bank Austria that was selling SDP to

Stronach. When Vranitzky left politics in 1997, Stronach invited him to join the Magna International board. He'd also developed a connection with Gerhard Randa, chairman and CEO of Bank Austria. Randa had been on Magna's board since 1995, which put him on the boards of both buyer and seller of SDP when the sale occurred in January 1998.

Rudolf Streicher, a former CEO of SDP, had met Stronach in 1992 while serving as the Social Democratic Party's minister of transport and economic development. He'd worked with Magna to find subsidies for new plants and had developed a close friendship with Stronach, with whom he shared a technical background and a love of skiing and soccer. When Streicher lost a bid to become Austria's president in 1992, he resumed his job as boss of SDP, a position he held while Stronach was negotiating its purchase.

Streicher denied that he'd influenced the sale. In fact, he claimed that the deal was negotiated without his knowledge. But the link was difficult for Austrians to ignore, especially when Streicher left SDP to join Magna Europe's board. There were questions, too, as to the price Streicher might have paid for a unit in Magna's exclusive enclave of luxury homes within its Oberwaltersdorf compound, where his neighbours included a number of other politicians and high-ranking officials who had dealt with Magna Europe.

On their own, even a forest of Austrian eyebrows skeptically cocked at the political manoeuvring might not have had much impact on the SDP deal. The heavy state control of industry had almost necessarily involved politicians in business and business people with government. But Stronach had interpreted the positive response of business and government to his apparently successful enlivening of Austria's torpid economy as acknowledgement of the superiority of his theories and view of the world. Enjoying the status he'd acquired in the eyes of the political and business establishment, he set out to win the hearts and minds of the general public as well, chasing the popularity that had eluded him in Canada.

"HOW LONG CAN YOU LOOK AT MICKEY MOUSE?"

Stronach's influences were many, and in the mid 1990s they included the technology boom that had launched the era of Internet-inspired dot.coms. Frank, of course, had been committed all his life to making things that could hurt when dropped on a toe, but he didn't necessarily ascribe to the notion that Magna was "old economy." A technophile in manufacturing, he'd been impressed by the growth of so-called knowledge industries and the service sector that technology gurus were confidently forecasting would lead to greater leisure time for all.

On that basis, Stronach figured Magna's diversification into entertainment – a knowledge industry if ever there was one – would be no bad thing, and that Austria was ideally located to catch a new market he foresaw emanating from newly democratized Eastern Europe. Hungary, Slovenia, Slovakia, the Czech Republic, and Poland, abutting or close to Austria's eastern border, already had car assembly plants that were current or future customers of Magna's factories. As Eastern Europe shed the inefficiency of Communism, an emerging middle class would have money to spend, more time to spend it, and a growing appetite for Western culture, fantasy, and entertainment. Disney, the quintessential purveyor of American culture, proved Stronach's point: Disneyland Paris opened in 1990 and at first struggled, but by the mid 1990s, it had successfully overcome even France's renowned cultural xenophobia to become a major European attraction.

Convinced there was room for at least one more theme park in Europe and that Austria would be the perfect location, Stronach began thinking of himself as a latter-day Walt Disney, only a quicker study. As with everything he'd tried, from politics and auto parts to horse racing and economics, he felt qualified to point out Disney's mistake: the world's biggest entertainment colossus had built too many hotels when its market was day-visitors. It wouldn't have happened, Stronach believed, if old Walt had still been around. "How long can you look at Mickey Mouse?" he asked. "People just go for a few hours with the kids."

The attraction Stronach had in mind was nothing if not impressive. The original configuration of his proposed Magna Globe Resort theme park planned for Vienna featured a 200-metre-high globe, or *Weltkugel* as it had become known locally. The 60-storey sphere would house amusement rides, displays, and interactive entertainment that followed evolution from the Big Bang all the way to space travel. A line from Magna's promotional material suggested, with a perhaps unfortunate Teutonic nuance, the theme of the park: "On a perfect little planet, a race of beautiful people has built a utopia." Lest anyone doubt that Stronach was personally involved, the theme park would also include a horse museum.

Stronach also approved, as an architectural tour de force, the inclusion of huge statues of the Greek god Atlas, on the same scale as the globe and attached to its base as though supporting it. But the project's designers somehow failed to note that statues tend to depict Greek gods naked. On a model of the project that Stronach kept in his Oberwaltersdorf office, the statues seemed like demure little figurines. But rendered in the dimensions Stronach was proposing, mischievous locals pointed out, the genitalia of each Atlas would be about seven metres long, perhaps not an ideal image for the family audience that was targeted. Stronach promptly downsized the globe and replaced the statues with plain columns. But even at its new height of 140 metres, the globe would have been an attention-grabbing 40 storeys high. This was rather more than Vienna's town fathers felt appropriate as a neighbour for the Gothic twelfth-century St. Stephen's Cathedral in the ancient Austrian capital.

Stronach wasn't alone in his belief that Vienna was ready for a theme park. A group of investors that included the U.S. investment house Morgan Stanley (and, improbably, the former United Nations secretary-general Javier Perez de Cuellar) proposed building

Ultrapolis 3000, a $560-million (U.S.) multimedia theme park with an Asian theme, adjacent to Shopping City Sud, a suburban mall that was one of Europe's biggest. A German group got into the act with a proposal to develop a park, which included a permanent home for the Cirque du Soleil, in the Prater, a historic downtown Vienna landmark whose traditional amusement park and ferris wheel were featured in the 1949 movie classic *The Third Man*. As well, the head of the local chamber of commerce, wanting to stop the hollowing out of Vienna's downtown as projects sprouted on the city's outskirts, proposed yet another Prater development, a new commercial and entertainment centre. He hoped the Prater's racetracks and its soccer stadium would tempt Stronach to consider the site for the Magna Globe Resort Park.

Stronach expressed interest in Vienna's suggestion, and even pledged $1.13 billion in development funds if the project took root. But he shunted the Magna Globe Resort project out of town to Ebreichsdorf, a few kilometres from the Magna Europe head office, and renamed it World of Wonders. He'd already invested $29 million in 667 acres of land in Ebreichsdorf in 1996, although Magna hadn't showed the purchase in any of its financial filings. Stronach now claimed that the tract had initially been purchased as a potential site for an auto-parts plant, which justified its being paid for with some of the proceeds from the $149-million sale of Magna's air-bag manufacturing operation. But according to the mayor of Ebreichsdorf, Stronach had told him of the land purchase and his theme park plans six months before the air-bag operation sale. Stronach had even gone so far as to drum up local enthusiasm by whisking the eleven-person town council on an expenses-paid trip to Disneyland Paris, so that the councillors could see the potential economic benefits of theme-park tourism. It had worked. The mayor and council were onside. The local provincial government, however, balked at the project on environmental grounds, stalling approvals.

EXIT ROBERT GRUBER

Stronach's zeal to diversify into non-automotive ventures, meanwhile, had repercussions at Magna Europe. Robert Gruber, whose
financial expertise had been invaluable in setting up Magna Europe's
automotive business, had hoped that with the addition of SDP/SFT
he'd be given more operating responsibility. Stronach, though, was
now favouring Siegfried Wolf, a boisterous machinist and native of
Steyr whom he'd hired from a munitions company in 1994. He tried
to persuade Gruber to take over the running and development of
the non-automotive business, hoping his credentials and reputation
would legitimize it. Gruber, who felt that his expertise was in automotive, not only didn't want anything to do with Stronach's other
projects, he objected to allocating resources from the automotive
business to them. "I still don't know why he wants to do that. I'm
not convinced the globe project is a good one," Gruber said after
leaving Magna in 1997 to join Porsche's Austrian operations.

GEORGIA ON STRONACH'S MIND

Stronach appeared to believe that it was only the lack of exposure to
horses, and especially to racing, that prevented an explosion of
global fascination with the animals that matched his own. As a con-
sequence, a constant in his theme-park proposals was an insistence
that whatever got built, wherever, had to somehow have an equine
component. Even in the city that preserves the spectacle of the
famous Lippizaner horses strutting their stuff, it struck the Viennese
as odd. But odder still was his attempt to spread the message in
Atlanta, Georgia. In September 1997, armed with a ten-minute video,
Stronach pitched World of Wonders/Georgia Globe to the press, and
civic and state legislators.

Stronach, as usual, mentioned a possible Magna auto-parts plant
in the area. But the theme park he had in mind, he told Atlantans,
would generate about 4,000 jobs, depict the evolution of the world,
and fill the gap left by the 1996 Olympics as a tourist draw. That the

entire development was contingent on permission to build an accompanying horse-racing track, was a not inconsiderable hurdle: Georgia law prohibited live racing and parimutuel betting. Stronach, though, was unfazed. "Since Georgia doesn't have horse racing, you could start out with a clean sheet," he said. As for gambling's "very minute negatives," he believed a PR campaign would placate anti-gambling religious groups such as the Christian Coalition. "We would issue warnings to people: 'Don't bet the grocery money,'" he said. Ah, well, that's all right then. Problem solved.

The evanescent Georgia proposal slid into oblivion before he got around to explaining how its theme of evolution would play in the heartland of creationist theorists who were heavily committed to the notion of "intelligent design" and Adam and Eve. But the exercise demonstrated Stronach's avid belief that the revival of horse racing depended on its being linked to other modes of entertainment, preferably with a family orientation, and on the introduction of more casino-style gambling. Later he would add technology such as television and the Internet to the mix, and as the concepts coalesced in his mind, they would colour his future Magna projects for years to come.

"A HUNDRED PROJECTS AND IDEAS"

Back in Austria, at the end of 1997, the $787-million Ebreichsdorf World of Wonders remained mired in bureaucracy. To demonstrate the economic benefit of the park, Stronach breezily forecast it would attract 15,000 to 20,000 visitors a day. Big mistake. Regional politicians, horrified at the potential traffic congestion, balked at approving it until it was determined who would pay for the required roads. For their part, environmentalists objected to the destruction that the park would inflict on woodlands. Stronach, still confident the project would go ahead, was certain the public would come around. "It will be like the Eiffel Tower," he told the *Financial Times*. "At first they [Parisiens] were all against it but now 99.1% are for it." Stronach refused to apologize for the scale of the project relative to, say, the

Prater's traditional amusement park. "Nobody comes to Vienna for another merry-go-round," he said.

Stronach's profile in Austria, raised in the business pages by the Steyr-Daimler-Puch deal, rose still higher as the general news media began focusing on him with the same intensity as the business press had. Since 1996 Magna had been operating Magna Air Luftfahrt GmbH out of Vienna's Neustadt airport. The idea had been to get full utilization of Magna's Dassault Falcon 900, the latest plane that Stronach used, as well as a couple of Cessna business jets. In February 1998, Stronach elevated the jet rental business up to airline status. Magna, he said, had leased two Airbus 319 jetliners that would be configured with only thirty seats. The rest of the space would consist of amenities such as offices and sleeping accommodation to appeal to high-flying executives like himself, who regularly worked on two continents.

The same month, he revealed plans to build a retreat and "sports hotel" on a lake in Carinthia in the south of Austria, as well as an executive retreat on the site of an old hotel in the pine-and-lakes cottage country of Muskoka, north of Toronto. Stronach, Austria's honorary consul in Toronto, also hoped to attract the Austrian consulate in Canada to one of the two downtown Toronto buildings Magna had bought (for $4 million, too trivial to be considered material enough to bother shareholders with, the company said).

Management back in Aurora often first heard of Stronach's latest "vision" or statement from reporters calling for a comment. Graham Orr, frequently the designated Frank comment–deflector at Magna, struggled gallantly to explain his boss's latest ideas. The theme park, he said, was one of Frank's visions that hadn't yet been subjected to feasibility studies or board approval. But in Austria, according to the media, Stronach was telling another story; a four-man team, he said, was on the job, and $1 million had been spent on feasibility studies.

And the airline? The airline, said Orr, was the sort of thing that might be held in a venture division made up of non-automotive assets, but was still conceptual. Conceptual or not, it didn't stop Stronach from waxing enthusiastically in Austria on the airline's potential. "We have ordered only two Airbuses and will start small," he told an Austrian newsmagazine in an article entitled "The crazy projects of Frankie S." "Magna Air will fill a market niche," he said. In the same article, Stronach admitted that "I constantly have 100 projects and ideas ready for examination on my desk. Ninety-nine percent of them are junk."

Investors began to view Stronach's assessment as bang on. Recalling that Magna had almost hit the ditch the last time the driver was distracted by non-automotive flyers, they reached the conclusion that the man at the wheel was suffering another brain cramp. By the end of January 1998, Magna's stock, which had steadily climbed to over $100 a share, had fallen to the low $80s. Impressed by the drop in market capitalization, Stronach uncharacteristically began calling analysts to reassure them that any non-auto investments would be managed separately from Magna. He also angrily denied that the current diversification was a reprise of the one in the 1980s that many felt had contributed to Magna's near-death experience. "That's bullshit," he told the *Globe and Mail*. The previous diversification into media, restaurants, and a ski resort, he said, "was only half a percent [of Magna's business]."

Still, investors' concerns began to have a direct effect on the acquisition of SDP and SFT, the biggest automotive deal that Magna Europe had yet done, the one that would put it into the forefront of the industry.

A DEAL UNDONE?

Under normal circumstances a plunge in stock price might not have bothered Stronach, who professes to manage for the long term, paying little attention to short-term fluctuations. But the agreement with Creditanstalt, the bank from which Magna was buying SDP and SFT, forced him to pay attention. In early January 1998, Magna had agreed to pay for SDP and SFT with a combination of cash and stock. At the time, Magna's stock was trading at about $91 a share. Magna had intended to make the stock portion of the payment with about 3 million Class A shares that would give Creditanstalt a 4 per cent stake in Magna International. But the January sell-off of Magna stock had represented a loss of around $23 million to Creditanstalt. Stronach's telephone effort to calm investors had temporarily boosted the stock price by $5 or so, but Creditanstalt still stood to see about $7 million less than it would have under the original sale agreement.

The changing value of the deal had another effect. Some members of SDP's board had thought from the outset that Magna was getting the company too cheaply. When the Magna stock that Creditanstalt was to get began dropping in value, they started to push their case again. Sensing that the state-controlled SDP and SFT might be in play once more, new bidders appeared, forcing Creditanstalt to postpone closing the Magna transaction while it considered the new bids.

It was about the last thing Magna needed: not only was its own stock price dropping, but three new potential buyers on the scene were now driving up the price of SDP. The unwelcome combination made it seem inevitable that Magna's final cost would be higher than it had intended.

UNUSUAL TIMES PRODUCE UNUSUAL MEASURES

Somewhat unconventionally, Stronach included a letter to shareholders with the quarterly report when it was mailed in March 1998. Whatever the press might claim, Magna had not spent money on non-automotive projects, he said, and he reiterated his promise not to do so in the future, except through a new venture capital company that Magna planned to create, to isolate non-automotive ventures from Magna's core automotive business. Investors seemed to accept Stronach's promise, despite the fact that a few weeks earlier the Austrian media had declared that he'd spent $1 million on the theme-park development alone. Magna's stock price immediately popped up $9 to $99 in response to the letter.

Damage had already been done on the SDP deal, however. The arrival of new buyers on the scene – among them yet another high-ranking Austrian official, Hannes Androsch, a former Austrian finance minister, who had also previously served as chairman of Creditanstalt's management board, and BorgWarner Inc., a U.S.-based Magna competitor – embarrassed Creditanstalt and Bank Austria. They were left to explain why they hadn't put the company up for auction in the first place.

The Austrian public was asking the same question. But before it was answered, Magna's biggest customer came once again to its rescue. Chrysler, as a 50 per cent partner of SFT in Eurostar, had a contractual right to be consulted in the event of any change of ownership of SDP. What with SFT being a part of SDP, and Magna being a reliable, high-quality supplier on whom Chrysler depended, it decided to support Magna over the other bidders. In the end, the deal was saved. Magna wound up paying a combination of cash and convertible debentures worth $438 million for the SDP/SFT package.

It was difficult to say whether the price of the purchase, which had appeared to have been falling apart in March, was a good one. Magna never revealed its original price, rumoured to be about $400 million. According to some reports the price had gone up by more than $30 million as a result of the complications arising from the falling stock price.

Then, just when Magna thought it had steered out of trouble, another pothole appeared in the road ahead. As part of the final deal, Magna had negotiated to pay *more* for the SFT part of the package and *less* for the SDP portion. In doing so Stronach had by definition devalued SDP's shares and increased the value of SFT's. But in order to sell off the parts of SDP he didn't want, Stronach needed to own 100 per cent of the shares, which meant buying the stock of minority shareholders. Magna ultimately paid $145 million for the 33 per cent minority stake. But while it was a premium over what Creditanstalt had received, it was still a considerable discount from what some analysts were suggesting the Steyr stock was now worth. Small investors who owned the minority stake complained loudly that they'd been shafted, and Creditanstalt and Magna continued to attract flak. Of special interest to the protesters was the dual role played by Gerhard Randa as both an SDP and Magna director.

For Magna, though, the deal proved an excellent one, even if it was perhaps more expensive than intended. The final cost of SDP/SFT, including the minority interest, was $584 million. But Magna had made a huge move toward being a full-vehicle manufacturer, the first time a parts maker had integrated so far into the auto business.

By the summer of 1998, it seemed that Magna had survived Stronach's shot to the foot. At the conclusion of the SDP deal its stock was back trading at more than $100 in Toronto. Stronach himself, appearing none the worse for wear, evidently assumed the stock rebound was a mandate to carry on his diversification initiative. In September he found yet another field that aligned with his personal interests.

SOCCER KICKS IN

The way Stronach related the tale to European reporters, he had been flying back from a business meeting in Russia accompanied by Rudolf Streicher, the former SDP executive now on Magna's payroll, when on the Vienna cityscape below he noticed a floodlit playing field. Streicher, Stronach's skiing buddy and president of the Austria Vienna professional soccer team, told Stronach that the game was an exhibition one between Austria and the U.S., who were still regarded as novices in the round-ball game. When Stronach learned the next day that Austria had lost 3–0, he said, he was appalled at how far Austrian football had slid. He committed himself on the spot to restoring its reputation.

Whether or not the story is apocryphal, the subsequent invest-ment by Magna in Austria Vienna, known as the "Violets" for the team colours, was real. As usual, Stronach was happy to make use of the handy provision in Magna's corporate charter that dedicated 2 per cent of pre-tax profits to "charitable, educational, political, cul-tural and community activities." This vague definition gave Stronach licence to invest Magna's money more or less where he pleased in support of "the basic fabric of society" without having to report to shareholders. In 1997, Magna's $836-million pre-tax profit meant that the 2 per cent amounted to a hefty $16.7 million. So in September 1998, apparently identifying Austrian soccer as the somewhat tat-tered warp and woof of his homeland's basic fabric, Stronach dipped into the Magna fund, and pledged $750,000 to become the "sponsor" of Austria Vienna in Austria's top professional *Bundesliga*, the national soccer league. The investment gave Magna television and marketing rights to the fifth-place team's games. But its size also gave Stronach a significant voice in the operations of the club – too much say, it would later occur to fans.

As he was investing in the Violets, Stronach resurrected his belief that appropriate training could groom carefully selected youths into top-flight athletes. He pledged $1.6 million to the creation of a soccer school to prove his theory. The idea was that the academy would subsidize and train academically qualified youths whose ath-letic and psychological profiles demonstrated their potential as future soccer stars.

Somehow, when this public-spirited money was being spread around, Stronach didn't bother differentiating between himself and Magna. Although the money for the school was Magna's, the company name was nowhere to be found on the Frank Stronach Football Academy. And since the funding came from Magna's charitable pool, the expense didn't turn up anywhere in the company's financial reports. Neither, for that matter, did Stronach's declaration that he intended to spend still more on Austrian soccer in order to build an elite team that would compete in a proposed European Super League. "I am prepared to invest between 500 million and 800 million Austrian schillings [about $63.7 million (U.S.)] in Austrian soccer if the system and structure are correct," he told the *Kurier*, an Austrian daily.

It was probably just as well that little of the stir Stronach was creating in Austria made it to North America. He soon created enough there with another acquisition. In October 1998, when Santa Anita Park in California went up for sale, Stronach quickly had MI Developments (formerly MI Realty, the internal real-estate-development subsidiary of Magna), grab it for $126 million (U.S.). Magna's leap into racetrack ownership was a jolt to Magna International shareholders, who were already concerned that they seemed destined to own a theme park and a luxury airline. Stronach did his best to allay their fears by pointing out that the three hundred or so acres surrounding Santa Anita in northern Los Angeles were eminently developable by MI Developments and alone justified the price. The argument might have been more acceptable had MI Development's experience not been entirely in industrial properties – specifically in Magna's auto-parts factories.

Meanwhile, the non-automotive, sports-related projects kept coming. In Austria, he floated a proposal to meld elements of soccer and theme parks in a $100-million (U.S.), 20,000- to 30,000-seat stadium in Salzburg. In addition to being able to host games between *Bundesliga* teams, he hoped the stadium would attract the 2004 European Cup soccer tournament whose television rights also appealed to him. According to *Die Presse*, Magna agreed to handle 51 per cent of the stadium's operating costs using revenue from the 1.5 million visitors he forecast would visit an adjacent theme park that focused on opera and the Brothers Grimm fairy tales.

By December 1998 Stronach had come to view the financially perilous state of the *Bundesliga*'s ten teams as an obstacle to his plan to resurrect Austrian soccer. Making good on his promise to invest in the sport, he bought marketing rights to two other Austrian teams for $10 million – he already controlled Austria Vienna – and declared his intention to buy the rights of the rest as well. In February 1999, he went further and offered to spread 1 billion schillings (about $122 million) across the entire league in exchange for marketing rights, which included the right to televise games. He hoped the teams would use the money to encourage top Austrian players to remain in Austria rather than head off to other leagues in Europe, and to buy better players that would raise the level of play generally.

This time, he said, the soccer investment would come from Magna's Ventures division. But Magna, he added, wasn't about to shell out that kind of cash without a degree of control over the league's affairs: a condition of the investment was that Stronach was to be elected president of the entire league. It was a measure of how needy Austria's soccer teams were that they agreed.

Forty-five years after abandoning his hopes of becoming a professional soccer player to instead become a tycoon, Frank Stronach, then sixty-seven, had become president of the highest-level league in Austria.

THE CONVERGENCE FAD CONVERGES ON MAGNA

Consciously or unconsciously, Stronach seemed to have been influenced by the claims being made for convergence, a business strategy that became fashionable during the technology bubble of the mid to late 1990s. Convergence involves collecting content such as programming, then adding a channel for delivering it to mass audiences, and an interactive means of receiving payment – often through advertising, or in some way using the Internet or telecommunications. In the U.S., the merger of Disney, a content creator, with the ABC television network, a delivery channel, was one of many examples of convergence. In Canada, BCE Inc.'s convergence strategy was to combine the content of the *Globe and Mail* newspaper with the CTV television network and the Bell Canada Sympatico Internet service provider, to deliver information to consumers.

The purchase of Santa Anita had been a seminal part of Stronach's global convergence plan. Horse races held at the famous track, soccer games televised from Austria, and Formula One car races – in fact, any sport on which punters could bet – would become content. Magna also intended to own the channel, a satellite television station that beamed programming into the homes of gamblers. Magna – or whatever vehicle it set up to hold the operation – would take a piece of all bets placed via telephone, the Internet, or in off-track betting parlours. A key part of the Santa Anita strategy was that the racetrack would be redeveloped as a theme park, with shopping, entertainment, and restaurants, but with horse racing, and gambling, as its focus. "To me, it's quite clear specialty tourism and gaming will be consistently growing markets," Stronach said.

It wasn't all that clear to investors or analysts. Or at least if it was, they decided that soccer, and especially racetracks, were signs of a continuing drift of attention away from Magna's core automotive business. Despite a 20 per cent sales hike in 1998 to $9.2 billion from $7.7 billion in 1997, analysts who'd been reading of Stronach's European plans and who were dubious about where the Santa Anita purchase fit into the company's overall picture, downgraded their forecasts for Magna's stock on the basis of what David Olive, the *Toronto Star's* astute, long-time Magna watcher, called "the Frank Factor" – the unpredictability of the chairman. Stronach answered his critics by announcing that Magna was considering spinning off MI Developments as a real-estate company that would hold the non-automotive assets.

Austrians, meanwhile, had begun thinking of Stronach less as a repatriated prince of industry with millions to spend on his homeland, and more as an opportunistic bully using cash as his pulpit. A columnist for an Austrian newspaper compared Stronach to an evangelical preacher, saying, "Stronach is a patriarchal, authoritarian, self-made man who has designed his own philosophy." Writing in an Austrian magazine that cheekily commissioned him to explain Stronach in the context of Austria, the respected philosopher Konrad Paul Liesmann described Stronach's speeches as "a mixture of naked calculation and utopian statement which makes even the most stupid and incomprehensible schemes (such as the World of Wonders theme park with its 80-metre globe) appear as a work-creating project worthy of discussion."

Although Stronach's master convergence plan was a little hazy, the government-owned broadcaster Österreichischer Rundfunk (ÖRF) saw enough in it to stage a protest against his effort to lock up Austrian soccer rights, which it had previously owned. ÖRF had a plan of its own for a sports-gambling channel. Austria's one hundred or so independent licenced bookmakers, who already opposed ÖRF's plan, also objected to Magna's proposal, which would eat into their business. Magna responded by taking out its own bookmaking licence, which made Stronach the world's wealthiest bookie.

A FEW STAFF PROBLEMS

Back in North America, in the interim, the Frank Factor again kicked in. In January 1999 Stronach made the surprising revelation that he had hired Garth Drabinsky to advise on the entertainment prospects of a proposed development of real estate around Santa Anita. Drabinsky, a Toronto impresario who had moved on from founding Cineplex, a chain of multi-screen movie theatres, to start up Livent Inc., a live-theatre company that was now insolvent, was undeniably an expert on entertainment. But he came with unfortunate baggage: he'd been suspected of cooking Livent's books and was under investigation in the U.S. by both the Securities Exchange Commission and the Department of Justice. Within a week of his hiring by Magna, the U.S. federal government filed a fraud indictment against him. It was a regrettable coincidence, and Stronach fired him.

The ill-advised hiring of Drabinsky was not an isolated example of Stronach's dubious personnel decisions or mishandling of employees and associates. In fact, it was almost part of a pattern, as though he deliberately sought controversy or made contrary decisions to prove that he wouldn't be swayed by public opinion or convention. Austrian soccer fans were enraged by Stronach's revolving-door style that replaced team management on at least an annual basis. That Austria Vienna's payroll dwarfed that of other teams, without producing a winning side, proved equally irksome.

No less perplexing to some were Stronach's personnel choices at Magna itself. In selecting a European CEO, he had chosen the flamboyant Siegfried Wolf – later famous for insisting on addressing the Magna AGM in Toronto in German – over the steady, capable Gruber. The decision had divided the office and ultimately induced many employees to bolt the company. "It was hard to take Siegi seriously," says a former executive who describes Wolf's relationship with Stronach as excessively ingratiating. "I don't know many people who like him . . . I think Frank has the wrong guys around him. He doesn't judge character very well." The executive goes on to say he tends to hire only those who tell him what he wants to hear.

Two star executives, who likely told Stronach things that he didn't want to hear, but whom he went back and forth on, were Jim Nicol and Fred Jaekel. By 1997 Stronach had hired Nicol for the third time after he had twice departed. In 1990, Stronach had also fired and then rehired Jaekel, who went on to involve Magna in the supremely successful and profitable hydroforming technology. (The two would later get into a duel of lawsuits.)

But perhaps the best example of Stronach's lack of foresight when it came to selecting staff was his hiring of Karl-Heinz Grasser. In 1998, he engaged Grasser as SDP's new communications director to fill a gap left by staff who had quit when when Siegi Wolf was promoted. The scion of a wealthy auto dealer in Klagenfurt, the capital of Austria's Carinthia province, Grasser looked like a catch. An able student of economics, he had a charisma that had already attracted the attention of Jörg Haider, Carinthia's governor and leader of the far-right Freedom Party of Austria (FPÖ). Haider had made him Carinthia's deputy governor, a position he held when Stronach first approached him.

Grasser left the government post after falling out with Haider when the latter shocked the world by offering the view that Hitler's "employment policy" was fundamentally sound and that veterans of the Waffen SS were "decent people of good character." Haider also downplayed the Holocaust and pandered to Austrian nationalism by promoting a xenophobic, anti-immigrant initiative that had unfortunate echoes of the "overforeignization" that Hitler had used to justify his fascist policies.

Grasser, only twenty-nine when he began his eighteen months as Magna's communications director, enjoyed a reputation as a ladies' man that clearly was not an obstacle for Stronach. (An enthusiastic heterosexual himself, Stronach later didn't seem to find anything particularly untoward in Siegi Wolf's widely covered dalliance with figure skater and Playboy model Katarina Witt before Wolf returned to his wealthy wife.) Stronach's hiring of Grasser – he'd made the offer before Grasser split with Haider – eventually gave him yet another protegé in government. When Haider's Freedom Party grabbed 27 per cent of the popular vote and shocked Europe by becoming part of Austria's governing coalition in early 2000, Haider put forth Grasser's name for the position of Austria's finance minister, forgetting their earlier differences. Grasser would later say that he took the job, becoming the youngest finance minister in Austria's history, only after gaining the approbation of Stronach, who, along with Haider, he proclaimed as the major influences in his life.

Most Austrians seemed embarrassed when the inclusion of the extremist Haider party in the governing coalition threatened to make Austria an international pariah. Stronach wasn't one of them. Whether because he wanted to demonstrate yet again that he couldn't

be cowed by public opinion or because he genuinely sympathized
with Haider's immigration policy, Stronach did remarkably little to
distance himself from it. Instead of criticizing the very restrictive
immigration strategy like most of the Western world, Stronach defended it. "It's like a canoe that has room for four people," he said,
doubtless sending Magna executives rushing to find the well-
thumbed "Bail out Frank" page in their procedure manuals. "At some
point there's no more room," he added. "You can't let in the whole of
China and the whole of Russia. It's not peaceable. It's not practical."

The resulting controversy inevitably dredged up other questionable politics. The *Globe and Mail* quoted the leader of a small
Austrian party who claimed to have been told by Stronach that his
objective in hiring Grasser had been to pick his brains for ideas to
help found a political party that Stronach had been contemplating,
to be based on the Magna charter and his Fair Enterprise manifesto.
Another political leader had led the opposition to the World of
Wonders theme-park project (in part because she objected to its
structure, a globe similar to one that Nazi architect Albert Speer once
proposed for Berlin). She also disliked the theme-park brochure's
ill-phrased claim that it would celebrate a "race of beautiful people."

The controversy would die down in Austria, only to be fanned
back into flames when Haider made an unannounced visit to Canada
in mid February 2000, claiming to be there to promote Austria.
Amid minor protests and a refusal to permit him to visit a Montreal
Holocaust museum, his connection to Stronach was again raised
when a published rumour, quickly proved unfounded, suggested
Haider was on his way to Aurora to visit with the Magna chief.

Most who knew Stronach found the contention that he had
extreme right-wing leanings or latent anti-Semitic tendencies simply
preposterous. It wasn't beyond belief, however, that he would welcome a close connection with the Austrian finance minister while
Austria was still privatizing state-controlled businesses, including a
steel company and a broadcasting unit, in which Magna Europe

might be interested. Still, it wasn't Stronach's proudest moment, and it contributed to Austria's growing wariness of Stronach, however altruistic he painted the benefits he promised to bestow – and indeed, had bestowed – on his homeland.

In 1999, Magna ran into a different kind of controversy when it fired a woman for allegedly encouraging a union to organize its factory in Stronach's hometown of Weiz. The Austrian metal workers accused Magna Europe of violating Austrian law and went to court to force Magna to reinstate the employee. Conscious of public sentiment, not to mention the fact that 60 per cent of private-sector workers and 85 per cent in the public sector are unionized, the Austrian government joined the fray, saying that until the dispute was settled it would withhold $98 million in aid promised to Magna companies. Stronach countered by once again brandishing his ability to create jobs, the same club he'd used in North America to wangle out of governments everything from zoning changes to grants.

Somehow it all sounded different now, five years after Stronach had begun to rise to prominence in his native land with bold promises. His bluster sounded less like Frank the messiah, ready to lead Austria out of the wilderness. In fact, in sharply warning Austrians that he'd build Magna's plants over the border in Slovenia if they weren't grateful for the jobs he was creating, he sounded more like Frank the disgruntled industrialist, who had huffily departed Canada complaining that his efforts hadn't been appreciated. Under-appreciation of Frank Stronach, it seemed, had spread.

12

MAGNA'S MIDDLE-AGE SPREAD

Despite promising for nearly a decade that he would spin off some of Magna's groups as clones – the strategy was first approved in 1982 – Stronach had always found a reason not to do so. Magna had come closest to executing the strategy in 1989, when Jim McAlpine had Cosma and Decoma teed up for an IPO to raise $114 million to help pay down the company's debt. Stronach's yanking of the public offering, which meant postponing the debt repayment, had contributed to the company's near-collapse. He'd since mused about selling shares of a number of Magna subsidiaries, including Magna Steyr, Tesma, and Decoma (again).

The idea behind spinoffs was to clone Magna's structure in publicly traded companies in which Magna would remain the majority shareholder. Instead of competing with other subsidiaries for capital from Magna, as public companies they could raise equity according to their needs – and according to investors' confidence in such things as their business plan, management, and competitive position, the usual stuff. The connection with Magna, of course, would help, but the debt they incurred, or the profit they made, would only be shared by Magna in proportion to its ownership of the spinco. Magna would also collect an "affiliation fee" of 1–2 per cent, which entitled the subsidiary to access to corporate resources.

The concept was based on Magna's bedrock belief that profit-sharing and stock-ownership plans were an incentive to employees to work harder and smarter. As Magna grew, workers were more likely to feel a disconnect between their individual efforts and the value of Magna's shares or the size of its profits. But, the theory went, subsidiaries spun off as publicly traded companies – mini-Magnas – would reaffirm to employees that their efforts affected share-price and profits.

In 1995, Magna finally decided to take the spinoff plunge using Tesma as its test case, with Fred Gingl at the helm. Gingl had done well with Blau KG, the $75-million-a-year Austrian fuel-handling company he'd bought in 1993 (with Magna as a 45 per cent share-holder) after a European contact had tipped him that its seven ageing owners wanted to sell. Gingl indicated he one day hoped to take Blau public. But before he could do so, Stronach approached him to run Tesma.

The opportunity to raise its own capital had attractions for Tesma, Magna's power-train operation. As the smallest subsidiary, it was often at the end of the line when capital was being forked over to the subs by Magna. Gingl's appointment as president and CEO fulfilled his ambition to run his own show, not to mention Magna's equally strong desire to have a trusted soldier as the boss of its first spinco. Magna paid Gingl $400,000 plus 740,000 Tesma shares for Blau, which was renamed Blautec when it was folded into Tesma. Gingl couldn't complain: at an IPO price of $10.50, the shares alone were worth $7.8 million, giving his total package a price of $8.2 million.

Magna, which controlled 82 per cent of Tesma's B shares, was happy as well. Despite the relatively small float of shares sold to the public, the spinoff generated $28.9 million. As well as any additional capital gain it might make on its shares in Tesma in the future, Magna also received an annual affiliation fee of 1 per cent of sales. Stronach, as usual, did best of all: for spawning the deal, he rewarded himself with 750,000 options on Tesma shares, exercisable at the issue price of $10.50. By the end of 1996, they'd risen $3 in value, giving him a $2.25-million gain on paper.

By rights, the Tesma success, and the promise of a Decoma spin-off in 1998, should have earned Magna coverage in the financial press. And they did. But not nearly as much as the story of an embarrassing sex-and-sales scandal that broke in the fall of 1997, and went on to feature Magna in salacious front-page tales more typical of the *National Enquirer* than the *Wall Street Journal*.

SEX AND SALES AT MACHO MAGNA

Stronach proudly claimed to be the progenitor and sustainer of Magna's "unique entrepreneurial culture" – indeed, this cultural nurturing was routinely cited in annual reports as the reason for his enormous consulting fees. Unfortunately, neither he nor the corporate charter had been particularly successful at transforming the company into a model of sexual equity. Like many companies in the male-dominated automotive sector, Magna was fuelled as much by testosterone as it was by profit-sharing.

Stronach's own wandering eye and his admiration for beautiful women may have had something to do with why little had been done to modify the macho corporate culture. Tom Dillon is an MEC executive vice-president as well as president of Aurora Hospitality, the Magna Entertainment division that oversees catering operations at its racetracks and golf courses. He first met Stronach in the late 1970s when he was a frequent patron of Siro's, the landmark restaurant in Saratoga Springs, New York, which Dillon has run at the centre of the social scene for twenty-six years. Dillon says that his friend's reputation for being "a bit of a rake" is well deserved, and at times inconvenient, such as when Stronach took off with one of Dillon's employees. "My hostess was there and Frank would say, 'I'm going to take [her] away to Paris,'" Dillon laughs, shaking his head. "I'd say, 'It's a big weekend, Frank, I can't lose my hostess,' and he'd say 'Don't worry.' Frank's about sixty and the girl's twenty-two, and she'd come back and be useless for a week after being in Paris."

The boss's rakish behaviour was noted by Magna's European employees, as well. Austrian office staff accepted as a given that the secretary Stronach hired would typically be a beautiful woman in her twenties, according to a former manager in the Magna Europe office. One such hire, says the manager, was incapable of the simplest filing chore: "She wasn't even capable after three months to put all the press releases together the right way." Female employees discreetly warned younger women on staff to beware the boss's behaviour at events such as the office Christmas party, to the point of describing, from experience, the "moves" to expect from the boss. Even male managers would sometimes alert new female hires about the chairman's louche tendencies. "It was the first time an executive told me before I started [a job], 'Be careful, he's a womanizer,'" says a woman who worked at Magna Europe.

Although many of Magna's plants employed women on assembly lines, and as clerks and secretaries, few women had made it to the upper echelons of management. In the company's twenty-eight years leading up to 1997, only 5 of the 122 directors and senior executives named in its annual reports had been women. One was Heather Reisman, the future CEO of Indigo/Chapters, who sat on the board for three years. Three others achieved the elevated status for only one year: Judi Decker, as Controller; Jean Fraser, a lawyer who sat as a Magna director; and Christine McAllister Wardell, who was CEO of a company Magna had taken over. The fifth woman was much more successful. Her name was Belinda Stronach.

In 1997, at the age of thirty-one, Frank's daughter had already been on the board nine years, longer than all the other women in Magna's 28-year history combined, and she deserves an introduction here. Since choosing auto parts over education and bailing out of York University in 1985 after a year – her father was a York trustee when she enrolled, and left shortly after she did – Belinda had rocketed through Magna's organization. Her decision to enter the business world looked brilliant in 1989; at about the time her former university class was graduating and hunting for jobs, she was appointed to the board of Magna, at the age of twenty-two. Six years later she was made vice-president of Diversa, a group within Magna responsible for non-automotive businesses.

She also administered Magna's charitable pool, identifying worthy causes for donations. Despite her success in turning the corporate ladder at Magna into a high-speed escalator, however, few doubted that she owed her rise more to pedigree than to any demonstrated talent for advising management on the intricacies of the auto-parts industry. "Giving away money's easy," chuckles Burton Pabst, Magna's seventy-four-year-old co-founder who has known Belinda since she was born. "Even I could do that, but I wouldn't say Belinda knew which end of a screwdriver to use." But Belinda's ascent hadn't noticeably affected Magna's approach to sexual equality, nor done much to alter Magna's behavioural culture, nourished for years by the frat-boy atmosphere that defined the masculine car world.

If her surname insulated Belinda Stronach from the macho culture, the experience of Lorrie Beno, another Magna employee, was markedly different. In March 1996 Beno sued Magna for sexual discrimination and sexual harassment. The ensuing publicity painted Magna as an active participant in the tawdry practice of wooing auto-company clients with booze and sex at local strip clubs.

Unlike Belinda, Beno wasn't in line to inherit control of Magna some day, or even related to anyone at the company. Also unlike Belinda, she had completed several years of higher education; she brought an engineering degree with her in 1994 when she joined the Detroit-based sales department of Atoma International Inc., Magna's door-module and closure-systems group. According to her legal suit, Beno soon encountered some difficulties when she declined to entertain potential customers in the fashion that her male Magna colleagues did. Whether buyers from the Big Three auto companies demanded sex and booze, or whether they had been offered them and accepted, it had become a matter of routine that Magna's salesmen ply them with both at local strip clubs on the company's tab. Beno, who refused to participate in the practice, claimed that Magna responded by reducing her expense budget to a fraction of what her male colleagues spent, limiting her effectiveness. When she objected, Beno was fired. She answered by suing Magna for $23.25 million (U.S.) in punitive damages.

The size of the lawsuit alone was enough to earn Magna some unwelcome publicity, including front-page treatment in the *New York Times*. Beno's charges gained credibility when Judith Copeland, a female employee in Atoma's accounting department, launched a separate suit in 1997, claiming she was an indirect victim of the sex-for-sales approach to doing business: alcohol-charged salesmen returning from lascivious lunches, Copeland said in her filing, sexually harassed females in the office.

Magna naturally denied endorsing or even permitting the use of liquor and lap dances to win contracts. But it couldn't deny that the practice went on: a paper-trail of expense-account records and credit-card receipts were entered into evidence to support Beno's claim that $300-plus lunches at local topless bars were more the rule than the exception. One Magna sales executive's yearly lunch expenses topped $40,000. Things became sticky when Magna indicated that its employees were merely providing what customers were demanding. That defence threw the spotlight, and the blame, on its customers. The Big Three automakers, all Magna customers, had been discomfited at being dragged into the case in the first place. Now they, not to mention a fair number of wives, were even less pleased at being caught in flagrante delicto and having to admit that their representatives had been accepting gifts of *any* kind from suppliers, much less booze and strip-club sex.

As was its practice, Magna settled the Beno and Copeland lawsuits out of court, with the usual condition that neither party discuss the details. The company also announced an in-house program to educate employees about inappropriate sexual behaviour in the workplace. At the very least, the response was tardy for a company that prided itself on its ability to adapt with lightning-like speed to the mere hint of a shift in a business condition that might affect its profits, or the well-being of its employees.

A POLICE CHIEF ON THE PAYROLL

In 1997, the same year Magna was dealing with fallout from the sexual harassment charges, its connection to another unsavoury character was questioned. Bryan Cousineau, the chief of the 700-officer York Region police force, was suspended during an investigation by the Ontario Provincial Police into a variety of corruption charges. The nine-month OPP probe uncovered the existence of a $125,000 interest-free loan made by Magna in 1995 to the chief, supposedly an advance payment for services Cousineau would provide to Magna following his retirement. It struck the OPP as passing strange that Cousineau, forty-nine, had given no indication that his retirement was imminent, yet had been on the payroll of York Region's richest and biggest employer. That Magna's luckless executive vice-president Graham Orr couldn't, or wouldn't, explain exactly who had negotiated Cousineau's deal, or for what reason, only piqued interest in Magna's role after Cousineau was charged with breach of trust and bounced from the force.

STRONACH LOSES AN ARGUMENT

These uncomfortable peripheral matters in Canada must have left Stronach eager to tend to his various non-automotive projects in Europe. But in the mid to late 1990s he had a new incentive to spend more time in Aurora, as plans for Magna's new corporate campus were unfolding. Or failing to unfold. In the spring of 1993, Stronach had seemed to be caught off guard when proposed local planning regulations caused the postponement of, and almost thwarted, the development. His concern was personal as well, since the regulations threatened to devalue the six-hundred-acre farm he'd owned since 1978 and currently lived on. Stronach's reaction had been to marshal all the forces he could to derail the plan.

The town of Aurora's land-use plan, two years in the making, was about to be approved by the province. The plan designated the land around Aurora for various uses in order to sustain orderly development. But Stronach's property, which fell just to the east of the planning area, would, logically enough, have remained zoned as rural-agricultural. Once the province accepted the Aurora plan, zoning of vacant land around Aurora, including Stronach's, would have been unalterable for at least five years. Stronach had tried to sell the property in 1989 for $57 million to developer Alfredo deGasperis, but the deal had fallen through. In the meantime, he had decided it would be an ideal location for Magna's new international head-quarters, the centre of the corporate campus. To make that happen, he proposed severing some of his land and selling it to Magna. But to do so, he needed zoning changes.

Aurora had reservations. It didn't want to be gulled in a bait-and-switch manoeuvre similar to those Magna had used in neighbouring communities, where, once Magna's land was rezoned for a head office, it was promptly sold. The town also had some planning objections to Stronach's proposed development of the farm into a corporate campus, where his notion was to add housing to the development. Aurora argued that this would contribute to urban sprawl and increase pressure for growth. When the town demanded a written commitment that Magna would actually build a headquarters, as a condition of its being included in the land-use plan, Stronach adopted the role of the aggrieved local benefactor being thwarted by red tape, and called the request "an insult."

In the spring of 1993, mere days before the Aurora land-use plan was to be approved by the Ontario Ministry of Municipal Affairs,

Stronach escalated the dispute by filing an objection with the government body. Incensed, Aurora mayor John West requested that the ministry reject the objection as frivolous. Not wishing to irritate one of Ontario's biggest employers, however, fence-sitting provincial politicians passed the decision off to the Ontario Municipal Board, a tribunal that rules on real-estate disputes in the province.

While everyone was waiting for the OMB to decide, in early September Stronach unveiled his grand plan to the Aurora council. Stronach showed up in person, accompanied by a bevy of consultants and advisers intended to overwhelm the municipal politicians. In his retinue was the former Richmond Hill mayor Al Duffy, with whom Stronach had had an on-again, off-again relationship, once flying Duffy and his teenaged daughters on a ski vacation in Colorado; Duffy, in his role of incorruptible public servant, had repaid him by abandoning his cause to join the winning bidder. Since retiring from politics, Duffy had become a consultant and land assembler. In any event, Stronach wasn't in a position to hold a grudge against Duffy, given his own list of broken promises to municipalities. Obviously, he thought Duffy had good enough credentials to shepherd his Aurora property proposal through whatever channels necessary.

Stronach also had some heavyweights on his own board he could call on. Former Ontario premier Bill Davis, a Magna director, lent his gravitas to the proceedings by noting somewhat portentously that the development was important "in view of the very competitive global economy." Stronach himself proclaimed that his sale of land to Magna for the corporate campus was a favour to Aurora, a town of about 32,000 at the time: Magna, already the employer of some 10,000 in York Region, would create direct employment for 1,000 and indirectly add 10,000 more jobs around the region and in Aurora. Had Magna considered its development anywhere in the U.S., he griped, "a thousand mayors" would be grateful. "They would try to cater for us, and that's the difference between Canada and the United States."

The scale of the $200-million development Stronach unveiled at the September meeting was undeniably ambitious. It included a four-storey Magna head office and administration building, a research centre, an auto-parts plant, a medical clinic, an arts and education centre, a seniors' residence, an eighteen-hole golf course with a clubhouse, and 237 "estate" lots for "manor-style" homes. As well, land was set aside for baseball, soccer, and other playing fields that would be available for use by the municipality.

The council, though impressed by the firepower Stronach had assembled, was unimpressed by the proposal. Indeed, there were indications that Stronach may have – not for the first time in his life – oversold his case. The OMB still had not ruled on his objection, and since its land-use plan wouldn't be reviewed for eighteen months, Aurora declined to offer an opinion on the presentation. Even the newly acquired clout of Dennis Mills, Stronach's friend and former Magna vice-president, did not achieve anything. Mills, who had left Magna's employ when elected to Parliament in the election Stronach lost, was now secretary to the federal minister of industry, as well as chair of the Ontario Liberal caucus. Stronach saw him as a proxy for his own failed political ambitions, a role that Mills seemed willing to play. Although his riding was nowhere near Aurora, he seemed happy to lobby local politicians on behalf of his old boss, warning them that Stronach had no intentions of breaking the Magna development into separate components. His message was that the project would only go ahead on an all-or-nothing basis.

The threat didn't work. Following a March 1994 town hall meeting, Aurora approved an exemption for the office buildings, factories, research centre, medical clinic, and arts and entertainment facility, all of which would occupy about 73 acres. But it would reserve its judgment on the 237-acre golf course until more environmental studies were done. The approval of the homes that Stronach planned on another 464 acres was also shelved pending review, a process expected to take a few years. Irked that things had not gone his way, and that many of the three hundred or so local citizens at the four-hour meeting thought he'd been trying to bull-doze the town, Stronach peevishly reissued his usual threat when challenged: he might still move the entire project elsewhere, then everyone would be sorry.

(There was an interesting side issue in all this. Magna sharehold-ers might well have had questions about the $10.9 million the company paid for the land for its campus. Magna, of course, owed a fiduciary duty to shareholders to buy the land at the lowest price possible, and claimed that it had. But it had bought the land from Stronach, who naturally wanted the highest price. And he happened to control the company. The price was, however, approved by the independent direc-tors on the board, who in turn relied on three independent valuations.)

Meanwhile, the town of Aurora didn't much care what Magna had paid Stronach for the land; but it was pretty sure he wouldn't reverse the sale and give the money back (unless, of course, he had given Magna an exceptionally good deal and could get far more for the land elsewhere). The town called his bluff and ignored his threat to go elsewhere. Nothing happened. For good measure, Aurora got in a parting shot: it insisted that Stronach withdraw the objection he had filed with the Ontario Municipal Board. Otherwise the deal was off.

Stronach complied. And by 1995, lo and behold, he was posi-tively conciliatory. Construction of the approved part of the campus was underway and Cam-Slide, a Magna factory just to the north of Stronach's home and stables, was already cranking out car-seat rails. At the official opening of the factory, he offered an olive branch to Aurora, now led by a new mayor, the manager of a tennis club where Stronach played regularly and a supporter of Stronach's development plans. "If I've been too pushy over the years, I'd like to apologize," Stronach said. "I came down too hard at one council meeting."

VERSAILLES COMES TO AURORA

Beside the factory, Magna's research centre, administration building, and headquarters were almost finished. The stunningly impressive complex, which had an unmistakable similarity to Magna Europe's headquarters near Stronach's medieval castle in Austria, was rendered in a faux-chateau style reminiscent of Versailles, the French palace built by Louis XIV. The Sun King, whose fifty-four-year rule epitomized absolute government, has been credited with developing France's cultural roots; Magna's long-time absolute ruler was clearly Louis's equivalent, the formulator, champion, and protector of Magna's culture.

In his tours of the project during construction, Stronach missed few opportunities to impress on those around him, including the press who were invited along, that he'd accept nothing less than perfection in the construction of his legacy in which he was taking a personal, hands-on interest. That interest, naturally enough, wasn't particularly welcomed by the architects, contractors, or workers who'd been working to the design specifications, and from a budget he'd already approved. Unrestricted by any such details as budgets, Stronach's attention ranged from the smallest details, such as selection of doors, to major systems that he demanded be redone. Change orders, which tend to increase the costs of completed work, typically happen here and there on construction projects; at Magna, a tour of the site by the boss could elicit as many as fifty at a time.

For example, when he decided that the conventional air-conditioning and heat venting marred the look of the green slate roof, he ordered it removed; re-venting the HVAC system added nearly $1 million to the building's cost. Reversing a stairway in the research building to open to the opposite direction cost almost as much. Stronach, in his role as Sun King, was unapologetic for the initial $200 million budgeted for the complex or for the added costs his changes had caused. "A hundred years from now," he told reporters invited on one tour, "when people see it, I want them to say, 'Great building, great foresight.'"

The town of Aurora didn't have to come up with street names for the Magna campus. For one thing, it was private property, as the guard houses and security cameras reminded visitors. For another, Stronach had already picked them. Stronach Drive, the tree-lined road leading to the main headquarters, was changed to Stronach Boulevard, perhaps because the chairman felt that name had a grander ring to it. But that there would also be a Magna Drive was a foregone conclusion. In the residential area and around the golf course, he named the streets after, you bet, his winningest horses: Glorious Song, Awesome Again, Touch Gold, Macho Uno, and Red Bullet.

1997 – A GOOD YEAR FOR MAGNA, AND FOR FRANK

The revelation of Magna's involvement in the liquor-and-ladies scandal in Detroit and the unexplained payment to York Region's police chief were public relations irritants that took some of the shine off the move into the new quarters in Aurora. Strange tales from Austria of Stronach's theme park and the planned airline project elicited growing curiosity as well, and Stronach's compensation also came in for its annual scrutiny. It was in fiscal 1997, it will be recalled, that the $26.5 million Stronach pocketed exceeded the combined total that the chairmen of GM, Ford, and Chrysler earned. The 750,000 Tesma options that he'd been granted at an exercisable price of $10.50 were looking good by November 1997, too. Tesma's shares were trading at $22, giving him a paper-gain of about $8.6 million.

Magna's performance in 1997 sparkled as well. Sales of $7.7 billion had produced a profit of $603 million, almost double 1996's profit of $319 million. The earnings included a $148.7-million gain from divesting the air-bag business and $41 million from the sale of Tesma shares.

NICOL'S RETURN – BUYING A COMPANY TO GET ITS CEO

More significant than Tesma's contribution to Magna's profit was the fact that it was a spinoff that had actually happened. In March 1998 the Decoma subsidiary (with $951 million in sales of plastic components and exterior trim) became the second subsidiary to be gently, and profitably, eased from the Magna nest. Decoma netted the parent company $39 million.

As well as generating money for Magna, the spinoffs heralded yet another of Magna's restructuring phases. And in anticipation of it, Stronach had been trying to rehire Jim Nicol, who had already put in two tours with Magna, most recently as chairman of the team that had engineered Magna's spectacular turnaround in 1990.

In one respect, Nicol had already created a Magna clone before Stronach got around to executing his plan to do so. Along with Magna CFO David Copeland and lawyer David Hughes, Nicol left Magna in 1992 with fat settlements as a reward for their salvage job. Following the expiry of their non-compete clauses in the fall of 1993, they had put up $1.4 million of their own, found private backing, and, in 1994, created Triam Automotive Inc., a publicly traded auto-parts business. Triam had kicked into life by acquiring a $62-million-a-year manufacturer of transmission components.

If it was Stronach's capricious management style that had helped drive Nicol from Magna, Nicol himself never said as much and, in any event, he was no bridge-burner. Triam's business model, he said, was based on Magna's, which he and his partners, including Dan Chicoine, former head of Magna's Atoma division, and John London, another ex-Magna executive at Triam, greatly admired. Rather than build organically, Triam intended to consolidate profitable small-to medium-sized parts suppliers, improve their functional operations, and then "put them under an umbrella of sophisticated management."

As a public company, Triam hadn't set the world on fire, but it had acquired some auto-parts contracts, and its laser-welding technology gave promise of winning it more. Prospects were good enough that Nicol wasn't initially interested when Stronach started feeling him out about returning to Magna for a third time. To Stronach, however, "No" generally means "How much?" In 1998, when Nicol indicated that he didn't want to move unless other Triam shareholders benefited as well, Stronach promptly put up $77 million in cash and Magna shares and bought Triam.

Getting a 30 per cent premium for their stock appealed to Triam shareholders. It met with Nicol's approval, too; Triam options plus payment under a contractual guarantee saw him collect a $3.4-million package, plus whatever he made on his Triam stock in selling it to Magna. It was a little more difficult to weigh the merits of the hard assets Magna got for its money, although it naturally claimed that the Triam plants were a good fit with its own. Magna also took over a Triam contract to supply components to GM's Saturn Corp. But a Magna insider at the time says Triam was encumbered by dubious financing for tooling for the Saturn contract, a detail that had been buried in Triam's financials. If Magna bothered to exhume the matter, however, it quickly reburied it within Magna, and never was heard a discouraging word about Triam.

In any case, Nicol was the asset Stronach wanted most from Triam. Stronach had thought enough of his restructuring skills that he'd paid him $87,000 a month for a year, *after* he'd departed Magna in 1992. And while Nicol rejoined Magna after the Tesma and Decoma spinoffs, his imprimatur was on the changes to the Magna organizational chart that occurred as it geared up for the next phase of its evolution, which now included building entire cars.

DETAILS, DETAILS – PRODUCE MANY MILLIONS OF BUCKS

The speed with which Magna's research and development teams could now invent methods of doing things and develop new products made the company that Nicol returned to different from the one he'd left six years earlier. In 1998, Magna still had the most diverse range of products in the auto-parts industry. There was no part of the automobile – front end, rear, chassis, roof, exterior, interior, engine, electronics, or doors – that Magna was not manufacturing parts for. Its myriad innovations ranged from a standardized, integrated child's

seat system used throughout the industry, to methods of manufacturing gears used in starter motors and on flywheels. Magna's more
than thirty product development centres around the world turned
'out countless items that, after being prototyped and tested on proprietary Magna equipment, became items used daily by virtually
every driver on the road.

Magna's move into plastics in the 1980s had been behind
Decoma's growth into a $1.2-billion company that made convertible
top systems and exterior trim. More recently it had expanded into
sealing systems; adapting its method of making door-sealant systems
had recently resulted in a one-piece window module that reduced
not only wind noise and leakage, but also customer costs. Tesma sales
had grown to $646 million largely on the basis of power-train prod-
ucts, unseen by most motorists but essential to the comfort of all. In
addition to offering customers the gold standard for automotive
pulleys, for example, Tesma had refined belt-driven accessory systems
under the hood to reduce noise and vibration. And following the
acquisition of Steyr in Austria, it acquired four-wheel-drive technology that was ideal for the coming SUV boom.

No less innovative were the subsidiaries still under the corporate wing. Atoma, a $910-million lock-and-latch specialist, had
graduated to manufacturing fully integrated door systems that
incorporated electronic, keyless-entry modules. It also had developed a power sliding door capable of stopping in the event that an
object was detected in its way, a powered lift-gate used as the rear
door of minivans and SUVs, and sensors that automatically adjust
opening of doors according to weather, vehicle age, and incline.
Magna Mirror Systems (MMS) had turned the simple, one-trick exterior rear-view mirror into a marvel of self-adjusting, automatic-
defrosting capability. Its patented pickup truck mirrors could extend
outward for visibility around wide loads. Interior mirrors automatically compensated for intrusive high-beams. When MMS was through

tinkering with the simple sun-visor, it might incorporate a lighted vanity mirror or a programmable electronic garage-door opener. In 1998, MMS sales reached $423 million.

Technological innovation, imagination, and the incentive of profit-sharing had created new divisions that launched Magna into entire new businesses. Take Fred Gingl's foam-in-place seating technology, for instance. First explored in 1984, it had integrated the previously separate manufacturing of the cushion and seat frame. By 1999, the foam-in-place process had been merged with other seat-system processes, so that hardware such as heating elements and power adjustments could be built into the seat modules. The seats could flip, fold, and recline, but most importantly be delivered to Magna's customers' production lines precisely in time for installation. Magna had learned to make and deliver seats so efficiently that Magna Seating Systems was contributing $1.7 billion to Magna's total sales. Magna Interior Systems (MIS), a new subsidiary that designed, engineered, and manufactured complete interiors, continuously investigated potential new fabrics, features, and materials that met Stronach's goal of producing "a better product at a better price." MIS added another $286 million to overall sales.

Meanwhile, Cosma, Magna's metal-stamping group, had refined its production lines to become the most efficient manufacturing process of its kind in the industry, able to supply a complete "body in white," the sheet-metal framework of an automobile, to car makers. It had also advanced the use of hydroforming, the method of shaping metal using water pressure that Fred Jaekel had fought to adopt in 1993. Cosma's engineers and technicians, driven by the technology's potential to lower costs, and hence increase profit in which they would share, had since refined the process to the point that a 700-person plant, the size of twenty-two football fields, was designed specifically to accommodate the hydroforming process. When it opened in 1998, the state-of-the-art Formet Industries facility in St. Thomas, near London, Ontario, was the world's largest fully automated vehicle-frame plant, capable of making one frame every eleven seconds. Even before Magna had a plant capable of demonstrating the benefits of hydroforming, Jaekel had sufficiently impressed GM with its attributes that it had signed a $400-million contract to take delivery of hydroformed pickup-truck frames for the 1998 model year.

The first chassis from the Formet plant was the beginning of yet another entirely new product line that innovation had founded: Magna had not previously been in the chassis business at all. By 1998, Cosma was contributing more than $2 billion to Magna's coffers, and the product lines from Magna's 159 plants around the world had become so diverse that there were very few cars built any-where in the world that didn't include at least a few Magna parts. Often a lot more than a few.

Stronach's attempt to establish the mirror image of Magna's North American operations in Europe had in some respects gone one better. The on-again, off-again acquisition of Steyr-Daimler-Puch, finally completed in June of 1998, extended Magna's capability to the assembly of complete cars, making Magna the first supplier in the world able to offer such a thing to OEMs. When Stronach was in full throat, he talked of Magna Europe becoming a spinoff that would trade on a European stock exchange, just as Magna itself did in North America.

The problem for Magna, however, was a long-standing one. The expansion and innovation that had been its stock in trade was a response to shifting customer demands. But the incessant need to evolve made it very tricky to develop a coherent, lasting organiza-tional structure that, theoretically anyway, would add to the com-pany's overall efficiency. The group structure of the 1980s, for example, had gotten out of hand, which led to different parts of the organization bidding against each other, depressing the value of winning bids and decreasing profitability. When Stronach dismantled that configuration in 1989, the one that replaced it had groupings along geographical and product lines. But as Magna embarked on its spinout strategy with Tesma and Decoma, and as Magna's remarkable R&D thrust developed new products and manufacturing methods that led to new lines of business – chassis-making, in the case of hydroforming, say, or the burgeoning seat-making operation, or assembling niche vehicles – it became clear that yet another organizational chart was required.

Nicol's challenge was to make sure that the new chart was clear and understandable, and that it facilitated co-operative ventures, stayed in step with the automakers' march toward globalization, and set up Magna's groups to thrive as independent spincos with motivated employees. But to meet these goals required changing responsibility for operations from one group to another. Inevitably, that meant toes would get stepped on. And at Magna toe-stepping tended to become messily litigious.

THE DAY OF FRED JAEKEL

Fred Jaekel was born to German émigrés in Argentina and trained as a tool-and-die maker before making his way to Canada, where he worked for nine years before joining Magna in 1982. Jaekel showed a rebellious streak early in his career there. Typically, equipment in Magna's plants was painted dark colours to hide dirt. In the factory he was managing, Jaekel had the machinery painted white to show up the dirt and thus prompt appropriate cleaning and maintenance. Stronach got wind of what he was doing and paid him a visit. "Frank told me it looked like a hospital – and told me he wanted me to do the same kind of thing in other Magna plants," says Jaekel. In 1984, when Magna was creating Atoma from a number of plants that made door latches, locks, and seat parts, he chose Jaekel to manage it. Within six years, Atoma's revenue had grown nearly ten-fold to $690 million, and Jaekel and Stronach had become friends.

Like Fred Gingl, another Stronach protegé, Jaekel had the technical background, inquiring mind, and willingness to take risks that both qualified and drove him to test new projects and processes. However, while Gingl tended to keep his counsel, the outspoken Jaekel didn't mind voicing his opinion, even if it meant opposing Stronach. Which had got him fired in 1990 when he refused to lay off staff. Rehired a month or so later to turn around what he says was a nearly bankrupt Tesma division, Jaekel says he accomplished the feat in less than a year, turning an $8-million loss at the engine and transmission group into an $18-million profit. Stronach, Jaekel laughs, couldn't believe it. "He sent in the accountants and accused me of cooking the books to get a bigger bonus," Jaekel says. "The accountants came back and said, 'It is what it is.'"

After Jaekel's two-and-a-half years as Tesma's president, Stronach offered him another challenge. "He came to me and said, 'Look, I need to give Tesma to Fred Gingl. Why don't you take over Cosma?'" One of the enduring mysteries surrounding Magna's spinoff strategy was why Cosma, a spinout candidate in 1989, never became one again. The answer, according to Jaekel, was that Cosma wasn't strong enough when he got there, and was too strong a few years after he did. Had it been spun off, Jaekel says, it would have revealed that it was accounting for nearly all the company's profits, which would have exposed the weakness in the other groups. "When I took it over, it had $300 million in sales, but wasn't making any money," he says. By 2000, Cosma had become Magna's biggest unit, its $3.1 billion in sales accounting for 30 per cent of Magna's total revenues and 70 per cent of its profits. "I introduced hydroforming to grow the company and to make new products and chassis and space frames and so on," says Jaekel. "In my last year there, Cosma made $725 million pre-tax."

Jaekel admits he was intemperate in gloating to the board. "I said, 'I know when we met last year, I promised $500 million [in profit]. I didn't do that. We made $725 million instead of $500 million,'" Jaekel recalls. "Frank got upset about that, because it was really saying the rest of Magna was falling. I didn't realize what I'd done and I ended my speech by saying 'I promise you a billion profit for next year.' After the meeting Frank started yelling at me because I was outshining the rest of the groups being run by Don Walker."

Stronach cooled down, perhaps seeing in Jaekel's efforts to develop hydroforming something of himself as a young man, determined to develop better ways of making superior products for less money. Jaekel was happy for the opportunity to indulge his creativity, and he was well remunerated. Within the Magna family of companies, only Stronach himself earned more than the annual $6 million or so Jaekel says he was pulling down at Cosma – no great shame, considering that the Magna chairman out-earned nearly every other executive in Canada most years. In 1999, for instance, Stronach topped the list with a compensation package worth $33.4 million.

Even so, Jaekel fully expected the gravy train would end as soon as Nicol's restructuring along global lines took place. And Belinda Stronach, who replaced her former husband, Don Walker, as CEO in 2001, in announcing Magna's intention to create five "supergroups" (a structure believed to be the brainchild of Nicol and Frank Stronach), did herald change: Magna decided to hang on to Cosma, but to spin off the seating and interiors division as Intier International, which Walker would run. The other supergroups would be Magna Steyr in Europe, as well as Decoma and Tesma, the two already publicly-trading subsidiaries.

No one doubted that Intier, under the well-regarded Don Walker, would appeal to financial markets as a spinoff. But Magna Steyr needed some perking up to attract investors. Jaekel, who sat on Magna's strategic-planning committee, recalls that he agreed to throw a few of Cosma's assets into Magna Steyr to sweeten the pot. "Frank wanted to give Siegi Wolf a portion of Cosma to straighten him out," he says. But Jaekel was incensed when he discovered that what Stronach had decided to give Wolf were some of Cosma's North American stamping plants that employed hydroforming, Jaekel's baby, instead of the original factories Jaekel had agreed to. Not only would Jaekel be losing money by giving up the profitable plants, but in future Cosma would be competing in the metal-stamping business with its own plants, now under Magna Steyr.

Jaekel saw the whole affair as Stronach's attempt to prop up Wolf, a favourite. He didn't shrink from pointing out to Stronach the stupidity of what he saw as the zero-sum game of pitting two divisions against each other, depressing the end price and Magna's profit margins. He also resented having built up the Cosma factories' business, only to have Wolf benefit. "I said I wasn't going to stand there and see someone . . . take a part of me and go into competition with me," Jaekel says. He also reminded Stronach that he had the right to reject any restructuring of Cosma, a claim Magna denied.

What happened after that can only be known for certain by the two men involved: "Frank said, 'Well, huh, you're fired then,'" Jaekel says. Stronach claimed Jaekel elected to resign rather than be fired, and advised Belinda Stronach accordingly. As Jaekel tells the story, the next thing he got was a letter from Jim Nicol accepting a resignation he hadn't offered, then a visit from Jack Taylor, another former York Region chief of police who had risen to the giddy heights of head of security of Magna, who escorted him out of the building.

Jaekel's departure in March 2001 was followed by the inevitable blitzkrieg of suits, countersuits, claims, and counterclaims. Jaekel sued Magna for wrongful dismissal, seeking $70 million, including unpaid bonuses ($5 million due in 2003), $10 million in aggravated and punitive damages, and another $10 million for loss of reputation. Magna's statement of defence denied Jaekel's entitlement to any compensation and contended that Jaekel actually *owed* Magna $1.5 million, for bonuses he'd already been paid and for which he became ineligible upon resigning.

The issue of whether Jaekel had been fired or left of his own accord took on a new twist in September after Jaekel and Nick Orlando, Cosma's CFO, joined Rob Wildeboer, a former Magna executive vice-president and legal adviser to Frank Stronach, at Royal

Laser Tech Corp., a small start-up with aspirations to grow its metal-forming business. Royal had been so eager to land Jaekel, widely acknowledged as one of the world's leading experts in hydroforming technology, that it offered him 9 per cent of the company and the position of CEO. Wildeboer was already chairman of the company and Orlando joined as CFO.

Soon Magna had a $55-million lawsuit going against Royal Laser and its founder Bill Iannaci, and Orlando, Jaekel, and Wildeboer. It charged that prior to quitting Cosma, Orlando had met with Jaekel and Wildeboer on at least five occasions, and that in one instance, he had spirited away "a bag of documents" that he copied prior to the meeting. The charges raised the question how Magna got wind of the meetings, unless it had had Orlando followed. Jaekel claimed publicly that he'd spotted gumshoes (possibly more graduates of the York Regional Police Magna training program?) tailing him on a couple of occasions. Magna refused to comment.

Eventually the charges were all settled out of court with the usual confidentiality provisos, leaving the truth unknown except by the participants. One of the more interesting sidelights of the affair, however, was Wildeboer's formal complaint that Magna had no right to enjoin him from working for Royal Laser. He'd never worked for Cosma. He'd had an $800,000 one-year contract with Magna to provide financial advice to Stronach. He'd quit to become chairman of Royal Laser after ten weeks, he said in his statement of defence, appalled that Stronach, who made $42 million in 2000, was mostly interested in how he and his family could extract more money out of the company.

TESMA – AVOIDING FRANK'S PLAN B

Jaekel, though gone from Magna, had the satisfaction of seeing Stronach in effect admit that he'd been right when Stronach took his advice and dropped the plan (Plan A) to graft Cosma units onto Magna Steyr. Instead, to beef up the Austrian company, Stronach decided to merge Tesma with it (Plan B). But a new Magna Steyr contract to assemble BMW's X3 SUV scuppered that idea, sending Magna and Nicol off to reshuffle the Magna assets yet again in an attempt to bring some order to the restructuring.

Although the BMW contract gave Magna's sundry groups an inside track to bid on components for the vehicle, the contract strained the capacity of Magna Steyr's assembly plant in Graz, Austria, already working full out on Mercedes-Benz models. It turned out that Tesma's European facilities could not provide the required room on production lines, so instead of merging it with Magna Steyr (Plan B), or building a new plant (Plan C) that might have delayed taking on the BMW contract, Magna Steyr bought DaimlerChrysler's nearby Eurostar plant (Plan D).

The outcome – Magna Steyr, a contractor, assembling both BMW models and those of arch-rival Mercedes-Benz – exemplified the future of the auto-supply industry. But it left hanging the (Plan B) merger of Tesma's engine and transmission group with Magna Steyr. Stronach still liked it on grounds that it "would have enabled us to build a better product for a better price," the simplistic mantra that he often repeated as his business goal. Tesma chief Fred Gingl saw synergies between his company's capability as a designer and manufacturer of engine, transmission, and fuel systems and Magna Steyr's capacity as a manufacturer of drive-train components and an assembler of niche-vehicles. Magna insisted the deal was merely delayed and would be revisited when the Eurostar purchase was tidied up.

Tesma shareholders, though, were okay with the delay; in fact they saw absolutely no benefits in a merger they felt would dilute their company's profits and increase its debt – which may in fact have been Stronach's goal, since the merger would also make Magna Steyr look better. Tesma, though smaller than Magna Steyr, had recorded sales increases in 25 consecutive quarters since Magna spun it off as a public company in 1995. Its profit margin of 10.5 per cent was also higher than Magna Steyr's. Post-merger it would be diluted to

5.7 per cent, according to one analyst's calculations. Tesma would have generated a disproportionate amount of the profit as well: in 2001 Tesma posted an $89-million (U.S.) profit on sales of $1.2 billion (U.S.). That was almost 70 per cent of the $129 million (U.S.) that, according to one estimate, would have been the combined profit had the companies merged in 2001. No wonder the delay was just fine with everyone associated with Tesma.

SOLIDARITY FOR . . . QUITE A WHILE

Restructuring wasn't the only challenge Magna executives were facing. In 1999, the antipathy of labour toward Magna in Austria turned up in North America as well. In the spring, the Canadian Auto Workers union, long stymied by what it viewed as Magna's active opposition, tried a new tactic. Union president Basil "Buzz" Hargrove tried to coerce the Big Three into using their leverage as customers to lean on Magna to permit organizing drives. The car makers' response was half-hearted at best.

Then, when more than half of the five hundred employees at Integram, a Magna seat-making plant in Windsor, Ontario, indicated they wanted to join the union, the CAW felt it had found a crack in Magna's armour. Although Magna fought the union – the plant manager allegedly warned workers that a DaimlerChrysler contract would be jeopardized by union-scale wages, since they'd bump up the price of the seats the plant made – the Integram workers voted to unionize.

The CAW saw this as a foothold it could use to attack the car makers' growing tendency to outsource work to non-union companies such as Magna. Pushing an outsourcing agenda was touchy for Magna and its customers; if they admitted that more outsourcing was likely, as indeed it was, they risked contract impasses and possible strikes; announcing that a non-union assembly plant was even in the planning stages would have been positively incendiary.

Magna's chairman himself managed to provide the spark. Speaking to reporters who had accompanied a trade mission to Austria led by Prime Minister Jean Chrétien in June of 1999, Stronach had taken pains to deny unequivocally that Magna planned to buy or build a North American assembly plant. Minutes later, while touring Magna Steyr's assembly plant in Graz with Chrétien, Stronach was recorded by a television reporter's open microphone telling Chrétien that Magna was indeed interested in assembling entire vehicles in Canada, as it was doing in Austria. "We just need an assembly factory in Canada," he told Chrétien, then added, *sotto voce*, "We're talking to GM about it."

It wasn't the first instance of Stronach saying one thing and doing another. He'd always claimed that he'd respect democracy if workers voted to adopt a union. But after the Integram workers did just that in the fall of 1999, voting 317 to 285 to have the CAW represent them, Magna launched a prolonged challenge of the vote before the Ontario Labour Relations Board, blocking the union from the plant in the interim. The delaying tactic eventually wore the CAW down. The union was so desperate to get a toehold in Magna that it agreed in February 2001 to forgo the right to strike for six years, provided that Magna promised not to lock union members out of the Windsor plant. It was a measure of how far the union would go to get a union certified at a Magna plant that it was willing to sacrifice its ultimate weapon, the right to withdraw its members' services.

13

MEC LEAVES THE STARTING GATE

Magna investors who thought they'd bought shares in a superb auto-parts business always got nervous when one of Stronach's visions seemed to be launching Magna into a risky venture that had nothing to do with cars. In his letter to shareholders in March 1998, Stronach had tried to reassure them that in the future, Magna's non-automotive flyers would be held within a new venture-capital group known internally as Diversa, of which his daughter, Belinda, was listed as vice-president. His intention, he said, was that Diversa would be spun out as a public company "completely removed from Magna's automotive operations, so that Magna's management team can continue to remain focused on the development and expansion of our core automotive business." But after the promise that Ventures, as the new company came to be called, would hold the non-auto assets, little had been done to create it. The delay, after the letter's clear commitment, raised investor concerns anew. Magna's stock, trading at more than $100 after he sent the letter in March, began slipping again. By September 1998, it was below $90.

A LOT OF HAY

Uneasy analysts and investors had seen nothing yet. When horses entered the equation, Stronach's flights of fancy could hit the stratosphere. In October 1998 he heard that Santa Anita, a storied California horse-racing track, was for sale. Churchill Downs Inc., owner and operator of the famed Louisville Churchill Downs racetrack, home of the Kentucky Derby, as well as other race courses, was considered by many to be the logical buyer. But when Stronach expressed interest, the *Daily Racing Form*, the industry bible, touted Magna as the likely new owner.

The DRF's speculation was largely predicated on Stronach's growing reputation as a free-spender of both his own and Magna's money. He'd personally made a massive investment in his thoroughbred ownership and breeding businesses. Though he hadn't had a huge winner like Glorious Song since the eighties, in 1996 he began hitting the winner's circle more frequently, coming third among owners in North America with total winnings of $4.2 million (U.S.). In 1997, he raised his profile still further: in June, his Touch Gold won the Belmont Stakes, the last of the three races in the famed Triple Crown in the U.S. In July, Awesome Again won Canada's Queen's Plate.

In 1998, his reputation for developing winners – at a high cost, to be sure – was burnished by a stellar year at North American tracks: no fewer than five of his horses were nominated for races in the Breeders' Cup series, considered racing's championships, held in October that year at Churchill Downs. One of his entries, Awesome Again, beat three winners of Triple Crown races to triumph in the $5 million (U.S.) Breeders' Cup Classic, the richest race in the world. The horse was favoured to win an Eclipse Award, the highest honour in racing, as Horse of the Year. Stronach, feeling his oats, was also promoting *himself* as an Eclipse winner in the owner category. "I'm the leading owner of race horses in the world this year and for the last few years," he told journalist Diane Francis of the *National Post*, a long-time admirer of Stronach's. "My horses have won $7 million this year. That's a lot of hay." He won the award, but the horse didn't.

Even with that kind of money in winnings and the $27 million that Magna paid him in 1998, Stronach was not inclined to use his own money to invest in a racetrack. A few weeks after Awesome Again's victory in the Breeders' Cup in the fall of 1998, the DRF's prophecy was fulfilled. MI Developments, Magna's real-estate arm, bought Santa Anita for $126 million (U.S.).

The famed track had a very romantic past – Seabiscuit ran at Santa Anita, and for many years it was the hangout of Hollywood stars. While admitting that this was attractive to him as a racing aficionado, Stronach insisted that the purchase was purely a business decision and that it would be one of the assets packaged in Magna's non-automotive Ventures group, when he got around to creating it. He allowed that Santa Anita, though a premier track in the U.S., was a little past its best-before date and could use a sprucing up – maybe an $18-million (U.S.) or so facelift to start with. But he believed that with appropriate development Santa Anita could become one of the draws in a family-entertainment centre that would include shops and a racing museum; the latter, at least, made more sense in conjunction with a racetrack than attached to a Viennese theme park. The fact that Santa Anita was situated in the foothills of the San Gabriel mountains north of Los Angeles and came with 305 acres made it a bargain for its real estate alone, Stronach said.

NEW VENTURES

Inevitably, the news that Magna now owned a racetrack brought the spinoff strategy back to the front burner. After Tesma and Decoma had been set off on their own, Jim Nicol had been brought back to schedule the spinoffs of other groups, including Magna Steyr and the Intier subsidiary. But by December 1998, those two had not been taken public. Furthermore, nine months after Stronach's letter to shareholders, there was still no decision about when, or how, or even *if* the new company, Ventures, would be spun off. Indeed, Stronach was floating a different idea: instead of creating a *new* company to hold the non-automotive assets, he suggested that Magna's MI Developments, the purchaser of Santa Anita, might be spun out as a publicly traded company to serve that purpose. At the time, MID was run as a separate entity within Magna. It owned the land under most of Magna's 155 factories around the world (which analysts estimated to be worth about $800 million), not to mention the gated head-office campus in Aurora, the Oberwaltersdorf European head-office complex (including its eighteen-hole golf course and perimeter housing), and a few Toronto office buildings. In an interview with *Forbes* magazine, Stronach said he saw MID as a repository as well for the Ventures grab bag of non-automotive properties.

Another difficulty stalling the spinout plans was determining what would be bundled into Ventures (or MID, if that route was chosen). Theme parks and an airline, though cheerfully tossed into the mix as possible pieces of the new enterprise, had yet to come to life except in Stronach's mind, or in lovely little scale models in his Austrian office. Formally valuing the businesses – a necessity before Ventures or MID could ever be considered as a separate public company – would have been nearly impossible, given their ethereal nature.

Stronach wasn't helping by musing about still more projects. In November he gave the impression of having full support within Magna when he told an interviewer that "we believe tourism is the next area Magna should be involved in and we are currently looking at sites for our first $1-billion theme park in North America." Worse, he told an Austrian interviewer that he saw a need there for a lifestyle magazine and possibly another daily newspaper.

And that wasn't all. The extent of his investment in Austrian soccer was coming to the surface. Although Stronach took the credit for pumping $750,000 into the Austria Vienna "Violets" soccer team to become a "sponsor," news that it was actually Magna's money caught investors off guard. To be sure, $750,000 amounted to a rounding error in the grand scheme of things at Magna; in fiscal 1998, the company posted sales of $9.2 billion. But the Austria Vienna investment was just a start. He'd followed it up with a payment of $10 million to two other teams in the ten-team league, and then offered to invest $122 million in the *Bundesliga* to lock up television rights.

All of which, it turned out, was part of his even bigger plan to roll out a new television enterprise. The purchase of television rights to Austria's games played by the *Bundesliga*, considered a second-tier soccer league in Europe, was a move to acquire broadcast content. Likewise, owning Santa Anita gave Magna racing fare to televise. "What we want to achieve," Stronach told shareholders at the Magna annual meeting in December 1998, "is a television station with a betting channel attached to it. That means you can sit at home and bet on soccer, on tennis, on skiing, on Formula One racing and so on."

This vision didn't quite fit with that of the investors who bought Magna for its ability to manufacture bumpers, dashboards, and the like. "If it's such a good idea, why isn't Time Warner doing it?" wondered analyst Gary Lapidus, who followed Magna for the investment firm Sanford C. Bernstein & Co. in New York. Following the meeting, Magna's stock (which at one point in 1998 had traded as high as $113) fell from $104 to $102. A week later it had dropped to $95, which prompted Andrew Bell, writing in the *Globe and Mail*, to have some fun at Stronach's expense:

> Memo to Frank: Why stop at theme parks and airlines? The market seems to be just loving this diversification gig! Probably because the synergies are so intuitively obvious. Auto parts, theme parks, auto parts, theme parks – the terms are practically interchangeable! My advice is not to let this

Internet thing pass by. Think: Captain Frank's Cyber Shop, car seats over the Net . . .

REVOLT OF THE TAME DIRECTORS

Not for the first time, Magna executives were caught short by their boss's latest schemes. The chairman's reverie put vice-chairman Nicol, who was structuring the spinoffs, into familiar damage-control mode. The notion of loading MI Developments with non-real-estate assets, he said, was premature. And though offering MID shares to the public was still in the cards, an IPO would be delayed until markets improved. Stronach, though, was serious enough about his convergence plan to have hired Toronto-based sports executive Brian Cooper as MI Developments executive vice-president, charged with packaging the TV channel's proposed programming.

Few of Stronach's ideas had been approved or even discussed by Magna's board and would probably have been strangled at birth at most companies. But Magna shareholders could not count on their board to overrule even the most hare-brained initiatives of the chairman, larded as it was with obedient family members and loyal associates. And he personally controlled enough votes to trump dissenters in any case.

By March 1999, however, investors had downgraded their own opinion of Stronach's plans even further. They'd sold Magna's stock down to $86 and change, which amounted to clipping about 20 per cent from its price a year earlier. (It had hit $108 on the TSE within weeks of Stronach's letter of assurance to shareholders a year earlier.)

It was too much even for Magna's tame directors. At a board meeting, significantly held in Arcadia, California, site of Santa Anita, they finally insisted that Stronach address shareholders' rancour. Following the meeting, Stronach made a landmark announcement: Magna had bundled its non-automotive assets, valued at $300 million (U.S.) – plus $250 million in cash – into a new company with the working name Ventures. The plan, he said, was to take it public as soon as possible, but in the meantime Ventures would be managed separately from Magna under the aegis of MI Developments. The key component of the spinout was a seven-year moratorium on *any* spending by Magna in Ventures, which was to say in any non-automotive businesses, until May 2006.

Stronach confessed that he wasn't entirely in accord with the terms of what would become known as "the forbearance agreement," or even that it was necessary. Pressed for the moratorium by the board "and shareholders," he said he'd sought to limit it to five years. To some observers, the board's uncharacteristic overruling of the chairman bore the fingerprints of vice-chairman Jim Nicol, who'd doubtless been frustrated by Stronach's dizzying new ventures hammering Magna's stock price at the precise time that he was trying to structure Magna's spinouts. In any event, Stronach did his best to portray himself as willing to go along with the rule out of sympathy for shareholders. "I fully understand that if investors want to buy apples, they don't want to buy pears," Stronach said.

For the most part, Magna intended to stick to the model it had used in transforming its Tesma and Decoma subsidiaries into publicly listed entities: it would issue subordinate voting shares in Ventures in the form of a dividend to Magna shareholders, then gradually reduce its initial control of the new company to a minority position. Gone was Stronach's plan to spin off MI Developments. Magna said it would retain 100 per cent of MID, which would hold its automotive-related real-estate assets, principally the land on which its plants sat. But *non-auto* real estate – such as the Toronto office buildings, land earmarked for the Austrian theme park, and the Santa Anita racetrack – would be placed in the spinout company, along with the soccer team and other odd bits that Stronach had acquired.

Whatever Stronach saw in the long term failed to impress analysts and investors. They welcomed the parent company's promise to quit taking non-automotive flyers, but were nervous at what

Stronach's next big idea might be. The $550 million (U.S.) in cash and assets that Magna was dumping into Ventures caught their eye as well. Notwithstanding the omnipresent Graham Orr's explanation that Magna didn't want to hamstring the new company by under-capitalizing it, it struck many observers that $550 million (U.S.) was excessive. Instead of improving Magna's share price, the announcement caused sellers to knock it down $2 to below $84 on the TSE.

HORSE RACING – A LOSING PROPOSITION?

Learning that Magna was now in the racetrack business might justifiably have given shareholders pause, such was the state of the racing sport. Its steady decline in the twenty or so years prior to 2000 was due to a constellation of factors, beginning with the fading interest in things agricultural that had begun in the 1950s alongside the urbanization of North America. Fan interest in competing sports, meanwhile, had grown. The accelerating popularity of NASCAR races, for example, had by the late 1980s eclipsed that of horse racing, and of many other sports as well.

As major-league sports expanded to accommodate new cities and increase their exposure, city fathers willingly spent public funds on facilities to house local teams. Cities often raised capital for stadiums and arenas through the issue of municipal bonds offering tax advantages to investors. The cost in terms of foregone taxes was borne by all taxpayers, frequently after a long public campaign about the (usually illusory) "spinoff" economic benefits claimed for the new facility.

Racing, on the other hand, failed to develop either a competitive product for television (except in the case of marquee races such as those comprising the Triple Crown) or to make its case effectively to government. The fault lay first with the industry's fragmented nature. Most tracks were still individually owned by racing enthusiasts (or their heirs, since many remained in family hands). Even more troublesome was horse racing's contradictory public image. Racetracks were seen as the milieu of the rich and famous, an aristocracy who showed up in garden-party dresses and top hats to watch million-dollar horses run. At the same time, racing involved gambling, and so tracks were also perceived as the habitat of touts, roguish railbirds, petty crooks, and the occasional mobster. Neither of these images provided much incentive on the part of government to fork over assistance. Indeed, government had a third view: racing was a cash cow that it regulated (as much as possible) to keep it clean, and then milked for a piece of the betting action. Taxes that applied to gambling, after all, like those on smokes and booze, were viewed as voluntary, only paid by sinners.

In truth, horse racing could argue a better economic case than most sports that were seeking government support. Breeding and owning racehorses supported a huge, and often hidden, slice of the local agricultural economy, ranging from jobs for stabling and training staff, to feed-growing and transportation. Anything that increased the "handle" – the amount bet – helped the industry: the better the horses in a race, the more competitive the racing, the greater the amount wagered, the bigger the purses available to be won by horse owners, and the fatter the profits to track owners. Bigger purses also attracted more owners and breeders, strengthening the infrastructure.

But the inverse was also true: smaller handles eroded the fortunes of the entire racing industry. And ironically, while government tightly controlled racing, it was government itself that became addicted to gambling. Racing's argument that at least gambling on horses took skill, as opposed to pushing a slot-machine button, fell on deaf ears in state legislatures. Lotteries, video terminals, and casinos, all of which poured more money directly and faster into public coffers than racing did, not only attracted the attention of cash-strapped governments, they also sucked gambling dollars from racetracks. And video terminal operators never asked for government subsidies, unlike racetrack owners.

The net result was that racetracks lost their monopoly on legal gambling. Their new competitors were the well-financed, government-sanctioned casinos – in effect, the government itself, sometimes the one that regulated them, but just as often one that didn't. Tracks that had relied on a local market in a state that didn't happen to have a lottery or permit casinos, for instance, lost gambling customers who could drive a few miles across a state line to wager at gaming tables in a neighbouring state that did.

In the circumstances, it was small wonder that owners of race-tracks that had been built close to fans in urban settings in the 1930s and 1940s, struggling to maintain their properties while competing with government, discovered that their tracks were more valuable to developers as real estate than as going concerns. According to the *Los Angeles Times*, parimutuel wagering (in which bettors backing the first three places in a race divide the pool created by losers, minus the track's commission or "takeout") in the U.S. grew by 34 per cent between 1982 and 1995. But this was hardly dramatic. In the same period, state revenues generated by lotteries rose by 602 per cent and the amount of money gambled in casinos increased by 329 per cent. Furthermore, much of the growth in parimutuel wagering had been due to the introduction in some states of off-track betting (OTB) parlours in which punters wagered on televised races.

Simulcasting – beaming races in real time to OTB parlours and other racetracks where gambling was licenced – addressed some of the difficulties of the industry. A portion of each off-track wager went to the track staging the race, broadening the track's reach beyond its live audience. Technology that extended simulcasting into the home, and where legal, permitted wagering by phone or the Internet, increased the potential market still further. By the late 1990s, it had dawned on the industry that its primary source of revenue was no longer at the betting wickets at the track. That realization began one of the most viciously fought battles in horse racing's long history as players fought to control each component of the converging industry, from staging races (creating content) to providing a simulcast service (controlling the delivery channel), to taking bets.

Churchill Downs Inc. (CDI) appeared to have been first out of the gate. But by 1999 Stronach had become one of the world's biggest breeders and winningest owners. Now that he, through Magna, had become a racetrack owner as well, nobody was counting him out as a serious contender.

JOCKEYING FOR POSITION

Arguably, Stronach spent more on his eight hundred or so horses and racing amenities than almost anybody in the world, with the possible exception of oil sheikhs who'd recently discovered the sport. His facilities were about as extensive as it got. Besides his 200-acre Aurora farm, by 1999 he'd grown the Adena Springs spread in Kentucky into 1,600 acres and added another 600-acre thoroughbred farm in Ocala, Florida. So he had an obvious self-interest in propping up racing, and he wasn't about to let the sport that he genuinely loved deteriorate to bush league status.

Stronach had forced the racing community to recognize his accomplishments as a horseman; his numbers as a leading owner and breeder spoke for themselves. He appeared unperturbed at not being accepted by the sport's establishment, seeing it as a patrician milieu of old money, more often inherited than earned, into which one was born or married and thence expected to comport oneself with lazy insouciance, however frayed one's tweeds. He, on the other hand, was a self-made entrepreneur and man of action whose yardstick of self-worth was the money he could earn. What had bothered him almost from the moment he got into racing was that the toffs' sensibility of effortless superiority appeared to hold sway in the sport.

In Canada, he identified the Ontario Jockey Club, operator of Woodbine, Canada's premier track, as well as three others, as the embodiment of all that was wrong with racing. The OJC's not-for-profit organization affronted his belief that monetary incentives elevated performance. Magna, where financial reward was a guiding principle, was his corroborating example. The directors of OJC, he complained, regarded their jobs as a casual exercise in noblesse oblige, and treated the racing world as though it were a country club. Undisciplined by a business's need to generate profits, it had failed to recognize and remedy the obvious slide in interest in racing.

As was his custom, Stronach presumed that his success as an owner and breeder qualified him to prescribe a cure. In his view, Woodbine would flourish if it became more businesslike and made profit its objective. By reinvesting the profits it would increase purses, stimulate racing, and build crowds. But even those who agreed with Stronach's assessment wondered at his motivation. It seemed a touch self-serving, inasmuch as his horses would be competing for the bigger purses he was public-spiritedly proposing. And of course the OJC resented the implication that it had failed out of ineptitude or a lesser devotion to racing than Stronach held. It was all for growing purses. But it wasn't especially enamoured of the idea of his secular, hard-nosed business approach displacing the emotional pageant and tradition that made racing the sport they loved.

Indeed, the only thing that he and the racing establishment seemed to share was a love of racing. And neither side wished to contemplate the terrible possibility that horse racing was an anachronism that had drifted too far out of the public consciousness to ever recover. Finally, tired of Stronach's sniping, and out of respect for his position as one of the sport's most important breeder-owners, in 1995, when his record as the province's leading owner and breeder made it impossible to keep him on the outside, Stronach was invited to join the OJC board.

It wasn't a happy experience. As it turned out, Stronach was no less irritating to the OJC when sitting across the boardroom table. And when the OJC board ignored his recommendation to privatize its operation, Stronach took his complaints public. In an August

1997 interview with a Toronto newspaper, he accused the OJC board of doing such "a lousy job" running its tracks that it had "screwed up a monopoly." If the OJC were willing to sell Woodbine, Stronach added, he'd buy it and manage it properly.

David Willmot was the OJC's widely respected president, as well as owner of the very successful Kinghaven Farms racing stable (a family enterprise that had been started by his father, as Stronach no doubt noticed). To his credit, Willmot resisted noting that "proper management" at Magna lately seemed to include paying police chiefs under the table and paying naked women to dance on top of it. He did, however, curtly invite Stronach to make an offer for Woodbine, adding that he'd personally sell every share rather than hold an investment managed by Stronach or Magna.

Stronach never did make the offer and the OJC promptly dumped him from its board in 1997. The OJC affair was a harbinger of things to come in the U.S., but writ much larger, as Frank Stronach took on not just one racing company, but the entire racing industry.

SHOPPING FOR RACETRACKS, SUDOKU STYLE

The 1998 purchase of Santa Anita finally did make Stronach a race-track owner, albeit through his control of MI Developments. And what looked initially like a capricious, one-off deal by Magna that played to Stronach's hobby became part of a consolidation strategy not dissimilar to that which Magna had successfully employed, most recently in Europe. Auto-parts plants it collected under its banner got the benefit of a central management, greater access to capital, and economies of scale that could lower the costs of such things as raw materials; yet by leaving as much autonomy as possible in the hands of the individual factories, their entrepreneurial dexterity and nimbleness were not harmed.

There had once been a reason that racetracks scattered about the U.S. tended to be individually owned; each was in a separate market. But television that beamed races everywhere had changed that.

Stronach saw the fragmentation of the industry as a consolidation opportunity that would give him control of their racing calendars – essentially, control of the programming for simulcast broadcasts. He intended to unleash the capital parked in Ventures and embark on a buying spree to collect a strategically located package of racetracks around the country.

The shopping was not unlike completing a Sudoku puzzle. Race meets, often regulated as to date and length by state racing commissions that licenced tracks to prevent overlap and to ensure the availability of horses for a competitive field, varied from state to state. Ideally, Ventures wanted tracks spread from coast to coast in order to offer racing over the maximum amount of time daily, and spread north to south to allow racing at least somewhere in both the winter and summer seasons. Once he had an appropriate mix, Stronach believed, he could impose efficiencies through economies of scale and professional centralized management that would reduce operating costs.

The second part of the plan was to expand the amount bet on races from the tracks by simulcasting races to other tracks and to off-track betting parlours licenced to take bets. Eventually, televised races would be carried on Ventures's own channel and be sold to subscribers at home who would bet by telephone or the Internet. Although the plan at times included a panoply of other sports on which viewers could bet – especially in the European version of the sports betting channel, where Magna had invested in television rights to professional soccer – horse racing was the prime content in the U.S. The exact technology was a bit of a moving target, as was the legality of telephone and Internet wagering in some jurisdictions. But the zeitgeist of the dot.com era in the late 1990s was that any technology hurdle could be surmounted.

The plan had some other things in its favour. The advent of casinos, lotteries, and video lottery terminals (a kind of poor-man's slot machine that some states permitted even in bars and convenience stores) had been contributing to the ebb of interest in racing.

Naturally, this had depressed the price of tracks. That, in turn, suggested that many of the available tracks had been poorly maintained,
and they were. But Stronach had an answer for that, too. The third
part of his plan was a redevelopment of racetracks along touristy
theme-park lines, complete with shopping, pubs, restaurants, entertainment, and, where permitted, slot machines, in an effort to attract
a new, younger crowd that would become, he was sure, entranced
by the spectacle and excitement of racing that so fascinated him.

To start the program, he would use the $250 million (U.S.) in
cash parked in Ventures. Once it was up and running, renovations,
redevelopment, and modernization would be carried on using the
cash that poured in from bettors as well as from other operations.
Meanwhile, Ventures – first renamed MI Entertainment, then re-
christened Magna Entertainment Corp. (MEC) – would pay lobbyists
to educate state governments about the no-strings-attached income
available to the state from slot machines at the track, where, when
you thought about it, gambling was already going on. The tracks,
mind, only wanted a slice of slot revenues; the bulk would go to government for schools and hospitals and all manner of things taxpayers couldn't otherwise afford. All MEC was looking for was a share of
slots proceeds to boost purses for horse owners. And the state would
win again as the trickle-down effect stimulated the entire economic
infrastructure that racing supported.

SANTA ANITA: TAKING ON A LEGEND

Although Magna Entertainment Corp hadn't yet been spun off as a
public company, Stronach had clearly shifted his attention from
Europe to the U.S. His first move as a racetrack owner was to
announce that Santa Anita was badly in need of an upgrade. Initially
he placed the cost at $18 million (U.S.). To kick-start the project with
a new dining room, he put in a call to Tom Dillon, the friend whose
restaurant-hostess he once whisked away to Paris.

It was an inspired choice. A lanky restaurateur and executive chef, Dillon has a relaxed affability and a professional host's talent for gliding through a full dining or reception room, casually greeting guests and employees alike by name. A Boston University graduate, he'd catered events as varied as a fund-raising dinner for J.F.K. and corporate hospitality at the Lake Placid Olympics, and had owned and operated as many as twenty fine-dining establishments at a time across the U.S. When Stronach called, he had cut back to just one, Siro's, the seventy-year-old institution within hearing of the Saratoga Springs racetrack's call to the starting gate, in his hometown in the foothills of New York's Adirondack Mountains.

A waiter once famously characterized Siro's as a place where *Goodfellas* meets *Gone With the Wind*. It only opens for the six-week Saratoga season, which is regarded in racing as the sport's nonpareil event of summer. But it serves as many as nine thousand diners during the season with a cuisine sufficiently haute (and prix to match) to preserve its four-star rating, and to generate about the same profit, Dillon says, as his twenty restaurants had year-round. One of those who could afford Siro's was Frank Stronach. Through Stronach's patronage and through horse racing, they became friends. When Stronach called on him to help with the Santa Anita restaurant, Dillon admits to being inspired by Santa Anita's museum-like qualities, which included a spectacular room with six chandeliers dating back to the 1930s, regularly rented out as a movie set. "The other thing," he says, "is that it was Frank asking. I love the guy, and he doesn't take no for an answer."

In addition to executing architect Steve McCasey's design for the new restaurant at Santa Anita, Dillon soon found himself acting as Stronach's wheelman, steering other proposed renovations for the track around local objections. On one side, traditionalists, including a local historical society, opposed any changes that failed to respect the hallowed track's art deco architecture. On the other, racing fans weighed in to complain that the alterations blasphemed Santa Anita's picturesque, if quirky, turf track. "I did all the alterations and went to every city meeting, state meeting, preservation society meeting," says Dillon. "I was the diplomat you need in those situations."

But the intervention of chairman Stronach complicated Dillon's efforts. On one occasion, when Dillon was close to getting the locals to approve alterations to the grandstand, Stronach managed to undo what it had taken Dillon months to achieve. "I took him to one meeting and he gets up in front of the preservation society – and this is after we had talked to them – and goes, 'Well, if you don't want anything in front of it, you're going to be looking at a rusting hulk,'" Dillon says. "This is Frank. I've been pulling teeth with these people and Frank tells them, 'You'll be looking at a rusting hulk.' Oh, they loved that. It took me a year to recover from that one meeting."

Dillon subsequently refused to let Stronach attend meetings. But the experience taught him a lesson that other Magna executives had learned the hard way – that "sometimes you have to protect Frank from himself," notwithstanding what Dillon describes as his uncanny ability to survive misadventures. "It's like he jumps off the roof, lands on the awning, goes into the pool where he lands on a rubber raft," he says.

Stronach is also persuasive, Dillon notes. Once he'd got the new Santa Anita restaurant up and running and the staff trained – at a cost of $40 million (U.S.), well in excess of the originally budgeted $18 million or so – Dillon told Stronach he was going home to his family in New York. "He said, 'What do you mean? We've got other things,'" says Dillon. Stronach appointed him executive vice-president of MEC and president of Aurora Hospitality, the group in charge of catering at all MEC's facilities. "Somehow or other, doing a three-month job turned into ten years," says Dillon, whose candour supports his view that he's one of the few executives ready to challenge the boss.

Stronach's abrupt HR policy at Santa Anita, however, didn't win any friends, and was a hint of things to come at MEC. He fired the track's president, along with nearly twenty administrative employees, to make way for his own appointees. Along racing's shedrows, the housecleaning came as no surprise to trainers who associated Stronach's what-have-you-done-for-me-lately approach with a high turnover rate of training staff, and a mean-spirited attempt to shortchange those fired. The split between Stronach and Patrick Byrne, whom he had hired in 1998, was a case in point. Byrne's two-year contract to train Stronach's horses exclusively called for payment of a $300,000 termination fee if Stronach let Byrne go in 1998, and $200,000 if he did so in 1999.

When Stronach lost faith in Byrne and wanted to let him go at the end of 1998, he would have triggered the $300,000 termination fee. Instead, he offered Byrne a new contract, promising that he'd continue to pay him and also put a string of top horses in his charge. According to Byrne, Stronach failed to deliver the horses for him to train, hoping that Byrne would quit and then no longer be eligible for the termination fee, saving Stronach $300,000. Byrne did resign, but he also sued Stronach, who, he claimed, duped him into a deal that had cost Byrne $300,000. The case, dismissed by Stronach as "nothing more than a difference of opinion," was ultimately settled out of court.

The plan Stronach had begun unrolling in the meantime for MEC's racetrack venture, sounded undeniably slick in the telling. This was especially so if you imagined Magna, by 1999 a $9-billion (U.S.) auto-parts colossus, behind the scenes backing it all. Even if the March 1999 forbearance agreement specifically forbade support from the parent company (at least for seven years), the perception remained that Magna was bankrolling MEC. Stronach, after all, was chairman of both companies. But funding issues aside, as Stronach began putting together his shopping list, he faced a much larger obstacle. It happened that Stronach wasn't first mover with the idea of consolidating racetracks.

CHURCHILL DOWNS FIGHTS FRANK FOR THE RAIL

Churchill Downs Inc. had had much the same idea as Stronach. The established, publicly traded racetrack company couldn't boast a Magna behind it or a Stronach up front. But it had a competent, prudent management led by CEO Tom Meeker, a more fully fledged (though money-losing) television strategy than Stronach, and support from the National Thoroughbred Racing Association (NTRA), a U.S. racing industry group. What was more, shortly after Stronach bought Santa Anita, Meeker, a lawyer and ex-Marine, served notice that he wouldn't shy away from a fight. Within weeks of the Ventures (sorry, MI Entertainment . . . no, Magna Entertainment Corp.) announcement in March 1999, both companies were out of the starting gate and going to the whip as the great racetrack derby began.

Like many sports-fan entrepreneurs, Stronach was soon living every railbird's dream – every diehard sports fan's dream, for that matter. He already owned the horses in races; now he was ready to jet about the United States shopping for entire racetracks. His first purchase was an inauspicious $6.4 million (U.S.) that he paid for San Luis Rey Downs, a California training track.

CDI, which also owned or had joint-venture arrangements with other tracks in Kentucky and Indiana, had wanted Santa Anita but had been outbid by Stronach. In early 1999 it answered Stronach's acquisition by acquiring Calder Race Track in Florida for $86 million (U.S.). The purchase gave Churchill Downs access to Calder's seven-month racing calendar, from June through December. Tom Meeker declared the move a big step toward building a simulcast "continuity that doesn't currently exist in the industry." A nine-year decline in attendance at Calder reflected the trend throughout North America, but Meeker shared Stronach's view that thoroughbred racing was on the cusp of a renaissance. Also like Stronach, he believed that slot machines, though useful in the short term to boost the fortunes of track owners, were far from a long-term solution, and that better racing was the answer.

In May 1999, CDI began negotiating the purchase of Hollywood Park in Inglewood, California, which would eventually cost it $140 million (U.S.) but give it a west-coast track from which to compete with Santa Anita. CDI had also recently invested in video-services and telecommunications in anticipation of creating a simulcast network. "With the recent acquisition of Calder Race Course in Miami and now possibly the Hollywood Park racetrack in Southern California, Churchill Downs will be positioned to be the premier racetrack operator and simulcast broadcaster in the U.S.," Meeker said. It was still after a big-name track whose schedule could fill in winter gaps so that it could sell a complete year of simulcast racing. Its pursuit of Gulfstream Park in South Florida, however, put it on a collision course with Stronach, who also had the track in his sights. Naturally the presence of two potential buyers edged the price up. Meeker, conscious of the consequences to CDI's stock price if his zeal to expand outstripped CDI's financial resources, blinked first. In September, unburdened by CDI's shortage of cash, MEC bought Gulfstream for $89.2 million (U.S.).

The acquisition made a splash in the racing world. Situated between Miami and Fort Lauderdale, Gulfstream's fame on the east coast was roughly on a par with Santa Anita's in the west. They were two of North America's best known racetracks and offered some of the world's most competitive racing. They also gave MEC two winter-season tracks in time zones three useful hours apart. And Stronach continued shopping for other tracks whose geographic location would help him blanket the U.S. with racing. In November, he added Thistledown in Cleveland for $14.5 million (U.S.) and Remington Park in Oklahoma City for $10 million (U.S.). In December he capped his buying spree by picking up Golden Gate Fields near San Francisco for $87 million (U.S.).

Stronach would have been hard-pressed to kick off MEC any more emphatically. In his year-long swing through the States, he'd signed MEC cheques to the tune of $206.9 million, against the

$250-million (U.S.) cash account that had been its original capital.
Renovations at Santa Anita were chewing through cash as well. At
the end of 1999, MEC was still privately held and operated under the
aegis of MI Developments within Magna, but as a separate entity in
anticipation of its going public in early 2000. Yet, even in limbo, it
had become the owner of four new racetracks – five, if San Luis Rey
were counted. Its acquisitions in 1999, plus the $126-million (U.S.)
purchase of Santa Anita in 1998, gave it racetrack properties that it
valued at $332.9 million (U.S.).

MEC's operating results for 1999 only added to its lustre, as
Stronach prettied it up for investors in anticipation of selling shares
to the public. Revenue of $187 million (U.S.) and an operating loss
of only $62,000 (U.S.) seemed to reinforce Stronach's confidence
that there was money to be made in racing. MEC's figures, Magna
pointed out, were misleading, inasmuch as they didn't include
income from the most profitable part of the racing season at some of
the tracks. Of course, they didn't include the more than $200-million
(U.S.) capital costs of the acquisitions, either. But the implication was
that things would improve when a full year's contribution for the
entire chain was calculated.

MAGNA AT THE MILLENNIUM

The truth of that remained to be seen. But Stronach had ample
reason for optimism as the world approached the new millennium.
For one thing, in 1999, the Canadian government (ignoring the fact
that he'd moved to Europe to escape taxes) finally awarded him the
Order of Canada, an honour given to prominent citizens, which
Sinclair Stevens had sought to have bestowed on Stronach in the
mid 1980s. Magna International, now an employer of nearly 60,000
in 174 factories and 33 product-development centres in 19 countries, had grown into a $9.4-billion (U.S.) giant that had graduated
from auto-parts manufacturing to assembling entire cars, the first

in the automotive supplier industry to do so. And it had done it in Stronach's homeland.

Using the enormous annual stipend he paid himself from Magna – $33 million in 1999 alone, not including the value of 500,000 Magna options he was granted (which added another $1 million to their value every time Magna's stock rose $2 higher than their $75 exercise price), he'd become one of the most successful breeders and owners in the horse world. He'd combined his business acumen and his passion for thoroughbreds, put them together with not a little of Magna shareholders' money, and astonished both the racing industry and his critics by creating – in little more than a year – the biggest racetrack company in the world.

There were no signs, as the millennium ended, that at sixty-eight Stronach was ready to yield his iron grip on Magna, its current and future spinoffs, or the spotlight. But his daughter, Belinda, fast-tracked to executive vice-presidency and being groomed to succeed her former husband, Don Walker, as CEO, was emerging as her father's equal for attracting headlines. One of Belinda's duties was to vet candidates for funding from the charitable and community service pool. While preparing to fund a group of former Olympic athletes who were setting up an institution to elevate the morality of the Games, she met speed-skater Johann Koss, a Norwegian Olympic hero and medical doctor. The two married New Year's Eve, the last day of the century. The marriage of the attractive blonde capitalist, heiress to an empire her father built, to a heroic athlete with a humanitarian bent, was the stuff of fairy tales. The wedding, a family affair that included attendance of Belinda's son, Frank Jr., eight, and her daughter, Nikki, six, took place in Beaver Creek, Colorado, at the luxury ski lodge Frank kept there.

Belinda (or her father) also showed a somewhat less than romantic side in having Koss sign a pre-nuptial agreement waiving rights to the family fortune. It would prove prescient. Although Koss moved into Belinda's home in the Magna compound with his new wife and her two children, he barely had time to get comfortable in his new surroundings. Within three years, Belinda's second marriage had collapsed, enabling her to portray herself a few years later, after leaving her position as CEO of Magna to run for office, as your average single parent with an intense interest in federal politics.

Frank Stronach, meanwhile, seemed happy that MEC was up and running. In addition to being a labour of love that satisfied his addiction to horses, it seemed to be a business to which his thirty-two-year-old son, Andy, something of a misfit in the auto-parts business but a virtual Rain Man or walking encyclopedia where horse pedigrees were concerned, might at last be able to apply his skills. Frank's wife, Elfriede, who shared his and Andy's interest in horses, seemed happy, too, spending half the year in Austria, her native land as well as his, where her down-to-earth personality and frugality charmed Magna Europe staff. A former female executive based in Austria notes that while clearly not in danger of outspending her VISA card limit, "Elfriede would go shopping in Vienna and then come back delighted to show us the bargains she got."

Her husband, who'd been snapping up racetracks around the U.S., seemed to believe that he'd got some bargains, too, creating a business foundation in the sport of racing. Stronach confidently claimed that racing and horses was something he knew even more about than he did auto parts. MEC, he maintained, had the potential to become even bigger than Magna International.

But if Stronach was feeling self-satisfied with what he'd accomplished at the end of the twentieth century, a year or so into the new millennium his latest business venture would show signs of coming up lame.

14

GOING TO THE WHIP: TAKING ON
THE U.S. RACING ESTABLISHMENT

The similarities between the U.S. and Canadian racing environ-ments made it only a matter of time before Stronach would confront the same shibboleths south of the border that he'd been battling in Canada since he first became involved in horse racing. While the U.S. racing community was initially respectful of his contribution to the sport as an owner and breeder, and welcoming of his money and his promises to rejuvenate racing on the basis of his vision, it was not long before Stronach's apparent belief in "creative destruction" had most in the industry characterizing him as more predator than prophet. "When there's no movement in the waters, the waters tend to become stale," said Stronach. "I'm here to muddle the waters."

The power in thoroughbred racing in the U.S. had traditionally been centred in Kentucky and New York, orbiting respectively around Louisville-based Churchill Downs Inc. (CDI) and the New York Racing Association (NYRA), operator of New York's Saratoga, Belmont, and Aqueduct tracks under licence from the state. Like most track oper-ators in the U.S., CDI and the NYRA were both backers of the National Thoroughbred Racing Association (NTRA). The NTRA was formed by a number of racing-interest groups in 1998 to be racing's national "head office," but whose mandate was mainly to unify the industry's marketing efforts. But the NTRA's board was largely made up of old-guard representatives of the U.S. racing establishment, many associated with either CDI or the NYRA, who typified the clubby cronyism that Stronach blamed for the sport's demise. When he found himself inadvertently supporting the NTRA through memberships he inherited with the tracks he'd bought, he started to squawk.

The NTRA's alliance with the Television Games Network (TVG) to handle its simulcasting brought things to a head in 1999. TVG intended to pipe content from NTRA-member tracks to licenced sites such as off-track betting parlours, other racetracks, and – where telephone and Internet betting was permitted – directly to home subscribers via cable or satellite television.

Stronach didn't deny simulcasting's importance. On the contrary. Even as track attendance had been dropping for two decades, the recent growth in the total handle (the amount bet) at racetracks was directly attributable to the tracks' ability to broadcast races and expand the betting on them. In light of that, he took a dim view of the NTRA's efforts to coerce its member tracks into giving TVG exclusive rights to their racing content. He had a simulcast strategy of his own, even if it was still an ill-defined one, which leaned toward a proprietary system, or a partner of *his* choosing. Until he could put it into action, he wasn't about to cede the racing content from MEC tracks to the NTRA-backed TVG Network. Neither was he willing to pay dues to a group whose policies he opposed. So in November 1999, he threatened to withdraw all of MEC's tracks from the NTRA.

The ultimatum was classic Frank. At a press conference he called the day before Gulfstream was to host the 1999 Breeders' Cup, one of racing's highest-profile events, he spent nearly an hour voicing his criticism of the National Thoroughbred Racing Association, and much else, before his handlers persuaded him to wind up his harangue. Oddly, though simulcasting rights was clearly his major issue with the NTRA, his principal grumble that day was that the NTRA appointed rather than elected its directors. "There must be a better process in choosing directors," he railed. "I don't like clubs that say, 'We're the directors, we know what's best for you.' I don't like that attitude." It was an interesting comment from the man who had blithely acknowledged that he would sack any director of one of his companies who didn't do his bidding.

His threat to withdraw his five tracks, including two of the biggest names in the business, Santa Anita and Gulfstream, shocked the racing world. MEC was estimated to be contributing $1.2 million (U.S.) of the $7-million (U.S.) total in NTRA membership fees. Now facing severe cinch-tightening in its $30-million (U.S.) budget, the NTRA agreed to "review how free enterprise can be better achieved in the industry." Satisfied that democracy had been served, Stronach withdrew his threat and granted the NTRA a reprieve for a year. But he'd opened a fissure in the industry that never quite healed.

In the fight to control both the content and the channel in the battle for simulcast supremacy, Stronach naturally identified CDI as his corporate rival. CDI saw itself that way, too. It had hijacked jargon from the dot.com-inspired convergence strategy to describe itself as an aggregator of content providers. But it had also done a reasonable job of keeping up with MEC through purchases and joint ventures to build a portfolio of tracks and content to fill out its simulcast race calendars.

Stronach, meanwhile, was not satisfied with duking it out with a corporate competitor with a well-established brand name. He also took a few shots at the referees – state regulatory agencies, which he felt were hobbling free enterprise by restricting each track's race dates so that there was no overlapping. In his Darwinian view of business, only the strong deserved to survive, and tracks should decide for themselves when to hold races and for how long. "When a municipality decides it wants to have a racetrack, then it should allow the [racing] meet to be as long as the racetrack wants," he complained to the Fort Lauderdale *Sun-Sentinel* after buying Gulfstream. It was a reasonable view: a facility forced to sit fallow for long periods couldn't be efficient.

He also thought states should legalize slot machines at racetracks. Like most horsemen, Stronach didn't much care for them. He likened governments' growing addiction to slots – basically gambling by push-button – as pandering to the dumb. "To me, slot machines and casinos are the worst form of taxation and there is very little spin-off effect for society," he told the editor in chief of *The Blood-Horse* magazine in December 1999. "I think it's a question of education – to make people understand that the chances of winning are very small compared to horse racing." But he also knew that governments, loath to raise taxes, were becoming politically dependent on the stream of cash from slots. Since they were going to be installed somewhere in most states, he reasoned, there was logic in putting them in racetracks, which could use a slice of the take to boost purses to benefit the sport and its spinoff economy.

MEC GOES PUBLIC, WITH A TILTED BOARD

Indeed, there was evidence that Stronach agreed with the conventional thinking, which was that tracks would inevitably become casinos, or racinos – racetracks with casinos, or at least slot machines, attached. When MEC was finally spun off as a public entity in March 2000, its board was tilted toward the gaming industry. Horse owner and breeder Jerry Campbell, former CEO of Michigan-based Republic Bancorp Inc. (and majority owner of Great Lakes Downs, which MEC was looking to buy), was the company's first president and CEO. Chief Financial Officer David Mitchell, a former executive of casino company Caesars World Inc., was joined on the board by Terry Lanni, the chairman of MGM Grand Inc., and Glenn Schaeffer, president of the Mandalay Resort Groups, a hotel and casino owner.

In the spinoff, Magna stockholders received one MEC share for every five Magna Class A or Class B shares they held. Magna held on to 80 per cent of the MEC stock but stated that its plan was to reduce ownership to 50 per cent, and eventually to less than 20 per cent. In other words, Magna was reinforcing its promise to separate the auto-parts side of its business from the horse racing side. In the first month of trading, MEC stock rose on the TSE from its initial $3.50 to more than $7 before retreating to $5.50. In New York, MEC's share price of $3.80 on NASDAQ in March gave the company a market cap of $306 million (U.S.).

Stronach, who received options on one million MEC shares, was jubilant. The $3 billion (U.S.) wagered at MEC's six tracks in 1999 had accounted for almost 25 per cent of the U.S. total, and the company hadn't yet fully developed its simulcasting network. In 1999 $11.4 billion (U.S.) of the total $13.7 billion wagered in parimutuel betting in the U.S had come from off-track simulcasts. Santa Anita alone, he exulted, whose brand name was "even bigger than Coca Cola," would boost MEC's market share when bundled with the likes of Gulfstream in a simulcasting package.

If there was a cloud in the picture, it was the parent Magna's stock price; it was languishing in the $60 range in Toronto after a high of about $96 in 1999. Some observers found it ironic that Stronach blamed technology stocks for sucking capital from manufacturers like Magna that actually made things – while it was technology that was driving MEC's fortunes in racing and entertainment. In fact, Stronach wasn't averse to trying to ride the coat-tails of the technology boom, if a little late; by the end of 2000, he was referring to MEC as "a dot.com company with solid assets."

A ROLE FOR ANDY

As well as combining his twin passions of horses and business, MEC seemed to resolve an ongoing personal issue for Stronach by employing his son, Andy. Unlike his self-starting and ambitious sister, Andy had stumbled on most of the paths Stronach had attempted to pave for him. He credited his mother, Elfriede, with whetting his interest in handicapping and thoroughbred pedigrees. She had sent him the *Daily Racing Form* while he was attending private school in San Antonio, Texas, he told the *Toronto Star* in a 2000 interview. After a brief stint as a touring tennis pro, he began a manufacturing-processes program at Bowling Green University in Ohio, but dropped out to enroll in a course leading to an apprenticeship as a tool-and-die maker, his father's craft.

This proved not to be his chosen career, however. But he had little luck translating his equine expertise into success as a thoroughbred owner. He was $200,000 in debt in 1999 after a couple of horses he bought looked unlikely to earn out the $600,000 he had borrowed to buy them. "My father told me he would take one of the horses to pay off the debt if I would come back to the farm," Andy told the *Star*. "I wanted to show my pride, but I was at a crossroads." He and his wife, Kathleen, a graphic designer, moved into a house in the Magna compound, where he was happy working in his dad's breeding operation before being made vice-president and director of MEC when it went public.

For a Stronach male, Andy exhibited no particular ambition to become rich. "I've seen people with a lot of money and they're miserable," he said. Of course, as a Magna heir, Andy was going to become rich one day whether he liked it or not. But his father was careful that it wouldn't happen sooner than its time. At MEC Andy received $100,000 a year to work on an electronic wagering concept and on real-estate deals. He also continued to develop his simulcast idea while encouraging his father to buy more racetracks to add to MEC's content. "Andy was responsible for three of them," says Tom Dillon, whose responsibilities were extended to overseeing catering at the new acquisitions.

While Frank seemed at last to have found a role for his son as well as his daughter in a Magna company, Andy's wife (no fan of her sister-in-law Belinda, according to a Magna insider) suggested that the Stronach males weren't much closer. "Most of the meetings are on the treadmill when Frank is doing his five miles," she said. "It's the only place where you can get him to stay in one spot."

THE RED BULLET AFFAIR

In 2000, Stronach's peripatetic multi-tasking hit the trifecta. He managed at once to alienate racing fans, antagonize another branch of racing's establishment, and, at times, confuse his own executives. In the spring, he'd kept his horse Red Bullet out of the Kentucky Derby, one-third of the hallowed annual three-race Triple Crown series; the other two races are the Preakness and the Belmont. Fans preferred that top horses run in all three races to provide an opportunity for a Triple Crown winner to emerge, something that many in the industry also saw as good for generating a buzz of excitement around the sport. When Red Bullet was not run in the Kentucky Derby but then won the Preakness, beating out the Derby winner, Stronach ended the chance of a Triple Crown winner in 2000. To make matters worse, although fans looked forward to the Belmont, as a rubber race between the Derby and Preakness winners, Stronach ended that prospect, too, when he scratched Red Bullet from the Belmont.

Fans responded with a storm of angry accusations that he had ignored what would have been good for the sport for purely economic reasons, and darkly suggested that had the race been held at an MEC track rather than at Belmont, operated by the NYRA, Red Bullet would have been entered, increasing the wagering to Stronach's benefit.

On the first count, Stronach could hardly be blamed. Risking injury to his horse in the Belmont, which was worth "only" $600,000 (U.S.) for a win, made no financial sense, given Red Bullet's earning-power at stud, where the horse might be paired with as many as eighty mares in a season at $100,000 a pop. The idea that he scratched his horse because the race was at an NYRA-operated track also seemed far-fetched, even for Stronach. But he admitted to aspirations to take over the running of NYRA's tracks, including Belmont, in 2007, when the

non-profit organization's contract with New York State expired. It
turned out MEC had already obtained a racing licence from the state.

TARGETING NEW YORK

Stronach's plans for reaching into New York's racing were wide-
ranging. In 2000, MEC's David Mitchell fuelled the hostility between
MEC and the NYRA when he declared that MEC would bid for New
York City's off-track betting operation (NYCOTB), whose $1 billion
(U.S.) in annual wagering made it a major contributor to the state-
owned NYRA's revenue. And if getting control of the NYRA's tracks, or
taking over the NYCOTB, didn't work out, Stronach had a Plan C.
Since 1998, Magna had quietly bought about eight hundred acres of
rural property on the south shore of Lake Ontario in western New
York. MEC executives were cagey about the company's intent –
options floated included everything from a car-parts factory to an
amusement and theme park – but Andy Stronach confirmed that
they were serious about building a thoroughbred racetrack on the
land, with an adjacent entertainment centre that would include a
high-tech simulcasting betting facility.

In the short term, none of the western New York projects would
get off the ground. But in announcing his quest to control racing
in New York State, Frank Stronach seriously antagonized Barry
Schwartz, yet another industry stalwart. A respected horse owner,
multi-millionaire co-creator and CEO of the Calvin Klein fashion
empire, and volunteer CEO of the NYRA, Schwartz was apoplectic at
Stronach's carpet-bagging attempt to grab the NYCOTB. Its profits, he
felt, should accrue to the NYRA where they could contribute to racing
in New York, not to the corporate treasury of foreign-owned MEC. In
Kentucky, meanwhile, CDI's Tom Meeker, who sympathized with
Schwartz, seemed more mystified than cowed by Stronach's constant attacks on the industry and his disruptive baiting of various
racing groups. "He keeps wanting us to roll grenades across the floor

at one another," Meeker shrugged in April 2000. "We're not going to get into that."

The cloud of controversy that Stronach towed behind him as he jetted around the U.S. also dumped a little rain on MEC itself. His colleague Tom Dillon, a thirty-year veteran of the horse business in New York, his home state, tried to get Stronach to back off from irritating CDI and the NYRA. He believed that it was logical that the NYCOTB and the NYRA would at some point be merged with a combined annual revenue of about $6 billion (U.S.) a year. He advised Stronach to create a partnership with CDI to bid for the business instead of quarrelling expensively with his rival. "Six billion is a lot of money in a year," Dillon says now. He recalls that he admonished Stronach, "You're not satisfied with half of that? You're going to spend $2 billion to push them out of business and *you're* going to go out of business at the same time? It's not making any sense to me."

CHURCHILL DOWNS WINS ARLINGTON

The newly public MEC's executives, meanwhile, were hard pressed to implement Stronach's three-pronged approach to dominating the racing industry: acquire and consolidate as many racetracks in North America as possible; bundle the races run at those tracks into a simulcasting package to rival CDI's; and upgrade and revitalize all the tracks as entertainment complexes to draw in new audiences. MEC's activities seemed manic in comparison with the more measured, corporate approach of CDI.

True, CDI had fewer goals to pursue: its simulcasting channel through the TVG Network was already up and running, and its tracks didn't require renovations to the extent that Stronach's did. It was still in the acquisition game with MEC, however. Chicago's Arlington Park, a modern facility in a big market, had been seen as a logical complement to both MEC's and CDI's simulcast plans. But Stronach professed to have removed it from his need-it list on the grounds that its operating dates were too restrictive. "When you are over-regulated owning a racetrack, it's as if you buy a very expensive machine for your business and then are told that you can only [use it] three months out of the year," he said. "That's just not a good business environment to go into."

Arlington's market price, said to be in the $200-million (U.S.) range, may have also braked his enthusiasm. Although he'd used shares in two instances to purchase tracks, making their sellers tiny MEC shareholders, doing so in the case of the more expensive Arlington (assuming its owner was willing to take a big piece of MEC in partial payment) would have meant diluting his own position as the controlling shareholder. The practical CEO Meeker had no such compunction. Although he also didn't have $200 million handy to buy Arlington outright, he merged CDI with it in a $71-million (U.S.) transaction that made the track's former owner, the well-respected Richard Duchoissis, a 30 per cent shareholder in CDI.

BINOCULARS AND BOREDOM

In contrast, MEC's track renos were proving tricky, and Stronach's avowed commitment to live racing, confusing. The nip and tuck at Santa Anita, which had run to $40 million (U.S.), played to mixed reviews, emphasizing the polarization of the markets MEC was chasing. Traditional racegoers were appalled that the new 2,150-square-foot infield screen that displayed races as they were being run blocked about forty yards of the backstretch where the actual race takes place. Lonny Powell, whom Stronach had hired as track manager after purging the track's front office, seemed surprised that fans might attend a day of live races to *see* live races. MEC, he explained, was being leading-edge, substituting far-away live with close-up electronic. "You don't see many people watching the races with binoculars any more," Powell said. "We've all become fans who look at the screens."

CEO Jerry Campbell told the *Washington Post* in 2000 – doubtless to the horror of dyed-in-the-wool racing fans – that MEC was aiming for an environment "with a Disney World feel." Inasmuch as Stronach himself admitted to boredom between races, Campbell acknowledged, MEC recognized that the family market it hoped to attract to its racetracks would similarly find the amount of actual racing competition – which took up little more than half an hour for a typical nine-race daily card – a touch light in entertainment value. MEC's goal was to attract fans with shopping, dining, concerts, and whatever else it could come up with, then entice them into the stands for races that were being simulcast because "a TV product doesn't work if no one is in the stands."

Campbell wasn't around long enough to see whether the theory held. In July, after just five months on the job, he quit as CEO (he remained as vice-chairman). His replacement, Californian Mark Feldman, had a background as an executive with *E! Entertainment Television* that seemed appropriate, in light of all the screens in MEC's business plan.

McALPINE RETURNS TO MUCK OUT THE STALL AT MEC

By the time the Breeders' Cup races rolled around at Churchill Downs in late fall of 2000, Stronach was withdrawing his seven tracks from the National Thoroughbred Racing Association, supported by 15 other tracks who also objected to the NTRA's simulcasting strategy, and felt MEC was their champion. The remaining NTRA/TVG supporters, including 56 other member-tracks, saw his act as ruining the sport. Stronach, of course, was happy to raise the temperature of the feud after two of his horses won races in the prestigious day-long series, earning him a cheque for $1.2 million (U.S.) from the Breeders' Cup Ltd., the corporation that staged the series. Stronach, though he knew better, couldn't resist antagonizing CDI, making it look as though the host track was paying him. "I love taking money from Churchill Downs," he told the media after the race.

It was a measure of racing's decline that almost no one outside the industry was aware of the conflict, or seemed to care. The Breeders'

Cup was billed as the pinnacle of racing and held at the most famous racetrack in the world. But its television ratings in 2000 tumbled to their lowest point in sixteen years.

Far from believing MEC's entry in the racing business was tantamount to whipping a lame horse, Stronach began making changes so he could pick up the pace. Tired of flying cross-country to tend to the company's affairs in California, he moved MEC's head office to Magna's Aurora headquarters, where he said he'd be able to play a more active role in running it. The switchover wasn't cheap. After only four months on the job, CEO Mark Feldman quit rather than move to Canada, and got a $1.28-million (U.S.) package, including a $150,000 (U.S.) signing bonus and $900,000 (U.S.) in severance. Stronach briefly became MEC's third CEO in less than a year, then persuaded Jim McAlpine to become its fourth. But, again, at a cost. McAlpine negotiated a compensation wad worth $1.2 million (U.S.) – almost three times MEC's net income in 2000.

Stronach's choice of McAlpine to head up the racetrack company appeared to be an attempt to improve MEC's credibility. Although Stronach had never completely absolved him of blame for the near-ruinous debt that almost killed the company in 1989, in the decade since leaving Magna, McAlpine had remained friendly with Stronach, and earned his entrepreneurial spurs by founding a hugely successful Ford dealership in Aurora. A tall man with a penchant for cigars, McAlpine's irrepressible personality seems more characteristic of a car dealer – or perhaps a racetrack habitué – than the skilled accountant he is. He also owns a small stable of thoroughbreds. To Stronach's way of thinking, he seemed perfect for MEC on all counts.

McAlpine had his work cut out for him. Even before he arrived, insiders were worried that MEC was galloping out of control. In mucking out the stall at MEC, he'd be coping with the cost of the eight racetracks MEC had acquired since 1998, including, in 2000, $2 million (U.S.) for Great Lakes Downs and $24 million (U.S.) for Bay Meadows. The $357-million (U.S.) bill for Stronach's spending spree was equal to 86 per cent of MEC's total revenues in 2000. In fact, it exceeded them, if the $58 million (U.S.) from one-time real-estate sales was removed from the income total.

Though there was a division of opinion among his executives about the next steps, Stronach wasn't finished buying. Tom Dillon, who had completed the Santa Anita project and been assigned to upgrade the catering and hospitality aspects of MEC's existing tracks, believed attention to customer service was the answer to attracting live crowds back to racing. Stronach, too, acknowledged that live audiences were critical to maintain excitement, even in the televised product.

But Dillon says Andy Stronach, who was infatuated with technology and its application to simulcasting, had his father's ear, and he persuaded Frank that MEC needed to buy more tracks in order to get the necessary *volume* of content to fill out a round-the-clock simulcasting schedule, without considering the *quality* of the racing they expected to sell. "He was like 'Let's buy Portland, let's buy Michigan,'" Dillon says of Andy. "They thought content was content. But they found out very quickly nobody [bettors or other tracks buying MEC's simulcast signals] cared about Portland Meadows, nobody cared about Great Lakes Downs. Anybody buying a telecast only cared about something good to bet on."

"YOUR EGOMANIACAL ATTITUDE IS DISRUPTIVE"

Stronach's ham-handed approach to public relations didn't help. The better his horses did, the more he seemed inclined to stir up controversy and pick fights. At the end of 2000, he had reached a pinnacle in the thoroughbred world when he won three Eclipse awards, one in the category of Best Two-Year-Old Male for his horse Macho Uno and one in each of the breeder and owner categories for himself. The awards fed his belief that he could repair racing. To that end, he boldly invited the industry to a January "Racing Summit" at his Gulfstream track in sunny Florida to brainstorm on racing's future.

One of McAlpine's first duties was to deal with the manure-storm the invitation initiated. In light of Stronach's encouragement of defections from the NTRA, many were disinclined to make nice with the person they saw trying to wreck racing. John Gaines, the founder of the Breeders' Cup, likened Stronach to former U.S. presidential candidate Ross Perot, saying both were power-hungry "manipulators of the media, charismatic leaders . . . driven by their own views of the world" who were "absolutely convinced of their rightness." In a full-page letter published in the *Daily Racing Form*, Ed Friendly, the respected founder of the Thoroughbred Owners of California, charged that Stronach's "greed and zest for power outweighs what is good for racing." Grousing that MEC had reneged on its promised improvements at Santa Anita, and then tried to divide the industry with his greedy power play, Friendly told Stronach, "Your egomaniacal attitude is disruptive to the well-being of the industry. You are hell-bent on controlling racing and are trying to destroy anything that stands in your way."

The thick-skinned Stronach, sixty-eight, riposted that Gaines (a mere four years his senior) was "very old, very feeble and semi-senile," and that Friendly's comments were possibly libellous. Meanwhile, he was also in discussion with the NTRA's commissioner, Tim Smith, regarding a possible return of MEC's tracks to the fold. The dissident tracks that had followed MEC in withdrawing from the NTRA discovered to their horror in mid January that the biggest company in the industry, MEC, which they thought was championing their cause, was more interested in its own welfare. The NTRA and Breeders' Cup Ltd. had reached an agreement that only NTRA members could host the Breeders' Cup series. Perhaps mindful of that, Stronach accepted a seat for MEC on the NTRA's board and committed MEC's tracks to the NTRA until 2002, when, conveniently, the highly profitable Breeders' Cup was scheduled at Santa Anita.

Stronach's objections to the NTRA's undemocratic method of appointing directors were quietly dropped. Which surprised no one.

Most had found it laughably disingenuous in the first place, given that Stronach had structured every one of the companies in the Magna ambit – including MEC – as an autocracy in which he alone determined board and executive makeup.

In February 2001, as though to underline his power, at Magna – now a $10.5-billion company with more than half a billion in profit in 2000 – he promoted Belinda, thirty-four, to CEO (suitably propped up by vice-chairman Jim Nicol, who actually knew something about the auto industry, and who Stronach put at her side as president and COO). She replaced her former husband, Don Walker, who was going off to manage Intier, Magna's proposed interiors-division spinoff.

GOING FOR LADBROKE

After taking the reins at MEC at the beginning of 2001, Jim McAlpine had little to work with to put Stronach's plan in effect. Although MEC had been profitable in 2000, its net income of $441,000 (U.S.) on revenue of $413.6 million (U.S.) represented a paltry 1 per cent profit margin. Pushed by Stronach's ambition, however, any thought of caution McAlpine might have had was soon swept away. MEC promised to renovate the somewhat faded Gulfstream track in Florida. And Stronach had no intention of fooling around with a minor facelift, either. "It's going to be knocked down completely and rebuilt from scratch," the chairman announced.

He followed that with an April 2001 deal with Ladbroke Racing Corp. that gave MEC a television product to compete with the NTRA's TVG system. Ladbroke was a partner in The Racing Network (TRN), a satellite-based simulcast network, and owned Call-A-Bet, a complementary telephone service that took bets. The $53-million (U.S.) deal made Ladbroke a 2 per cent shareholder in MEC and added The Meadows, a harness track near Pittsburgh, to MEC's stable of tracks.

In terms of Stronach's overall plan, and industry analysts' views, the money that went into the Ladbroke deal was well spent. In a 126-page report called "The Sport of Kings – A Guide to the Pari-mutuel

Horse Racing Industry," New York investment house Bear Stearns
& Co. forecast that new media and account wagering would be the
handmaidens of racing's rebirth. With TRN, Stronach finally had a
simulcasting channel through which he could pipe the MEC racing
package.

As Dillon saw it, though, MEC was getting ahead of itself in
emphasizing broadcasting over the racing. McAlpine, he says, came
to the job with little experience in horse racing, but an even stronger
conviction than Andy Stronach's that technology was the answer to
distributing races to a broader betting public. McAlpine, like Dillon,
knew which buttons to push to get Frank Stronach fired up about
an idea: tell him the result would be the world's first or biggest. "Any
time I say, 'The world's largest,' he gets enthusiastic," Dillon says. "Jim
talked Frank into being the world's largest electronic and media and
wagering company."

The fact that there were now two competing simulcast systems
only heightened the tension in racing in the U.S. Paradoxically, each
system's programming approach seemed better suited to the other
side's business style. Stronach's TRN took a statistics-laden, just-the-
numbers-and-facts approach that targeted experienced horse-players
and hardcore bettors with wall-to-wall racing; TVG's casual style, for-
tified by flashy graphics and colour commentary from racing celebri-
ties, was designed to entertain and attract new racing adherents.

For all that, taking on the established TVG to create a second
24-hour horse-racing television channel struck Dillon as dumb. "A
24-hour television station [TVG] on horse racing had already been
done and executed and failed miserably for 17 years . . . and lost $28
million (U.S.) the year before Jim decided to go into competition
with them," he points out. Once committed to the idea, however,
Stronach chose the strategy of his friend Jim McAlpine, a businessman with little experience in the horse business, over the advice of
his friend Tom Dillon, who had been involved with racing for more
than thirty years. "I know Frank won't like it, but I don't care about

all that," Dillon says of his candour. "The pure fact of the matter is [that] that absolute idiocy cost Frank."

CHASING CASH

To help pay for assets, track renovations, and other costs in getting MEC going, McAlpine intended to go to the market with a stock issue. But MEC's unstable stock price put the offering on hold. In the meantime, it seemed to McAlpine that a safer bet to generate revenue was to add slots to its racetracks. In its report, Bear Stearns agreed that slot machines and video lottery terminals as a gaming alternative at racetracks were critical to the success of racetracks in the future. Stronach appeared to know it too. He had bought tracks in states where slots were already legal – or were likely to be soon. MEC wasn't above leaning on governments to speed the process.

McAlpine and Stronach discovered that lobbyists were just the ticket for all sorts of things. In New York, MEC hired William Powers, a former Republican party leader, and Alfonse D'Amato, a former Republican senator, to massage city and state officials on behalf of an MEC-led group in the bidding for the New York City off-track betting (NYCOTB) prize. Initially, the money spent on the lobbyists looked like good value. Stronach and McAlpine were ecstatic when Mayor Rudy Giuliani accepted their bid over that of a combined CDI and NYRA, ignoring suggestions by the *New York Times* and other papers that the MEC consortium included some shadowy partners.

(One of MEC's cohorts in GMR-NY LLC, the official bidding group, was Greenwood Racing Inc., owner of a Philadelphia track and string of OTB outlets. Robert Green, a former U.K. bookmaker, and minority shareholder in the track, bought his stake in 1989 from a former business partner who was subsequently investigated and jailed for fraud. The biggest Greenwood shareholder was Watche "Bob" Manoukian, a mysterious London-based Armenian who was once the Brunei royal family's business agent. In 1989, the *Philadelphia Inquirer* claimed Manoukian was using the racetrack investment as a tax avoidance scheme. MEC's other partners were New Yorkers William Mack and Robert Baker, politically connected real-estate investors. The *New York Times* noted that the pair owned a couple of horses, including a Kentucky Derby candidate, in partnership with Robert Cornstein, the head of the NYCOTB.)

In any case, MEC's victory proved short-lived when the New York state legislature quashed the sale of the NYCOTB to the Canadian-led consortium. As it should have, noted a relieved but still irate Barry Schwartz, CEO of the NYRA. He had called the idea of selling to Stronach in the first place "a stupid decision." Even stupider, Schwartz opined after state politicians nixed the OTB sale, would be giving MEC a shot at taking on management of the NYRA's tracks (Saratoga, Belmont, and Aqueduct), as Stronach had indicated he would like to do in 2007, when the existing contract expired. "I haven't seen one racetrack that he's improved since he started buying them," Schwartz told *The New York Daily News*. "It would be a complete, colossal disaster for him to take over the NYRA."

Indeed, any sigh heard from McAlpine when the NYCOTB deal was scuppered might have been as much from relief as disappointment. The estimated $390-million (U.S.) all-in price would have been a mouthful for MEC. As well, McAlpine's comment that MEC offered "extensive operating experience" struck listeners as audacious overstatement. Being in the racing business for only two years hardly qualified as extensive experience.

Or expert, for that matter. MEC's flagship Santa Anita track was on its third president in three years, and Gulfstream was on its second; in MEC's own executive suite, McAlpine was the fourth chief executive in just over two years. Other than Stronach's son, Andy, not a soul who had been on the MEC senior management team in 2000 when it went public was still in the executive suite.

Even so, MEC's 2001 results suggested that it was finally making some progress toward the sort of profitability Stronach had envisioned. Its nine racetracks controlled 26 per cent of the parimutuel wagering in the U.S., and sales of $519 million (U.S.) constituted a decent jump over $414 million (U.S.) in 2000, even if much of the revenue increase had come via acquisitions. As well, MEC raised $41 million (U.S.) by selling surplus land, a more or less one-off income stream that nonetheless led to its first decent profit – $13 million (U.S.). Unfortunately, it would also be its last for a while.

CDI AND MEC, NECK AND NECK

In early 2002, the forces vying to control the U.S. racing market were well established. The corporate powers were neck and neck: CDI had six tracks and an alliance with the NTRA and its TVG Network; MEC owned nine tracks and a television connection with The Racing Network (TRN). The NYRA, though restricted to operating in New York State and on a non-profit basis, was almost as powerful by dint of its three tracks, two in the huge New York City market. Off to the side, but still a factor, were about fifty independent tracks.

All the players knew that simulcasting of races had become the most important source of income in the industry. About 80 per cent of the total amount wagered at races in the U.S. was off-track, which explained the dropping attendance at live racing.

There were two ways that simulcast races could reach bettors. The first was on screens at racetracks around the country and at licenced off-track betting parlours that paid a fee for a feed of the races, and shared in the amount bet on the race. Thus, for example, an NYRA-owned track might broadcast races taking place at MEC tracks, in between its own races or on a "dark" day at the track.

The second place a gambler could watch and bet on races was in his home. A horse-racing channel, either TVG or TRN, piped the simulcast races to the racing enthusiast's television via cable or satellite. Having established an account with a "betting hub," a company licenced to take bets, such as MEC's Call-A-Bet, the bettor then wagered on individual races against his account, either on the telephone or through the Internet. The total amount bet on the race, minus the purse, was shared by the racetrack, the simulcast channel, the betting "hub" company, and the government. Though the bet was theoretically only legal if the bettor's state permitted account-betting, there were always ways around that fussy technicality. What the bettor could not bypass was the fee he had to pay to receive the simulcast feed at home. Unfortunately for the consumer, in order to get all races, he had to subscribe to both TVG's and TRN's services. And unfortunately for TVG and TRN, the market for even one of them was slim, which had been Dillon's point to Stronach.

To market its product, CDI had taken a conservative, corporate approach. In addition to integrating its operations to wring economies out of their operation, it had begun packaging races from its tracks with the Churchill Downs brand. MEC hadn't gone quite that far. Although its Santa Anita and Gulfstream tracks were already two of the best brands in racing, the rest of its chain was a mixed bag. But instead of integrating operations – difficult, given its constantly changing head-office executive group, and the disappearance of key management personnel at each track – Stronach and McAlpine continued to prowl the U.S., adding new tracks to fill out racing slots for simulcasting. Failure to address some of the problems that had turned up, however, proved very costly.

A STUMBLE IN FLORIDA

Stronach had been braying to the Florida authorities for permission to lengthen Gulfstream's winter and spring meets. He eventually got the okay to do so, but the extended dates turned out to be a disaster. Historically, Hialeah, a smaller Florida track famous for its infield flamingos, held meets that had been an extension to, rather than in conflict with, Gulfstream's. Hialeah had also traditionally provided valuable stable space for owners who moved their horses south for the winter, including some who raced at Gulfstream. But Gulfstream's expanded racing calendar squeezed Hialeah's available dates. Rather than compete with Stronach's bigger Gulfstream with its overlapping program, the Hialeah owner closed his track in the winter of 2002.

It was, of course, exactly what Stronach said should happen in free enterprise: the strongest had survived. But the loss of Hialeah's 1,000 to 1,200 stalls had severe ramifications for Gulfstream. Without adequate accommodation nearby, leading owners decided not to move their top horses to Florida for Gulfstream's winter or spring meets, depriving it of the one commodity that a racetrack can't do without, horses.

Stronach had seen the problem coming. MEC had spent $22 million (U.S.) for forty-four acres fifty miles north of Gulfstream where it intended to build Palm Meadows, a new state-of-the-art training centre complete with stabling for 1,424 horses and accommodation for stable crews. But the training centre wasn't due to be completed until 2003. In the meantime, Stronach tried to milk his Gulfstream brand by operating six days a week with ten races a day, twelve on weekends, with a small and inferior crop of entries.

The idea stumbled out of the starting gate. Serious racing fans scanned the daily race card, determined that the quality of horses was miserable, and stayed home. Stronach tried out his entertainment-at-the track theory, with rock concerts featuring Styx and Bryan Adams and boosted attendance at the track those nights. But it wasn't a crowd that bet on horses, and it alienated the hardcore few who'd gone to the track in spite of the lousy horses and paucity of entries in races. By March 2002, the handle at Gulfstream, one of America's premier tracks, was down by $1 million (U.S.) a day. Average daily attendance had dropped below 10,000 for the first time since World War II.

Stronach blamed the sparse crowds on the drop in tourism due to the September 2001 terrorist attacks in New York. But the excuse didn't wash with the folks who ran tracks that subscribed to MEC's simulcasts, whose locations were unaffected by tourism. They'd noted that the wheezers Gulfstream was running were a cut below the top-flight horses, whose records and performance were consistent enough for punters to handicap and bet on. Simulcast betting on Gulfstream races, which accounted for about 80 per cent of the total bet at Florida tracks, fell off precipitously. The NYRA, a major market for Gulfstream races simulcast on days its tracks were dark, went so far as to quit paying for the signal, claiming "short fields, cheap horses, and no depth" had led to a 29 per cent drop in betting on races from the Florida track. Naturally, the NYRA's Barry Schwartz found it easy, maybe even satisfying, not to send money to Stronach, who'd earlier vowed to take over his tracks.

THE "QUESTIONABLE QUALITY" OF MEC'S TRACKS

The racing from MEC's other tracks didn't exactly pit Seabiscuit against Secretariat, either. The Wall Street investment house of Dresdner Kleinwort Wasserstein observed in an industry report that "the quality of Magna's tracks is very mixed . . . what we see as questionable quality and limited simulcast potential." The perception grew that Stronach, for all his efforts to paint the entire U.S. with MEC race coverage, had spread MEC's level of operations too thinly and left plenty of brush strokes.

The theory that Stronach had paid too much for tracks during his initial buying binge also began to take hold, particularly in light of the poor performance of his smaller properties. In some cases, he'd been saddled with owning tracks he didn't want, but for public relations reasons couldn't peddle them. He hadn't particularly been chasing the money-losing Remington track in Oklahoma, for instance, but paid $10 million (U.S.) for it in 1999 because its owner insisted that it had to be bundled with Thistledown, a $14-million (U.S.) Cleveland, Ohio, track that Stronach *did* want.

When he bought Lone Star, a track in Texas, in 2002 for $81 million (U.S.), one of its attributes, he said, was its geographic proximity to Remington, permitting integrated management and cost-savings. But the idea that Oklahoma and Texas would constitute an efficient integration program seemed a pipe-dream, given MEC's failure to achieve economies of scale elsewhere. When *Business Week* compared its financial performance in 2001 to that of CDI, admittedly a more mature public company, the magazine noted that CDI's $22-million profit was about 69 per cent better than MEC's $13 million, despite the fact that CDI's total revenue of $427 million was almost 18 per cent less than the $519 million MEC had generated (all figures in U.S. dollars).

As much as anything, the disparity pointed to MEC's struggle to carry out the necessary upgrading of tracks MEC already owned, many of them run down, while simultaneously integrating them into an efficient operating system. Yet new ones kept coming. McAlpine, now enthralled by television and technology that could push racing to bettors, according to Tom Dillon, saw each new track in terms of its racing licence, which meant content for his twenty-four-hour racing television channel. "Essentially, McAlpine would have run races in a studio in Phoenix, Arizona, and just telecast them all over the world," says Tom Dillon. That vision differed from Dillon's belief (and the one that Stronach publicly endorsed) that customer relations and creating a better track environment were needed first, to revitalize interest in live racing, before concentrating on simulcasting. "In many ways, Jim was very right," Dillon acknowledges, "except for the basic principle of business: have a good product before you distribute."

Stronach's vanity was fed by the idea that as the creator of a global network that beamed horse races around the world, he would be hailed as the man who rescued the sport. But in the meantime, little was being done to address the slipping attendance at races, the element that Stronach acknowledged as critical.

Dillon attributes the new MEC management's apparent blind spot to its lack of racing experience. The near-religious devotion to the corporate culture that Stronach had bred throughout Magna International, he says, became a liability at MEC, under CEO McAlpine, a former Magna CFO who was supported by vice-presidents Graham

Orr and Don Amos, two other Magna alumni. "These men grew up as execs in manufacturing, in the Magna culture, and never dealt with the public," Dillon says, warming to his theme. "They never made anything that wasn't already sold . . . There was no public relations. No marketing. None of those things are involved in manufacturing, and all of the hierarchy moved from Magna and had an unbelievable lack of understanding of retail, which is what this is. You've got to draw 20,000 people. You can't come in and cut every advertising budget and have no marketing, no nothing, because that worked for you making a carburetor. That does not work here."

THE SECOND JEWEL IN THE TRIPLE CROWN

McAlpine, however, was still riding the previous year's performance and, anticipating proceeds from the share offering, indicated that MEC was back in predatory mode. It was looking to add four or five more tracks. It also planned to double the number of off-track betting outlets it controlled and swell the number of home-account subscribers from 30,000 to 200,000 in the next few years. All of which would result in a gusher of revenue. In theory.

In 2002, Lone Star in Texas had been the first track purchase, followed by Flamboro Downs in Ontario for $56 million (U.S.). Shortly thereafter, Stronach took another scoop out of McAlpine's expansion pool by paying $90 million (U.S.) for controlling interest in the Maryland Jockey Club, the company that owned Baltimore's Pimlico racetrack and its smaller, sister track Laurel, which became MEC's twelfth and thirteenth tracks.

Pimlico's primary attraction was the Preakness, the second jewel in racing's Triple Crown that it hosted each spring, an event that Marylanders venerated as an untouchable part of the state's horsey history. The growing outrage of fans at MEC's shambolic operation at Gulfstream nearly wrecked the deal when news spread that MEC was looking at buying Pimlico. "Why would Maryland approve an operator that runs a premium racetrack into the ground?" wondered

Terry Saxon, a member of the Maryland racing commission that had to okay track ownership changes.

One reason that it eventually did, apparently, was that no one else was profligate enough to pay what MEC was offering, then promise to fix the broken-down track, located in one of Baltimore's seedier districts. CDI had looked into buying Pimlico, which would have given it two-thirds of the Triple Crown (it owns the Kentucky Derby), but had bowed out of the running, well short of Stronach's $90-million (U.S.) finish line. The NYRA, CDI's ally and owner of the Belmont, the other third of the Triple Crown, thought CDI prudent in walking away from Pimlico. "They [MEC] spent a lot of money for what they got," Barry Schwartz said. "Those properties [Pimlico and Laurel] have no value other than the Preakness."

Tom Dillon, in California when the purchase was announced, was inclined to agree with Schwartz when, at Stronach's request, he flew to Baltimore to assess Pimlico and put a number on renovations required to make it more customer-friendly. Met at the airport by a limo, he became increasingly alarmed on the thirty-minute pre-dawn drive to the racetrack. "The Pimlico sign came into view and we're now driving by lit trash barrels and roving gangs and kids all over the place," he recalls. When his driver casually warned at a stoplight that on any future trip Dillon should never take a left turn at that intersection, Dillon inquired why. "He says, 'Well, we had 84 murders here in Baltimore last year and 63 of them took place on that street.' So no left turn. I remembered that."

His assessment of Pimlico's prospects was less than glowing. "I called Frank about 7:30 that morning and said, 'Are you out of your frigging mind? We'll have to buy the whole town.'" Stronach, though, was undismayed, and MEC did exactly that, Dillon says. "We bought four surrounding blocks which are all going to be stripped out if we ever get permission. His whole thing there was ownership of part of the Triple Crown. The racetrack is a dump. We'll have to tear that down."

The DeFrancis family, who controlled the Maryland Jockey Club (MJC) tracks, was happy to sell to Stronach, who they believed was the Daddy Warbucks of racing, ready to spend millions to salvage Pimlico and save the Preakness. It was a role Stronach didn't appear to mind playing. But MEC's ownership of Pimlico promised an interesting time when the three Triple Crown partners had a sit-down to talk business. Tom Meeker, head of Churchill Downs, and Barry Schwartz, the NYRA's chief, seemed to regard Stronach as an arrogant blowhard whose perversely disruptive ways had damaged the industry. Stronach thought of Meeker and Schwartz as archetypal denizens of the barnacle-encrusted establishment that he blamed for the decline of racing. A bettor would have been given long odds on the probability of the three ever having a civil conversation, much less a productive business partnership.

There were plenty of good business reasons for Stronach, Meeker, and Schwartz to bury the hatchet, however, even if only just below the top soil. In addition to being the most watched series in racing, the Triple Crown was one of the most profitable. Triple Crown Productions LLC had a television contract with NBC worth about $10 million (U.S.) a year. Sponsorship from VISA kicked in another $3 million (U.S.) annually. In the end, the money won out and the three worked together. "We all have had a different view of racing," said Schwartz after Stronach's Pimlico purchase. "Frank's view is Frank's view. Tom is running a public company that is interested in the bottom line. I am running a state organization that is trying to make New York racing the best in the world."

STRONACH'S FAILED PROMISES

By August 2002, McAlpine was willing to take cash wherever he could find it. He announced that MEC would take a breather to digest and wring some operating efficiency out of the $640-million (U.S.) worth of tracks that it had swallowed. Among the plans put on hold was a proposed $140-million (U.S.) renovation of Gulfstream, one more in a string of Stronach's failed promises. At Santa Anita, where he'd promised a complete remake, with shopping malls, hotels, and the like, not much had happened since the quick once-over that produced a new high-end dining room, despite MEC's claim that it had sunk $40 million (U.S.) into the landmark track. In northern California, where its lease to operate the Bay Meadows track was due to expire, it had done nothing about building the promised $150-million replacement track at nearby Dixon. Stronach, however, promptly contradicted his CEO's parsimony, with a raze-and-rebuild plan for Pimlico that he claimed was in accord with his dedication to live racing. "We would flatten it completely," he said.

If his intention was to ingratiate himself with locals, his custom when moving into a new market, it had the opposite effect. Worried that the razing might take place, but the rebuilding might not, Marylanders were horrified that the revered Preakness might be given a new home at another of MEC's tracks. *Washington Post* columnist Andy Beyer, widely considered the best race handicapper in the world and the most influential racing journalist in the U.S., pointed out that even without taking into account Stronach's past failure to come through on promises, his plan for Pimlico, which would have meant investing a minimum of $100 million (U.S.) to rebuild a track in a crummy neighbourhood, was impractical for a company with a market cap of less than $300 million (U.S.). Stronach's live-racing strategy, Beyer added, was "out of wack" with the reality of racing and that even Arlington, which he considered the best track in the world, had been a financial flop.

MEC had already by the end of 2002 addressed one of the new realities of racing when it launched XpressBet, its home-account and Internet wagering platform that replaced Call-A-Bet, and HorseRacingTV (HRTV), a twenty-four-hour-a-day cable television network that focused on racing and covered all MEC's tracks. But buying tracks for content had been costly, and integrating them for efficiency more difficult and expensive than forecast. Furthermore,

Stronach's racetrack-as-theme-park-as-mall approach was still un-proved, and surprisingly and annoyingly time-consuming to execute.

PERSONAL DIFFICULTIES

While MEC struggled in 2002, Stronach had some personal issues to deal with as well. Two years after finding a place for his son at MEC, he got into a dispute with him, allegedly over ownership of tech-nology for electronic betting kiosks that Andy had been working on. Only when journalists noticed the younger Stronach's name absent on regulatory filings was it revealed that his father had fired him.

Then there was Frank's sexual harassment suit. In the summer, he'd allegedly tried to date a twenty-two-year-old York University nursing student who had been working as a waitress in the Magna Golf Course clubhouse in Aurora. She'd said in her statement of claim that she turned him down, but had to quit her job out of embar-rassment at the kidding she got from fellow employees for having attracted the unwanted attentions of the big boss. Stronach denied the allegations, claiming in his statement of defence that he'd merely been trying to set up a tennis game. The details of the out-of-court settlement – love all – had admitted no wrongdoing by Stronach. But the fact that the student's lawyer observed that she'd been very happy with the financial conditions, suggested that in addition to perhaps shaming Stronach, the affair had cost him a pile.

MEC – RIDING FOR A FALL?

By the end of 2002, it was clear MEC needed cash. Racing revenues had grown from $519 million (U.S.) to $549 million (U.S.), but 2001's profit of $13 million (U.S.) had become a $14-million (U.S.) loss – a $27-million (U.S.) swing. The company had raised over $214 million (U.S.) with a share issue and then with a debt issue. But most of that was needed just to cover the three tracks bought in 2002. Even after raising another $54 million (U.S.) with a real-estate sale, MEC needed a bank loan for $49 million (U.S.).

Which all pointed, once again, to the need for slot machines at tracks as a source of revenue. Ironically, the exemplar that proved the case was the Ontario Jockey Club, which had tossed Stronach out of its boardroom in 1997, after he'd accused its management of doing "a lousy job." But now, while Stronach's chain of tracks in the U.S. was struggling, in part due to befuddled management, the OJC's Woodbine track, having introduced slots, was thriving.

Since installing 1,700 slot machines in a purpose-built facility in March 2000, Woodbine's 20 per cent share of the take had enabled it to increase purses by 60 per cent to an average of nearly $300,000 (U.S.) a day for thoroughbred racing and $130,000 for standardbreds. This was so noteworthy that many U.S. breeders had been sending mares in foal to Canada so their off-spring would eventually be eligible for a special bonus set up for Ontario-bred horses, paid out of a $10-million pool, one-third of which came from slots revenue.

The program, as well as the bigger purses, had noticeably perked up the interest of Ontario breeders. The 8 per cent increase in the foal crop in 2001 had been four times the normal growth rate. Contrary to the experience at other tracks, Woodbine had even managed to get crossover slots fans to put a buck or two down on horses, which critics of slots had said would never happen. Total wagering rose 11 per cent in 2001. Stronach had taken note, and spent $56 million (U.S.) to purchase Flamboro Downs, a harness track forty-five miles west of Toronto that operated a 750-machine slots facility that, like Woodbine's, was profitable. But the acquisition mystified some of MEC's own executives, who saw it as spending money MEC didn't have, and that had the effect of tweaking the OJC, Stronach's old foe, by encroaching on its turf. "That was . . . a lost proposition from beginning to end," says Tom Dillon of the Flamboro deal.

Not even Flamboro's slots made it a keeper, especially after the province banned smoking in Flamboro's gaming room, reducing revenue. Within a year or so, MEC was seeking to offload the harness track and the related debt on its books. Getting approval to install slots in U.S. tracks, however, had been proving problematic and achingly slow. Individual states' regulators had to give approval, and politics got in the way. So did growing opposition to gambling, particularly by the socially and religious conservative forces whose power had risen under the Bush government. McAlpine invested heavily in lobbying and in judicious campaign donations, hoping to persuade various levels of government of the merits of slots at racetracks. But paying for lobbyists and donations only added to MEC's financial woes.

As 2002 ended, Stronach appeared to be boxed in. Salvation from slots' revenue seemed only a distant possibility, while lack of funds was strangling his attempts to improve his tracks and the quality of races that would in turn garner more simulcasting income. Magna International, frustratingly, had plenty of money. But the March 1999 forbearance agreement specifically prevented the parent company from doling any of it out to MEC. Stronach had another card up his sleeve, however, another restructuring that he hoped would solve all of MEC's problems.

In the process, he exposed Magna – and his autocratic control of it – to the biggest legal challenge by shareholders that the company had ever encountered.

15

INCURRING SHAREHOLDERS' WRATH

Following the spinoffs of Decoma and Tesma in the 1990s, Magna had taken Intier public in 2001. But nothing had been done to further the promised IPOs of Magna Steyr in Europe or Magna Donnelly, the company's new mirror division, headquartered in Troy, Michigan. So it was somewhat of a surprise when, in July 2003, Belinda Stronach announced that Magna was spinning off MI Developments (MID), the industrial and commercial real-estate group that owned the land and handled development of properties for its automotive-related business. Up to this point MID had operated as a completely autonomous subsidiary within Magna. The extent of MID's real-estate holdings as Magna's in-house landlord was considerable. The company estimated that once it traded on its own, MI Developments would become Canada's fourth-largest public commercial real-estate business, with about $1.8 billion (U.S.) in assets.

At the announcement, Magna was far enough along in its plan that it had appointed Bill Biggar, an experienced real-estate executive, as CEO. John Simonetti was tabbed as the new company's chief financial officer, and Werner Czernohorsky was brought back into the fold as MID's deputy chairman. Frank Stronach, as usual, would be chairman of MID. In keeping with corporate practice within the

Magna group, the MID board of directors was to be rounded out by the presence of ex-Ontario premier Bill Davis (also an MEC director) whose statesman-like persona lent it credibility, and yet another ex-politico, former Newfoundland premier and federal cabinet minister Brian Tobin, who had recently left Jean Chrétien's government "to spend more time with my family."

MID TAKES MEC UNDER ITS WING

The MID spinoff was expected to be popular with investors, given the stability of its primary client, Magna, and the amount it earned in rent on its properties. In exchange for Magna's $1.5-million (U.S.) loss in equity that the spinoff would incur, shareholders were to get one share in MID for every two Class A or Class B Magna shares. One of MID's assets was its 59 per cent control block of MEC, which it valued at about $300 million (U.S.), and which had been under MID's wing within Magna to keep it separate from the automotive business. Belinda, no doubt relaying the message her father sent down from on high, declared MID a "natural fit with MEC and some of the unutilized lands that MEC has in its portfolio."

"Right now, a Magna shareholder has a piece of paper that has automotive assets, real estate assets and some horse racing assets," Belinda told analysts. "That shareholder will now have basically two pieces of paper, one that has automotive assets and one that has real estate and racing assets."

Magna shareholders certainly had no problem with the spinoff of MID. It made Magna itself more of a pure automotive play, neat and clean with no ragged edges, and the announcement in July immediately pushed Magna's stock price up $6 to $99 on the Toronto exchange. But the stated intention to keep MEC's racetrack and gambling business inside MID when it became a public company cast some doubts over MID's prospects. Stronach argued that the value of MEC's real estate was not accurately reflected while it was held within the auto-parts company. But many analysts thought they were properly valued, just not as highly as Stronach liked to think they were worth. They worried that once MID, on its own, was saddled with all the racetrack and gambling concerns of MEC, instead of being a pure-play, industrial and commercial real-estate company with prime, money-spinning assets that produced a steady yield, its focus would be lost.

A primary concern was the rate at which MEC's got-it, need-it approach to collecting racetracks had burned through capital. Its cash pretty much tapped out, and its debt growing, it was running out of steam at the first turn, well before the assets it had acquired were able to produce a payoff. In 2001, MEC had debt of $86 million (U.S.) and shareholder equity of $568 million (U.S.); by year-end 2002, debt had tripled to $255 million (U.S.) – equity rose to $721 million (U.S.) – and in 2003, debt would bulge to $405 million (U.S.) against shareholder equity of $657 million (U.S.).

The solution to the imbalance, the parent company's cash hoard, appeared tantalizingly close at hand. But MEC couldn't access it due to Magna's agreement to forbear dumping any more cash into non-automotive ventures for seven years. There were three years to go before the agreement could be altered or cancelled, but at the rate MEC was spending, it would be broke by then, a prospect that Stronach could not and would not stomach.

Given the fact that most of MID's annual revenue of $116 million (U.S.) came from Magna in the form of lease payments, it didn't take much analysis to see the entire restructuring for what it was – an inventive circumnavigation by Frank of the forbearance agreement, which applied only to Magna and not to MID, once it was spun off. That recognition soured many potential MID investors who tended to share the view of Sentry Select Capital fund manager Sandy McIntyre that MEC would impair earnings of the real-estate company. He described the spinoff as "just a clever way of getting the cash flow to build the entertainment business while maintaining control through subordinate shares."

MID's CEO Bill Biggar, in defending the thinking behind the MID spinoff, admitted that Magna had considered turning MID into a real-estate investment trust (REIT), a more investor-friendly structure that flows the bulk of profits after expenses to holders of its trust units. At the time of the spinoff, REIT yields were typically in the 10 per cent range. The MID spinout's proposed 36 cents-a-share dividend was well below that. But Magna rejected the REIT concept, Biggar noted, in the belief that MID's income would be better used to execute a growth strategy that would benefit shareholders with a higher share price. Almost offhandedly, Biggar added that "we're not ruling 'REITing out' some part of the company in the future." Although he couldn't have known it at the time, his casual observation would become pivotal in a shareholder assault on MID, Stronach, and on the very structure of Magna.

In the meantime, though, investors were indicating that they weren't as crazy about horses as Stronach was. Since July, when Magna announced that it was offloading its racetracks to MID, buyers had been bidding up the price of Magna's stock. By the time MID – now bearing the risky burden of the tracks – began trading at the end of August, Magna's share price had shot up to a fifty-two-week high of $114 in Toronto.

But if Magna investors were happy to see MEC towed out of their company and parked elsewhere, those at MID were about to experience the pain of having a wreck parked on their lot.

STILL SHOPPING FOR MEC

Feeling flush following a $145-million (U.S.) issue of convertible notes, and confident that a new source of cash would flow from MID's spinoff and adoption of MEC, Stronach returned to his strategy of acquiring still more racetracks. In particular, he was again eyeing the New York Racing Association's Belmont, Aqueduct, and Saratoga tracks. The NYRA's licencing agreement still had four years to go before it expired, but Governor George Pataki was growing impatient with the non-profit group. Barry Schwartz had corrected much of the mis-management that had plagued the organization, but it still owed $11 million (U.S.) in back-fees to the state, and was suffering from a scandal involving sixteen parimutuel clerks accused of tax evasion and three more of money-laundering. In addition to attracting the attention of New York's politically ambitious attorney general Eliot Spitzer, the NYRA was facing a possible federal criminal indictment.

None of which deterred Stronach. Much to the distress of Schwartz, he said that MEC would be glad to bid on taking over the NYRA's licence from the state. At the same time, both MEC and Churchill Downs – and surprisingly, Canada's Woodbine Entertainment Group – also expressed interest in neighbouring New Jersey's plans to privatize Meadowlands harness track and Monmouth Park, a package expected to be worth about $300 million (U.S.).

By late fall 2003, though, MEC was hardly looking like a company that could afford to buy more assets. It blamed a $15.4-million (U.S.), third-quarter loss on low attendance due to hurricanes that disrupted Gulfstream programs. But lobbyists hired to push legalization of slots in various states, and the decision to establish its own racing network, rather than hook up with TVG to broadcast races, was also costly. In a cost-cutting campaign aimed at slashing $5 million (U.S.) in expenses, McAlpine cut more than twenty-four head-office jobs at MEC, including most of the marketing department, and saved $700,000 (U.S.) by closing the Pimlico barn in Baltimore for the winter.

LOBBYING THE STATES TO LEGALIZE SLOTS

Now aware that slots were essential to rebuilding the horse racing industry, MEC pulled out all the stops to get permission to install them at its tracks. But for all the money it was spending on lobbyists, there was plenty of evidence that positive results were not going to come easy. MEC had bought Pimlico, and committed to upgrading it, on the understanding that the new Maryland governor would support slots at the track. Despite what local papers estimated to be $400,000 (U.S.) worth of lobbying by MEC in Maryland, however, the state had voted against their legalization. In California, gambling interests, which included MEC, hoped that the incoming Governor Arnold Schwarzenegger would reverse a constitutional ruling that gave Indian bands alone the right to operate casinos. Racing interests were lobbying for licences to install 30,000 slots at tracks in the state, but Schwarzenegger, whose main interest was increasing revenue from gambling, was negotiating with the well-financed Indians, seeking a percentage of their gambling revenue for the state. In spending $4.8 million (U.S.) to influence the state, McAlpine saw MEC's role as educating the governor to the greater contribution tracks could make to the economy if they were permitted to install slots. MEC believed its ace in the hole was Stronach's close friendship with Schwarzenegger, a fellow Austrian whose gubernatorial campaign he had supported.

In Michigan, a couple of factors were confounding MEC's plan to build a new $350-million (U.S.) racetrack complex in Romulus, near Detroit. Chief among them was the question of whether or not slots should be allowed at tracks. MEC had been lobbying not only for slots, but also for account wagering and off-track betting. Andy Stronach, estranged from MEC since his father fired him, had complicated matters in the state for his old company, by turning up as a new competitor. A day after MEC filed for its Michigan racing licence in Romulus, EQTAH Ltd., a company Andy had formed, applied for a racing licence for a proposed $10-million track in Lansing. The operation's name, created from EQTAH, the first letters of equine, quarterhorse, thoroughbred, Arabian/appaloosa and harness, reflected the mixed-breed racing the company had in mind, along with what a company spokesman described as an "equine Disneyland."

EQTAH ultimately withdrew its applications in the face of local opposition to its proposal, but Stronach senior had evidently viewed it as a threat to MEC's plans. Reminding the state that Magna International was an employer of some seven thousand in the state, he adopted a time-honoured strategy to get locals onside: Magna promised Romulus citizens plenty of jobs at a plant it would build if they voted to give the new track the go-ahead. Later, agitated at the state's delay in granting him a racing licence, he called on the clout of Magna International as a Michigan employer to complain personally to Governor Jennifer Granholm that the racing commission was "jerking us around." But there were other opponents to MEC's plan to build a so-called "racino." Casinos in Detroit, already competing with those over the Canadian border in Windsor, objected to the Romulus project on grounds that still more gambling dollars would be diverted away from Detroit.

Both MEC and MID shareholders anxiously watched for signs of a return on the lobbying dollars being spent in various states for the legalization of slots. Whatever Stronach might say about live racing's importance, the general perception of investors was that without slots at the tracks, any dream of building the world's biggest horse racing empire would fizzle, along with their investment.

AN EXPENSIVE MANAGEMENT SHAKEUP AT MID

Belinda Stronach's reign as CEO at Magna ended in January 2004 when she resigned to launch her political career by running to become a Conservative Member of Parliament. Father Frank, supportive of her decision to run for a seat in Parliament, a goal he had failed to achieve in 1988, took over her responsibilities until a suitable replacement could be found. But Belinda's stepping down at Magna overshadowed another CEO's resignation in the same month: Bill Biggar's at MID. Stronach left the MID CEO's chair vacant for the moment and moved his nephew, Werner Czernohorsky, from vice-president for construction and vice-chairman at MID, into the president's chair. (Any MID shareholder who'd watched Czernohorsky's career might well have had concerns about what this might end up costing them, in light of the way Magna's money seemed to find its way into his pocket. When he left Magna International in 1992, Magna had given him a $3-million retirement benefit and then retained him on a five-year consulting package at $250,000 annually.)

Biggar claimed that, after half a year, he was moving on to new challenges, and that he'd only planned to stay at MID to oversee its launch as a public company. It strained the imagination to envision what sort of challenge might be greater than sorting out the mess at MEC that was now infecting MID. The fact that he hadn't signalled his intention earlier was also indicative of the opaqueness at Magna that Stronach liked to describe as transparency. Biggar's explanation was generally construed as code, suggesting he got a Czernohorsky-like package on the condition he maintain the *omertà*-like silence that accompanied most departures from a Magna company. In fact, his retiring allowance, after putting in a mere six months on the job, was $1 million (U.S.) plus 150,000 MID stock options.

Soon thereafter Czernohorsky also got a Czernohorsky-like package. He clearly had entertained private ambitions to move into the vacant CEO's chair at MID. Instead, Stronach promoted to the position one of MID's directors: Brian Tobin. Within two weeks, evidently miffed at being overlooked by Uncle Frank, Czernohorsky resigned from MID. His going-away gift was $1.5 million (U.S.). He also got 150,000 stock options that, like Biggar's, were exercisable at $6 less than MID's stock was trading at, giving him an instant $900,000 windfall, at least on paper. In the first quarter of 2004, MID took a $3.9-million (U.S.) hit for severance packages alone.

CAPTAIN CANADA TAKES OVER AT MID

Having spent most of his adult life as a politician, Brian Tobin had no real-estate background, and little more as a corporate executive. But he took his board responsibilities as a director seriously enough that he'd completed a course at the University of Toronto that aimed to educate company directors on corporate governance. Even as he was pinning his nice new diploma on his office wall at MID, however, he must have begun to wonder at the disparities between his course notes and what seemed to be the way things were done at public companies chaired by Stronach. It was rumoured that Biggar had suddenly departed when faced with growing pressure from Stronach to use MID's cash to redevelop commercial facilities at racetracks, which MEC could not afford to do on its own. The rumour reinforced the belief that the MID spinoff was an end-run around the forbearance agreement. Since MID wasn't subject to it, and held the control block of MEC, it could throw cash at the racetracks and related projects using money that Magna paid to MID in the form of rent. In effect, MID became the conduit to MEC for Magna's cash.

Very neat. The only problem was that, pretty soon, Magna shareholders were going to notice.

TROUBLES AT MEC, TOO

MEC unquestionably needed money from somewhere. Despite the raft of head-office firings, the company was having difficulty finding its niche. Its thirteen racetracks were supposed to supply content for its HorseRacingTV (HRTV) to home viewers who placed bets through its XpressBet (the former Call-A-Bet). But in an effort to push races from its top tracks onto its viewers via HRTV, it refused to permit rival TVG to simulcast them on its system.

In fact, MEC had not started the dispute. Before XpressBet and HRTV were on the scene, TVG had insisted on exclusive rights to races from tracks it signed up. MEC was merely fighting back with a similar strategy. But now bettors saw MEC as the heavy. Upset at having to subscribe to two separate broadcast systems to get all the races, and then being forced to use XpressBet – a system regarded by many as inferior to other phone and Internet services – about seven hundred bettors joined a website set up by Richard Bauer, a California horseplayer, to field complaints.

MEC's marketing strategy seemed so screwy that even Jack Liebau, a lawyer and veteran track manager who was president of MEC's California operations and an MEC director, sympathized with customers. Unable to convince head office that it was folly to withdraw races from all account wagering systems except XpressBet, he'd also had the temerity to disagree with Stronach on the need for more entertainment at race tracks to make the sport successful. "Scantily clad women is [sic] not going to save racing," Liebau told the *San Francisco Chronicle*. "What's going to save racing is changing the economics of the game so we can have large and competitive fields." When that protest, too, fell on deaf ears, Liebau quit. The CV of his replacement, Jack McDaniels, told the story as to why Stronach wanted him: McDaniels was hired away from Universal Studios where he was, here we go again, a theme-park specialist.

MEC's problems were clearly manifested in its 2003 results. Although revenue rose to $709 million from $549 million a year earlier, its $14-million loss in 2002 soared 645 per cent to $105 million (all figures are in U.S. dollars). The loss no longer directly affected Magna's shareholders, but it certainly got the attention of MID's.

NEW YORK, NEW YORK

At the end of 2003, while MEC struggled, things were looking up for the NYRA's racetracks. New York State approved slots at Aqueduct and certain other of its race facilities, a move sure to give profits a lift. As well, Eliot Spitzer lifted his threat to prosecute the NYRA after the association agreed to pay fines and offered assurances that it would clean up its accounting and organizational acts. As a result, chances were considerably slimmer that its three tracks would go up for sale, a disappointment to Stronach. Nonetheless, knowing that revenue from slots could only improve the financial performance of the New York tracks, Stronach publicly renewed his interest in going after their management when the franchise came up for renewal in 2007.

MEC's covetous eye had led to animosity between Stronach and

Barry Schwartz. The acrimony only promised to increase when Schwartz retired as CEO at the NYRA and, in July 2004, it looked like Tim Smith would replace him. As the head of the National Thoroughbred Racing Association, Smith had already gone toe to toe with Stronach in 2000 when MEC pulled its tracks out of the NTRA. Luckily for Stronach, Smith turned down the New York job.

The lobby team that MEC hired to press its case for taking on the management of NYRA's tracks was impressive; it included Pat Lynch, former aide to the state legislature's most powerful Democrat, assembly speaker Sheldon Silver; Kenneth Bruno, son of one of the state's most influential Republicans, senate majority leader Joseph Bruno; and former U.S. Senator Alfonse D'Amato, a close personal friend of Governor George Pataki. The lobby package was costing MEC about $400,000 (U.S.) annually. But, you know, when in Rome, do as the Romans do: New York State's racing market was potentially so lucrative, that Stronach seemed willing to do whatever it took to get hold of the tracks. And if the lobbying for the NYRA tracks failed (or even if it was successful), MEC still owned or had optioned six hundred acres on the south shore of Lake Ontario between Buffalo and Rochester, on which it could build a new racetrack/casino complex once slots were legal across the state.

MEC'S ACTIVITIES IN AUSTRIA

If and when MEC got around to building a "racino" in New York, it had a template of sorts – the North American–style complex that it opened in Ebreichsdorf, Austria, in March 2004. But the $90-million (U.S.) Austrian facility, on the site originally planned for the World of Wonders theme park near Magna's European headquarters, was hardly a triumph. It included three racetracks, stabling for six hundred horses, and a modern casino with all the audiovisual bells and whistles found in Las Vegas. But Tom Dillon had thought Stronach foolish to try to attract visitors to a jazzed-up facility that would appear garish compared with the magnificent old-world casino at Baden, only twenty-five minutes away, "that makes Monte Carlo look like a dump."

The location of MEC's racino didn't excite Dillon either. "It's in the middle of nowhere," he says. "I said to Frank, 'What are you doing? A person who grew up there couldn't find it.'" Stronach, who, of course, did grow up in Austria, carried on anyway. By 2004, it was evident that the Austrian racino had become another expensive money-loser in MEC's portfolio.

Exactly what else MEC owned in Austria remained a mystery. The Austria Vienna soccer team that listed Magna as a sponsor, for instance, still hadn't shown up in MEC's financial reporting. Stronach was also president of the Austrian *Bundesliga*, and had locked onto the idea of building a strong team for the European Championships that Vienna was scheduled to host in 2008. He also proposed buying another team in the league that he would stock with young players, which would ensure them more playing time and faster development than if they were on one of the better teams.

Although Magna owned the Vienna team, there was no question that Stronach pulled the management strings. It was also evident that his usual strategy of spending his way to success, which had worked so well in racing, hadn't worked out for him in Austrian soccer. Despite having the highest payroll in the league, Austria Vienna had won only one championship since Magna took it over in 1998. The steady shuttling in and out of coaches and players, reminiscent of the rapid arrival and departure of Stronach's horse trainers, reflected his impatience at losing. When he fired Austria Vienna's coach in March 2004, after the team lost four of its last six games, it brought to nine the number of coaches that he'd gone through since 1998.

Stronach's soccer adventure appeared to be an effort to win the hearts and minds of Austrians by rebuilding the sport in the country, somewhat as he had rebuilt the industrial base by broadening Magna International's operations. Instead of winning over his countrymen, however, Stronach's overbearing ways had made them at first wary, then downright dubious, about his intentions. Austrian author Martin Amanshauser expressed the growing suspicion in a satirical novel, *Alles klappt Nie* ("Everything never works"), published in early 2005, in which he portrayed Magna and Stronach as having bought the entire country.

ANNUAL MEETINGS IN 2004 FOR MEC, MAGNA, AND MID

In the first of the annual meetings for Magna Entertainment, Magna International, and MI Developments on consecutive days in May 2004, Stronach downplayed MEC's $105-million (U.S.) loss in 2003 as unimportant relative to the fact that he had recognized an opportunity to consolidate U.S. racetracks into an industry leader while Americans slept. "I don't want to brag, but I had a lot of good ideas," he bragged. Plans to improve the tracks in his chain, though, had depended on non-racing revenue. The purchase of the rundown Pimlico and Laurel tracks in Maryland, which Stronach promised to demolish and rebuild, had been driven by the expectation that extra revenue from the legalization of slots at the tracks would help finance renovations. But when the Maryland legislature nixed slots, MEC was left with decrepit assets for which it would ultimately pay $117 million (U.S.).

In fact, by 2003, only Oklahoma, of all the states in which MEC had tracks, had given slots the nod. In the others, McAlpine had lobbyists on the case, their meters purring expensively. The Canadian Broadcasting Corporation reported that MEC had spent about $20 million (U.S.) in 2004 pursuing what MEC called "initiatives related to the passage of legislation permitting alternative gaming at racetracks." Although it had little to show for the money, MEC vowed to stay the course. "What we are going to do," McAlpine said of the Maryland tracks, "is live up to the commitment we made to the racing commission and rehabilitate the facilities." But it was an obligation the company could ill afford. When it bought the tracks, it had agreed to $15-million (U.S.) worth of upgrades within eighteen months.

At the Magna International meeting the day after MEC's, none of the anticipated annual protest over Stronach's salary materialized. This was largely because major shareholders, aware that their votes were impotent, didn't bother to attend. Stephen Jarislowsky of the Montreal money management firm Jarislowsky Fraser, a charter member of the new Canadian Coalition for Good Government, whose members represented institutional investors such as pension plans and mutual funds, conceded that the group's objections were largely symbolic. Stronach "will still get what he wants, but he will at least get bad publicity," Jarislowsky noted. He declared that Stronach's $38.2-million (U.S.) pay packet, mostly for undefined consulting services, was an abominable violation of governance and a slap in the face to shareholders who were shelling it out.

The MID meeting, the third in the Magna series, was its first as a public company. The company's first-half performance since being spun off had not been auspicious and investors who had worried about the racetrack business it owned saw their fears justified. In the two prior years, operating separately from, but wholly owned by Magna, MID had shown decent profits, $33 million (U.S.) in 2001 and $10.5 million (U.S.) in 2002. In 2003, however, MID's share of MEC's $105-million (U.S.) loss had turned its profit from real estate into a $32-million net loss.

As a separate unit within Magna in 2002, MID's debt had been a mere $7 million (U.S.); in 2003, its total debt, including MEC's, was $402.6 million (U.S.). Meanwhile, Brian Tobin, handling his first meeting as CEO of anything, was to be paid over $1 million (U.S.) annually in salary and bonuses.

TOBIN TRIES TO PRIVATIZE MEC

Doubtless eager to prove himself worthy of the hefty paycheque, Tobin soon found that the strings that came with the job could be as constricting as a fish net. The Stronach-led board's edict that he privatize MEC as a wholly owned subsidiary of MID was the first big snag Tobin encountered.

He dutifully announced that MID intended to pay about $286 million (U.S.) for the 40.8-million Class A shares in MEC that MID didn't already own. Under the plan, MID would pay MEC shareholders $1.05 in cash and 0.2258 of an MID Class A share for each MEC share tendered. The way Tobin spun the deal to MEC shareholders, they would get a premium on the value of their stock as well as an opportunity to benefit in the future growth of both MID and MEC. He saw benefits for MID shareholders, as well, in cost savings of operating just one public company and in higher returns at MEC because of cheaper access to capital; instead of going to the market, it would simply tap into the real-estate money of MID. Both companies being under a single board would also eliminate the need to vet related-party deals.

Tobin immediately ran into a firestorm. In a conference call after the meeting, investors and analysts representing both parties to the deal pummelled Tobin, as well as Ed Hannah and John Simonetti, respectively MID's executive vice-president and chief financial officer. David Rocker, managing general partner of the New Jersey hedge fund Rocker Partners LP, an MEC shareholder, acknowledged that the proposed deal would give MEC access to cheaper capital for development of its racetracks. But he roasted the MID executives for being opportunistic. In Rocker's view, they were paying too little for MEC shares just as approval of slots at various tracks seemed imminent, which would finally generate some income for the cash-strapped racetrack and gambling company.

Poor Tobin. As though angry MEC shareholders weren't enough, soon MID shareholders and analysts were excoriating the deal for the opposite reason. Rossa O'Reilly, a real-estate analyst with CIBC World Markets, liked MID's investment prospects as a low-risk industrial real-estate company with a superb tenant, Magna, for its properties.

He wondered what the nearly debt-free company was thinking in even considering diluting performance by piling onto its balance sheet the debt from a high-risk gambling and racetrack operation like MEC. Larry Raiman, head of real-estate analysis for the investment firm Credit Suisse First Boston in New York, agreed with O'Reilly. He saw MID's "confused strategy" as ramping up debt and risk without much evidence of a commensurate reward.

It wasn't long before the writs were flying. MEC's minority shareholders got off the mark first in the United States, filing a class action suit seeking to enjoin MID from going through with the deal. Their chief complaint was that as 59 per cent owner of MEC, MID effectively blocked any other bid that might offer shareholders more for their MEC shares.

THE FIRST GREENLIGHT CHALLENGE

Tobin also got an earful when he went on a road show with Ed Hannah to try to sell the deal to investors. One fateful stop was the New York offices of Greenlight Capital Inc., the aggressive investment firm that handles institutional and private capital. Greenlight had bought 10 per cent of MID when it had gone public in 2003, and viewed its investment as a good industrial real-estate play, despite MID's 59 per cent ownership of MEC. (Although at one point Greenlight had owned MEC as well, part of its strategy to buy spinoff companies early, it had peddled the stake shortly afterwards.) MID, after all, had had a profit of $32 million (U.S.) on revenue of $814 million (U.S.). It also had 82 per cent of its properties leased until 2013, mainly to Magna, and no significant debt.

Greenlight president David Einhorn and his partners didn't much like the plan that Tobin and Hannah were trying to hawk. Indeed, they had an alternative suggestion for MEC. Instead of taking over MEC, they told Tobin, MID should cut it loose. Greenlight COO Daniel Roitman recalls being surprised at the response to their suggestion. Tobin, he says, indicated that the idea to privatize MEC was

Stronach's, not his, and that CEOs at Magna companies "are expected to follow the chairman's lead and that Mr. Stronach has a history of replacing executives that disagree with him."

Stronach would later claim the charge to be nonsense, but MEC's Tom Dillon recalls an incident that lends it credence. In the early days of MEC during a board meeting being chaired by Stronach, a former director, participating from England via conference call, began to object, over the speakerphone, to one of the chairman's ideas. "This guy in his British accent pipes up over the phone saying 'You can't do that,'" says Dillon. "Frank goes, 'Hang that up,' and two people pounce and hang it up, and cancel the open discussion at the board meeting."

Dillon admits he's in the minority in openly expressing his views, whether or not they jibe with Stronach's. "The man's presence is intimidating to presidents and popes," he says. And to directors, he adds. "Those men will all have something to say when they walk out of the room, but the next time they're in the room, it's 'Yes,' or 'No,' to him, no matter who you are."

Greenlight's principals, though, were neither directors, presidents, nor popes. So they weren't particularly intimidated. And they recognized that Stronach's control of MID meant that minority shareholders like themselves might not have a say in the proposal to privatize MEC. In August, Greenlight decided to force the issue by launching a legal challenge to block the MID plan to privatize. The way Greenlight described the deal in its regulatory filing, MID's objective was "clearly intended to further Mr. Stronach's personal passion at minimal risk to Mr. Stronach and has nothing to do with furthering the best interests of MID shareholders."

The Greenlight charge focused on a nuance of the privatization proposal that had almost gone unnoticed. Prior to making its offer for MEC, MID had paid Stronach $21.9 million (U.S.) – $3.3 million (U.S.) in cash plus 708,000 MID shares – for all of his shares of MEC. The deal had the effect of bumping MID's stake in MEC up to 62 per cent from 59 per cent. But in the event that the merger didn't go through, MID's board had given Stronach an option: he could reverse the deal entirely, or take back only the cash and buy the MID shares.

Stronach maintained that he sold his MEC shares at market price so he would be participating in the transaction solely as an MID shareholder and wouldn't reap any personal benefit from the premium offered to MEC shareholders for their stock. Greenlight, though, saw a more sinister motive. Had Stronach continued to hold shares in both companies, it argued, the takeover of MEC would have qualified as a related-party transaction, so under Ontario Securities Commission regulations, it would have needed approval of minority shareholders to be completed. Greenlight believed that Stronach wanted to avoid any vote that he didn't control, a not unreasonable assumption in light of the lengths to which Stronach had historically gone to control all parts of the Magna empire. Stronach's right to reverse his sale of MEC stock if the merger died, Greenlight noted, was an option that already set him apart from other minority shareholders. What's more, they argued, he still benefited from the merger inasmuch as his stock options in MEC would be converted into options on MID stock, a more valuable commodity.

Greenlight made sure to send a letter detailing its challenge to every MID director. The letter was also filed with the OSC, and as a so-called 13D public filing with the U.S. Securities Exchange Commission (SEC). Both regulators posted the letter on their websites upon receipt. It was serious stuff. Which was why Tobin stunned analysts and investors who connected to a morning conference call he set for August 11 to discuss MID's second quarter financial results, when he claimed that he hadn't seen the Greenlight letter.

At first, Tobin and Ed Hannah tried to stonewall, refusing to answer questions related to Greenlight's charge. When analysts and investors kept hammering away on the topic anyway, Hannah relented briefly to "categorically deny" Greenlight's claim that the purchase of Stronach's shares had been a ruse to avoid a shareholders' vote on the merger. He maintained that MID had insisted on it to ensure that Stronach wouldn't benefit from the deal and that, in any event, the privatization didn't require such a vote. But the conference participants weren't buying it. If preventing Frank from personally gaining from the deal had been the objective, one analyst wondered, why wouldn't MID put the whole question of MEC's privatization to a vote of shareholders?

Tobin may have been new in his job, but he had been around Frank Stronach long enough to know that such a thing wasn't in the cards at MID or any other Magna company. There would be no point in such a vote, since Stronach had voting control of each of them. Caught inexplicably unprepared for the conference call (if he actually was, and was not just claiming ignorance to avoid the subject), Tobin was clearly not pleased at having become Stronach's piñata.

POLITICIANS TO THE LIFEBOATS

Since the privatization had been announced in July, Tobin later said, MID's management had been spooked enough at MEC's spendthrift ways that "if MEC didn't raise significant new funds or cut back discretionary capital expenditures . . . it could possibly even run out of cash by the end of October 2004." Both the board and management team were split on how to proceed. Tobin thought it a no-brainer: kill the privatization deal. Not doing so risked turning MEC into a sinkhole for MID's cash. He appeared to have his supporters, among them Bill Davis, the seventy-five-year-old former Ontario premier who'd been on one Magna board or another, most recently MID's, since leaving politics twenty years earlier. Stronach, doubtless seeing himself left to go racetrack shopping with no credit card, was insisting that privatization should go ahead so he could load up his acquisition war-chest with MID's money.

Unable to persuade Stronach to pull the plug on what would be a decidedly good deal for MEC but bad for MID, Davis abruptly resigned for what he unconvincingly claimed were health reasons. He didn't give up any other of his directorships.

A day after Davis got off the Magna gravy train, and only a few hours after Stronach announced that he had hired the highly regarded Mark Hogan away from General Motors to become president of Magna International, Brian Tobin took the edge off Stronach's day. After just five and a half months on the job, he told Stronach he was following Davis out the door, the second MID CEO in a year to bail.

Stronach, in hiring mode anyway, hastily appointed CFO John Simonetti as Tobin's replacement, then set up a conference call with the media and investors. In retrospect, he'd have been better advised to delay the telephone press conference and to announce the changes to the executive and board first. Hogan's arrival was all but ignored as the press conference participants, naturally enough, wanted to know what the hell was going on at MEC, and why Tobin had jumped.

Stronach, who never understood public relations and never had much use for the press, obstinately refused to answer any questions related to Tobin. Incredulous, Ron Mayers, an analyst with Genoa Capital Inc., observed to Stronach, "When it comes to competition, democracy and unorthodoxy, you're unto yourself . . ." Other than to offer declarations about his dedication to corporate transparency, MEC's prospects, denials of personal profiteering, and a defence of his control of Magna companies – and of course the usual bland-ishments about Magna's unique culture and his role in it, which he feels obliged to deliver on any public speaking occasion – Stronach said nothing.

Neither did John Simonetti, Tobin's replacement. When ques-tioned directly, he either deferred to Stronach or Stronach intercepted the question with a curt "I called the conference call." Greenlight would later interpret Simonetti's deference as evidence of Stronach's control over the new CEO. It was a plausible assumption that may have been correct. But the fact that Simonetti was even participating in the call at all was not, perhaps, Stronach's best idea that week. When told of his appointment as CEO, Simonetti had been on vacation in Greece with his family. Hoping to give the impression of continuity, Stronach had had Simonetti participate in the conference call from his hotel room in Greece. It was a point that Stronach, the proponent of transparency, chose not to reveal during the conference call until he couldn't avoid doing so.

Simonetti was still out of the country as Stronach swung into damage-control mode. First, he set about looking for a way to save the privatization of MEC by making former federal transport minister Doug Young MEC's lead director, and then appointing him chair of a special committee to study the transaction. Young didn't need (nor did he have) special forensic accounting skills to add up (a) the impact of MEC's faltering finances, (b) a 15 per cent slump in MID's share price following the privatization proposal, (c) the pending challenge from Greenlight, and (d) assorted class action suits being threatened by shareholders if MID went through with it. Young came to the same conclusion that Tobin and Davis had, and told Stronach so: privatizing MEC was a lousy idea. Running out of politicians who'd support him, on September 16, Stronach reluctantly aborted the MEC takeover by MID.

THE FALLOUT

While it won't go down in Magna's corporate annals as a high point, the decision to cancel the privatization of MEC was nonetheless noteworthy. So far as anyone knows, it was the closest Stronach had ever come to capitulating to minority-shareholder pressure. Typically, the decision came with the sort of exorbitant costs that seem to accompany all high-level Magna departures. Staff turnover at MID, already approaching joke status after Werner Czernohorsky and Bill Biggar toted bags of money out the door with them in early 2004, resembled a full-scale comedy after subsequent changes at MID and MEC. In addition to the loss in August of Tobin and the loyal retainer Davis, COO Andy Blair departed the same month. At MEC, CFO

Graham Orr, a seventeen-year Magna veteran who'd spent many hard-working, imaginative years as a Stronach apologist, was moved back to Magna.

And there was more to come. At the time of Doug Young's appointment, Stronach had shored up the MID board with the addition of former MP and ex-Magna vice-president Dennis Mills, and Bill Sutton, a recently retired Scotiabank executive. Sutton sat on the board's special committee under Young, which had taken a second look at the merits of the MEC takeover. It turned out to be the last of his duties. The day Stronach called the takeover off, only sixteen days after he had joined the board, Sutton resigned for "personal and family reasons." Later in September, Ed Hannah, MID's chief counsel, left to return to private practice.

John Botti, a principal in Botti Brown Asset Management LLC, a San Francisco investor in both MEC and MID shares and an ally of Greenlight Capital in opposing the MEC takeover, summed up the general conclusion that most observers were drawing. "Every two weeks another board member and/or senior operating officer of this business resigns," Botti told the *Globe and Mail*. "We're not in the meetings, but from the outside, it looks to us like every person who is actually showing some spine and going up against Frank Stronach is being shown the door."

Along with the embarrassment, MID took a considerable financial hit from the resignations. After the $1.5-million and $1-million severances given respectively to Czernohorsky and Biggar, Tobin got a package worth $1.8 million, including $574,000 for less than six months' work. Nice work if you can lose it. Hannah's going-away gift totalled $1.4 million for nine months' work in 2004 as executive vice-president. Andy Blair got $1.58 million, including a $948,000 retiring allowance. In all, the slew of resignations cost MID $5.5 million (all figures in U.S. dollars). Stronach may have considered it money well spent; the accompanying non-disclosure agreements were effective at preserving the cone of silence around Magna's internal affairs.

Conversely, it wasn't all that uncommon for canned executives to have to go after Magna to get their due. Graham Orr felt he'd been given short shrift by Magna when he was inexplicably sacked after years of service that included such unaccountant-like activities as explaining to the press Stronach's schmaltzy Austrian theme parks and luxury airline plan. When Magna refused to pay a $350,000 (U.S.) termination bonus called for under his contract, Orr swung back at his former employer in 2005 with a $4.3-million (U.S.) lawsuit for wrongful dismissal.

GULFSTREAM, GHOSTZAPPER, AND GOLF COURSES

In the midst of the MID debacle, MEC was continuing its battle to get slots and other forms of "alternative gambling" legalized in the states in which it owned racetracks. In the summer quarter of fiscal 2004, spending on U.S. lobbyists contributed to a $50-million (U.S.) loss. It didn't get much value for its money, either. The U.S. presidential election in November included referendums related to gambling in several states of interest to MEC. Oklahoma voters elected to permit slots at racetracks, but Michigan and Florida voters decided to hold new referendums to get clarity on the issue. In Florida's case, each municipality would decide. For Gulfstream, it meant another year's delay before locals would give the okay to install slot machines at the track.

Californians also rejected slots and other new-wave gambling in the November referendum. Unfortunately for MEC and other race-track owners, Stronach's friend Arnold Schwarzenegger had seen the writing on the wall and cut a deal with California's native tribes, who had a monopoly on casinos in the state, to collect 25 per cent of their slots revenue. The double-whammy left racetracks with no chance of collecting revenue from slots, so they sued to have Schwarzenegger's deal with the Indians declared unconstitutional.

A few things did go well for MEC that year. Lone Star Park race-track in Texas was showcased the last weekend in October as host of the Breeders' Cup series. MEC used the occasion to unveil its new Horse Wizard betting machines that enabled racegoers to place bets electronically on races at a number of tracks. And Stronach personally was in the spotlight at Lone Star. His horse Ghoszapper, by easily winning the $4-million (U.S.) Breeders' Cup Classic race, immediately became the favourite to win an Eclipse Award as horse of the year. The Texas victory was especially gratifying for Stronach beyond the $2.08 million (U.S.) he got as his share of the purse. Ghostzapper was the son of Awesome Again, his horse that had won the same race six years earlier. It was the first time that a Breeders' Cup Classic winner had sired another winner of the race.

McAlpine wasn't in much of a celebratory mood, though. Responding a few days later to MEC's financial performance, he announced a cost-slashing program and a real-estate sell-off. The company's fourteen tracks, considered prime assets when MEC spent handsomely to collect them, had turned out to be mostly fixer-uppers. McAlpine's admission that "we knew we were buying old, rundown facilities" was in marked contrast to the enthusiasm Stronach had displayed at the time of the purchases.

MEC had also been bedevilled by the golf courses in Aurora and Vienna that Stronach threw into the company. It was doubtful that he would ever put up with anyone outside the Magna group owning them. In fact, he indicated that he intended at the first opportunity – which is to say, when the forbearance agreement ran out in May 2006 – to have Magna buy them from MEC to replenish the latter company's treasury. It would surprise no one if the price turned out to be considerably more than the book value of $80 million (U.S.). In the meantime, MEC was stuck with high-priced assets unlikely to ever earn out their value.

To help out MEC, Stronach had Magna paying MEC $9 million (U.S.), an exorbitant amount by any measure, to rent the courses. Magna justified (and still justifies) the cost to its shareholders on grounds that the courses and clubhouses are used for, er, corporate promotion and charity. It was a ridiculous claim, considering that $9 million (U.S.) would pay for at least 45,000 rounds of golf at $200 a round, which of course was a touch in excess of the number of rounds that would ever be played on the links of any two "exclusive" clubs. The golf courses, in short, were a boondoggle that enabled Magna's cash to cascade quietly into MEC without technically violating the forbearance agreement, or raising the ire of Magna's shareholders.

GREENLIGHT'S SECOND CHALLENGE

The aborted takeover of MEC by MID left MEC, in late 2004, about where it had been – a separate company with its own board and management, which had to make its own arrangements for any funding from its 59 per cent owner, MID, or from elsewhere. The awkwardness of two public companies complying with securities laws to do business with each other had been one of the reasons for proposing the merger in the first place. But the situation suited MID shareholders just fine, as it ensured that the movement of funds between MID and MEC would be reported instead of buried, as, say, MEC's actual lobbying costs were. Indeed, emboldened that their protests had helped to block MID's plan to swallow the racetrack company, institutional investors, led by Greenlight Capital, renewed their suggestion to MID that, rather than purchase MEC, it should sell its shares in the company and let it live or die on its own. Recalling that MID's first CEO, Bill Biggar, had admitted when Magna had spun it off that he wouldn't dismiss outright the possibility of converting the company into a real-estate investment trust (REIT), Greenlight, for one, thought that it was time to consider doing so. As a REIT, MID would pay out the bulk of its income to unitholders, or "create value for shareholders," as the phrase went in the world of hedge funds.

MID, considered a rock-solid earner compared with chancy MEC, nonetheless had a bad third quarter as well, almost entirely attributable to MEC. On its own, it had an $11.5-million (U.S.) profit. But princely retirement packages as well as the $2.7-million (U.S.) cost of the aborted deal, not to mention MID's share of MEC's $50.3-million (U.S.) loss for the third quarter, all that stuff totted up to a $16-million (U.S.) loss.

In the grand scheme of things, that loss wasn't likely to do serious damage. But it definitely caught the attention of shareholders used to seeing Magna's rent cheques converted into earnings and dividends. In particular, the principals of Greenlight, which owned 10 per cent of MID's stock, were fed up watching a wonky racetrack-and-gambling company squander MID's profits. They decided to do something about it.

When MID announced in September, after all the resignations and firings, that it had established another special committee to review MID's relationship with MEC, Greenlight jumped at this fresh chance to engage in "a constructive dialogue to identify value-creating alternatives for MID." The company called Doug Young to express its willingness to participate. Young told Greenlight, "Don't talk to me, my job is done, talk to the Chairman." So the Greenlight executives called Stronach, who agreed to meet them on October 13 at the company headquarters in Aurora.

GREENLIGHT GETS THE FULL FRANK

Even as sophisticated investors from New York City, Einhorn, Dan Roitman, and Vinit Setha were suitably impressed with the Magna complex, the plush furnishings of the corporate offices, and the sumptuous clubhouse dining room whose five-star service includes the "Frank salad." They were more amused than awestruck by Stronach himself. Arriving late and ducking in and out all day to take calls, Magna's chairman spent most of his time with them pontificating on his life and vision. What the New Yorkers got, in fact, was the famous Full Frank, including the signature felt-tip marker "illustration" that depicts Fair Enterprise, the foundation of the Magna organization. "Sure I took it," says David Einhorn of the finished work. "I said, 'Thank you.' It's in my permanent collection."

Stronach finally allowed the Greenlight partners to present their proposal. Their suggestion was to separate Magna Entertainment from MI Developments, convert the free-standing MID into a REIT and eliminate its dual-class voting structure. They felt that MID had historically been undervalued for a variety of reasons and traded at a holding-company discount because of its investments in MEC. As well, they told Stronach that investors were skeptical of the logic of diverting MID's stable, low-risk cash flows to finance the riskier, and very different, business of MEC, especially since MEC was losing so much money. They also contended that MID currently had an inefficient tax and shareholder structure that would be rectified if MID were converted to a REIT.

Stronach once confided to his chauffeur in Austria that he had seldom in his life sat through an entire movie without needing to jump up to address an idea he had just had about something. Had Greenlight's Power Point presentation been prepared by Steven Spielberg, it's doubtful it would have grabbed Stronach. Considering that it was diametrically opposed to his wishes, it was barely begun before it was over, Vinit Setha recalls: "Four pages into it he started objecting, but we kept going, and then six or seven pages in, there was a whole other conversation and the show ended."

During the Greenlight visit, only Stronach and Dennis Mills, executive vice-chairman of MEC and a director of MID, met with the New Yorkers. MID's CEO John Simonetti was only two tables away during their lunch with Stronach. The Greenlight executives found it odd in the extreme that the CEO of MID wasn't invited to hear a proposal by a major shareholder to restructure his company. But Stronach, Einhorn shrugs, had made his decision: "Frank made it pretty clear that he was the decision-maker in all things."

Something else the Greenlight group noted was that Stronach repeated himself quite a bit. During the meeting he didn't seem to remember what he'd already said or not said: "He told lots of stories from that time of his life in the 1960s when he was building the company," says Einhorn. "Those memories were very fresh in his mind. But what he had said an hour ago wasn't very fresh, and what he didn't remember, he repeated." But that was okay with him and his partners; they were happy to sit and listen.

Before leaving the meeting Stronach raised specific objections to Greenlight's proposal; in particular, he refused to consider any alteration to the dual-class voting structure or any transaction that would remove him from control of MEC or MID. When Einhorn pointed out that Stronach did not have direct control over MEC, which was controlled by MID, Stronach responded that it didn't matter: he controlled MID. Stronach also airily dismissed a Greenlight scenario in which Stronach could lose control of MEC if MID's board thought it would be in the best interest of MID shareholders to separate MEC from MID. That would never happen, Stronach said, because, "I would call a shareholder meeting and elect another board."

Greenlight's management left the meeting with the feeling it hadn't been particularly productive. But as the gregarious Dennis Mills walked them to the parking lot, Dan Roitman says, he told them he thought progress had been made: "He wasn't exactly clear *what* progress had been made, but he was sure *some* had been." Mills also opined that Magna was the most investor-open company in Canada. Then, Roitman says, almost in the same breath, Mills told the Greenlight executives that they were the first MID investors to actually come up and see Stronach at the corporate office.

It wasn't until more than two months later that Stronach, through Mills, provided the results of MID's study of Greenlight's proposal. As near as Greenlight could determine, Magna's "thorough analysis" consisted of general background material and news clippings on the subject of income trusts – surprisingly, compiled by a parliamentary librarian in Ottawa. On the basis of Mills's analysis, MID rejected the REIT idea, stating that the income-sharing structure would inhibit the ingenuity of the company.

Greenlight says that when it politely suggested to Mills that his and Stronach's conclusions about the REIT were not supported by the materials, Mills suggested a follow-up call to CEO Simonetti. Einhorn did so. When he finally got through, he was astonished when Simonetti told him that no one at MID had even showed him the materials that Greenlight had provided to Mills as a follow-up to the October meeting. Simonetti's comments throughout the conversation made it abundantly clear to Greenlight that, contrary to what Mills had indicated, MID had done little or no analysis of their proposal. Nor were Greenlight's attempts to engage Magna's special committee, which was supposed to be considering the future of MEC in dialogue during February and March, any more successful. Though Magna representatives agreed to meet with Greenlight's advisers and legal counsel, Einhorn, Roitman, and Setha themselves were not allowed into the meetings.

This proved the final straw for Greenlight. It gave up its attempts to work with Magna on restructuring MID. As far as its partners were concerned, Stronach and the Magna directors had displayed unbelievable rudeness by not giving their proposal serious consideration. They felt they'd been screwed over. Accordingly, in February, they issued a proxy circular to all MID shareholders, outlining their complaints and issues, explaining how their plan would benefit them and urging them to mail their proxy votes in.

In effect, MI Developments was about to become the first Magna-related company to face the wrath of dissident shareholders in a proxy challenge.

16

OH, AND ANOTHER THING

Dear Frank:

Do you mind if I call you Frank? Most people do – you're one of the few businessmen in the world who's recognized by his first name alone. It kind of illustrates the stature you've acquired over your career. I know you don't answer e-mails or letters. At least not mine. But I wanted to let you know it's been a phenomenal journey retracing your life and Magna's evolution from a hole-in-the-wall shop to a $23-billion (U.S.) enterprise and counting. And it's the counting part that is difficult. This exercise could go on forever. *You* could go on forever, come to that, a point you've made yourself on occasion. But the story has to end somewhere, and I've still got some bits and pieces to deal with. If it's all right with you, I'd like to do it with some observations and a few queries.

Full disclosure here, Frank: I'm a shareholder of all of Magna's companies. I bought the stock in hope of identifying with other owners of the company (and so that I could get into the annual meetings). I don't have a big position, mind. In fact, it's as small as I could make it – a single Class A share in each company. But then, you don't have much skin in the game yourself, at least as far as the common equity shares are concerned. Yours are all the super-voting Class B shares. As you've indicated (rather more often and forcefully than was perhaps necessary) investors know who's behind the wheel. I guess there's something to that. And despite any cavilling, at seventy-four, you've so far proved to be the Dorian Grey of industry, with an energy that shames younger executives.

Which has been one of my problems. This whole project would have been a lot simpler if it had just been about an auto-parts company and the tycoon who founded it and controls it. Instead, it ended up being about three different companies, some spinoff groups, and myriad side interests – the media company, the politics (in three countries!), restaurants, pro soccer in Austria, a tennis-equipment company, horse-stall and artificial-straw businesses, theme parks, racetracks, golf courses, luxury airlines, ski resorts, real-estate projects, and a sports academy for Austrian soccer players.

I'm sure that list isn't complete. But the point here is that any one of those ventures would constitute a fair-to-middling career for most of us; and even if some of them tanked, nobody can say Frank didn't take his best shot. Or that you didn't do it your way, which is to say first-class – *cum laude*, you might say.

THE MAGNA MODEL

There's not much question in my mind that the drama that's been your life is the stuff of legend, complete with its own Camelot up in Aurora and what I guess you could call the Spinco Camelot in a castle in Austria. Plus those multi-million dollar *pieds-à-terre* in Florida and Colorado. It's a magical existence, and the business that goes with it isn't far behind. In the 1960s, your unknown partner, Burt Pabst, got you a contract making sun-visor brackets for GM, one of the biggest companies of any kind, and for sure the biggest car maker in the world at the time. Flash forward forty-odd years, and Magna is putting together entire cars, using parts it mostly supplies. GM, on the other hand, after eschewing your strategy of not letting unions have their way with you, is trying to keep its hood above water while paying laid-off union workers not to work and being pushed around by an ornery corporate raider who owns 10 per cent of it.

·Magna, meantime, has become bigger than itself. Have former GM (or Ford or DaimlerChrysler) workers been so enchanted by their environment that they've gone off and started a car company using the same corporate structure? They have not. But all kinds of former Magna employees have done that.

Take Paul Shin, for example. A young engineer who joined the testing operation of Magna's Atoma group in the early 1990s as a university co-op student, he left when he bumped into a superior with whom he didn't see eye to eye. "Magna puts golden handcuffs on you," Shin told me. "The longer I stayed, the more I could see that it wasn't going to work out. As second in command you should follow the leader, but I'd been a leader."

In the late 1990s, he founded Paragon Systems, a testing, engineering, and prototyping business not far from Magna's headquarters. You'd like the atmosphere at Paragon, Frank. There's a hum of industry on the shop floor and in the office. Machines open and close car-doors endlessly, over and over, to test latches and hinges. Refrigerated chambers measure vehicles' and components' cold-weather performance. CNC equipment shapes metal.

It's entirely intentional that the place feels like a Magna factory. Shin says it will feel even more so as it grows. "For me Magna is a model," Shin said. "Our goal is to set up like Magna. The system works. It's excellent and I don't see why we shouldn't follow it. A lot of my friends who have come out of Magna are doing the same thing. They try to operate in a similar way or integrate a lot of Magna philosophies."

It's a testament to the efficacy of the Fair Enterprise you developed, Frank. The legacy of new businesses spawned by Magna serves Canada and other countries well. You should be proud. Still, I couldn't help thinking that a diaspora of ex-Magna people, who'd left what even they admit is one of the country's leading employers to set up on their own, suggested that some bright people think they can do things better.

Fred Jaekel certainly does. He's president, CEO and a major shareholder of Martinrea, the hydroforming company he helped create out of Royal Laser, the company he joined after you tossed him out of Magna after nineteen years. Martinrea, he points out, is already more profitable than Magna, though smaller. To offer one reason, he waves out his office window at a boxy industrial landscape that's markedly different from the country-club environment at Magna. "We have no toys, no golf courses, no Bavarian chalets and planes and all that," Jaekel says. "When customers see all that stuff, they know who's paying for it. They are. We're bare bones."

Not so bare bones, mind, that there isn't a Benz worth six figures in his parking slot, or that he doesn't collect more than $1 million a year. Jaekel's admittedly a guy with strong opinions, and I can see how you and he could clash. But he's an unabashed admirer of what he says Magna was in its halcyon days. He's paid Magna the ultimate flattery by deliberately patterning Martinrea after it, but without the excess and distractions that he says have corrupted the original Magna model.

It's hard to prove his case. But thirty or so employees have jumped from Magna to join Martinrea, which has the same pay structure, including profit sharing and bonuses based on profitability. It's not as though Martinrea, with eighteen plants around the world, is going to conduct wholesale raids on Magna or anything, Frank. But Jaekel's success as he chips away at Magna's market suggests that he's doing something right. "And when I quit doing it," he says, "shareholders can throw me out. We don't have all that dual-class share stuff."

THE SPIN ON SPINOFFS

Jaekel or anybody else who hopes to overtake Magna is going to have to step lively just to catch up. Your instinct for sniffing out the direction the auto business is steering, then restructuring Magna to be there ahead of it, has worked, even though the shuffles have occasionally come so rapidly they've overlapped. Sometimes it's difficult to determine whether the reorganization is to the benefit of Magna, you, or one of your pet projects – or all (or none) of the above.

Take the stunning announcement in 2004 that Magna was doing a 180, reversing a twenty-year-old policy of spinning off groups into public mini-Magnas. That was the boldest U-turn yet, and the most expensive. At first blush it made perfect sense from Magna's point of view, even if it put paid to the message you were zealously preaching only six months earlier. Suddenly, spinning off groups as public companies, which had been baked into Magna's culture, was passé. Now Magna was going to spend about $1.3 billion to privatize the three automotive spincos already out there, buying up the shares it didn't already own.

Your explanation was that the automaking environment had changed and the spinoffs didn't fit any more. Automakers wanted suppliers to provide bigger chunks of their cars, and Magna had become capable of quoting on total cars instead of just modules. But tighter corporate-governance regulations that were enacted to ensure deals were at arm's length and fairly priced were making inter-company transactions between Magna's public companies increasingly cumbersome. I kind of got your thinking, Frank: if Tesma, say, was beating up Decoma on price, Magna couldn't demand that Tesma reduce price so that Decoma could go after a big contract with a low bid; if it did, shareholders of Tesma would accuse its board and management of taking a beating on a related-party deal.

By privatizing Intier, Decoma, and Tesma, you erased their boards and pesky shareholders. Deals could be put together without having to clear a lot of fussy watchdog committees. Merely eliminating all the extra securities reporting required of public companies brought a cost saving. Sure, some Tesma shareholders beefed about the price you were paying for their shares, but since you controlled the spincos, there was never much doubt that the repatriation would get done, with a combination of Magna stock and cash.

Magna's braintrust had already determined that the change was due by the time you plucked Mark Hogan out of General Motors to become president in 2004. As a former Magna customer who (like a lot of us) was sometimes mystified by its organization chart, his endorsement of the restructuring was its seal of approval. In Hogan's view, the streamlined organization will permit bidding on bigger jobs, eliminate duplicate investments, and boost revenue and profits all round.

In the short term, Frank, I like what you did with the excess executive talent. Hogan figures he's odds-on as CEO, replacing Belinda? Not so fast. You craftily parachute in Siegi Wolf and Don Walker as co-CEOs, so Hogan is their subordinate. It seemed to work, too. Sales in 2005 rose to a record $23 billion (U.S.) from $21 billion (U.S.) in 2004, although it could be said, and frequently was during Belinda's term, that Magna's momentum is such that it doesn't matter who is at the top.

THE LUCK OF THE STRONACHS

I know you consider yourself Magna, and Magna you, Frank, and it seems churlish to bring this up. But I couldn't help noticing that the spinco privatizations weren't detrimental to your personal finances. It must have been annoying to hold all those options on the spincos' stock that you were gifted with for all your work when they went public. If you'd exercised them, the resulting stock would be relatively illiquid. You couldn't peddle, say, 750,000 Tesma shares, without drowning the market and pushing the price down. Ditto your options on Decoma and Intier shares.

As ever, you were handed a solution by the privatization plan. It made the options of all three spincos swappable for Magna options. Good news or what! When you exercise *them*, you get Magna stock – a lot easier to unload in the larger, more liquid market without dramatically affecting Magna's stock price. I wouldn't suggest for a moment that that was in any way a part of your decision to go with the privatization, Frank. I only bring it up as an example of your uncanny good fortune.

HORSING AROUND

Let's look at the horse hobby as another example. You buy a riding horse in the 1960s and in forty years it's a herd of eight hundred (or a thousand, or whatever) thoroughbreds, one of the largest in the world. Okay, forty years isn't exactly presto, change-o. But you've corralled some of the game's most celebrated winners, and your steeds reside in the Four Seasons of stables in Ontario, Kentucky, and Florida. When not training for races or mating, they live in an air-conditioned environment where light streams through stained-glass windows. The high-tech straw in their stalls is better than the real thing, and manufactured by one of your companies that spins straw into gold, kind of like the fairy tale. There's even automated equipment to process the inevitable manure. It might be worth looking into a broader market for that, Frank. I've come across offices in need of machines capable of that function. Maybe you know of some too.

But I digress. Your horse operation is what fables are made of, a tribute to your determination. All those accolades – the ten Sovereign Awards for racing in Canada, the six Eclipse Awards you and your horses have won in the U.S., your membership in the Canadian Racing Hall of Fame – are well deserved recognition for your dedication to the sport. You have to be superbly skilled and lucky just to break even in the horse game, and you seem to be both. Lots of the fabulously rich spend lavishly on horses without your success.

One of the more enduring conundrums to me is that you've never actually said how much the ponies have cost you. But a couple of horse-industry outfits offer some numbers for consideration (all in U.S. dollars). The operators of the Keeneland thoroughbred auction held every fall in Kentucky say the median price of horses sold in

2005 was $95,000. But as you well know, not all are champions. A *Thoroughbred Times* survey found that fewer than half of all thoroughbreds ever win a race. In 2005, 25 per cent won less than $1,000, only 17 per cent made more than $25,000, and a mere 2 per cent made more than $100,000. The average horse's winnings never cover its expenses, according to West Point Thoroughbreds, a New Jersey company that puts together ownership syndicates. It reckons the annual upkeep of a horse to be $40,000 to $50,000.

Talk about a mug's game! Even if only five hundred of your horses get the full treatment – $30,000-worth of training, $6,000 for the vet, $1,800 for blacksmith work, and $1,500 for transportation to tracks – that's $19.5 million (U.S.) in costs per year, right there. And that's not factoring in annual mortality-insurance premiums of about 5 per cent of the horse's value, upkeep of facilities, management salaries, and the like. Sure, you recover some of that at the track. But I suspect this hobby isn't a money-spinner, right?

Which brings us to those outsized pay envelopes you've been pocketing. Nobody's paid much mind to where the $300 million (U.S.) that Magna's board has awarded you over the last ten years has gone. But you've never struck me as being a conspicuous consumer, the nags excepted. By your own admission, you work 24/7, so when would you have time to do any other shopping? Most of your own living costs are likely covered by an expense account. And Elfriede, by all reports an absolutely wonderful woman and mainstay of your family, isn't a spendthrift, either.

So here's the first part of my theory: unless the account you have in tax-free Jersey is chock-a-block with bullion or cash, the addiction to horses seems to have soaked up a big piece of your $300 million. And here's the second part: while processing the visions that flit through your fertile imagination, it occurred to you that spending more on thoroughbreds than maybe anyone else in North America was futile if nobody bothered to watch or bet on horse races. The solution was what has become Magna Entertainment Corp., intended to revive the racetrack and gaming business. Am I close here, Frank?

Whatever your motive, I submit that MEC doesn't rank up there as one of your top-ten epiphanies. Not so far, anyway. The strategy – consolidating scattered tracks, spiffing them up with slots and all the electronic gizmos and plasma screens – is a spellbinder, and a cash gusher, in the telling. But the devil's been in the doing – or the not doing.

In fact, name the devil and it's visited MEC. Renos at Gulfstream fall behind schedule due to hurricanes; lousy weather hits Santa Anita; your lease expires at Bay Meadows; no-smoking regulations thin out Flamboro's casino crowd; and state after state is taking its time approving slots that virtually everyone sees as racing's only chance for salvation. Without slots, plans to pimp up decrepit Pimlico in Maryland have been dying. After suffering $8 million (U.S.) in start-up losses, the racino in the middle of nowhere in Austria is hurting from low attendance. There must be days when the old World of Wonders looks like a piece of strudel by comparison. Crowds at MEC tracks in the U.S. were so small, and betting handles so niggardly, that McAlpine was boosting purses with dough from MEC's own pockets. And *they* were so empty that, in 2005, Tom Hodgson, McAlpine's replacement as CEO, had to peddle Flamboro, one of the few money-earning tracks, after only a couple of years.

The response to the new Horse Wizard electronic betting consoles that Andy invented to create a crossover of customers from slots to horse racing – was that a $2.7-million (U.S.) bill I saw in the 2005 annual report? – epitomizes the mess: Tom Dillon installed Horse Wizards at Gulfstream with seats, and a staffer to help racing newbies learn how to bet. He's since got rid of the staffer due to lack of interest by the public. Not a soul sitting at the consoles pays them a lick of attention. Horse Wizard earns zippo, Dillon says. The *Washington Post*'s Andy Beyer says racing enthusiasts have dismissed them as a joke. And the expected users, those who typically find slots a welcome option to the mental anguish brought on by the complexity of bingo, haven't showed much interest in the Horse Wizard, either. So much for building a crossover.

Is there hope for MEC? I know you keep saying there is, Frank. You're nothing if not optimistic. But I worry. So here's an idea that might fly: run a lottery on how long the next CEO will last. It's not so crazy. There have been six in as many years, including your second shot at the job after sacking Tom Hodgson in early 2006.

To tell the truth, though, we shareholders prefer you keep the job. At least you don't take any salary from MEC. McAlpine, on the other hand, was drawing down more than $800,000 (U.S.), which had to beat hell out of selling Fords, his previous job. And it's costing MEC $1.3 million (U.S.) in severance to buy him out of the job (and keep his mouth shut). Hodgson came cheaper at $500,000 (U.S.). In fact, he got paid less than anybody else on the MEC executive except for CFO Blake Tohana. But he wasn't a very exciting guy, even if he made some recapitalization progress by paring back MEC's ungodly debt. With severance and various other payments, though, Hodgson will hoof it from MEC with $1.1 million (U.S.) for his year on the job, including $500,000 (U.S.) in severance. In other words, it cost MEC $1.8 million (U.S.) simply to fire its last two CEOs.

It could be they deserved to be fired. After all, they collectively racked up losses of $320 million (U.S.), including the $105-million (U.S.) bath MEC took in 2005. That performance doesn't augur well for fulfillment of your prediction that MEC and racing will one day be a bigger company than Magna and auto parts. Not unless the world suddenly gets as interested as farm folks used to be, back when there were farms. Of course, if MEC ever comes anywhere near Magna's success, you'll be acclaimed a certifiable business genius by someone other than yourself.

THE INHERITORS

The innovations you introduced to the car-parts business have set the gold standard for corporate organization, no question, Frank. Ignore critics who see greed as the soul of Magna. Keeping plants smallish to fend off unions (even if it was Burt Pabst's idea) has been effective. Sharing profits with workers, and even more of it with managers, has worked wonderfully. Apportioning pre-tax profit by percentage to specific purposes? A leap forward. Enshrining it all in a constitution that management and board are bound to uphold has worked brilliantly to create the "unique entrepreneurial culture" at Magna.

I worry, though, at the constitution's implied fragility. You got $40 million (U.S.) in 2004 and $33 million (U.S.) in 2005 for consulting services. The stalwarts on Magna's compensation committee claim the money is your due as Magna's founder, for instituting the culture that the constitution now defines, and as a kind of royalty for your ongoing efforts to sustain it.

I may be missing something, but isn't the board and management already pledged to uphold the constitution now and forever? Surely there's no danger it will all fall apart in your absence. If that's true, why the big bucks? I assume that Elfriede, Belinda, and Andy will inherit the family trust and take over your responsibility, even though it seems to duplicate that of management and future boards. Will they go on collecting the big payment in the future?

Those aren't unreasonable questions, Frank. And they bring Belinda into the discussion. For a while, it looked like she was favoured to become the new Frank – not physically, heaven forfend, but as chairperson-for-life. The genetic makeup that matters to you horsemen was there. Even her rebelling against book-learning in favour of hands-on experience at Magna might have appealed to you; it wasn't so different from your own view, that practical trumps theoretical.

Knowing your dislike of privilege and entitlement, and your belief in meritocracy, we outsiders naturally assumed that Belinda's performance in her first three years on the job at Magna so completely outshone that of anyone else in the company, and that the torrent of praise from managers, who only happened to notice her surname after noting her superiority on the job, was so overwhelming, that you were forced into promoting the young superstar.

In 1988, when you appointed Belinda to Magna's board of directors – only the fourth woman in almost forty years, and at twenty-two by far the youngest of either sex to achieve the honour – the die seemed pretty much tooled, as it were. In the course of a decade, she married Don Walker, gave birth to Frank Jr. in 1991 and Nikki in 1993, worked assiduously to "preserve the social fabric" by parcelling out the 2 per cent of pre-tax profit that Magna makes available for educational, charitable, political, and community purposes, divorced Walker, and got bumped up to vice-president. By 1998 she was executive vice-president. MEC should create tracks that are that fast, Frank. Horses would break records daily.

And Belinda wasn't finished. Saintly Johann Koss, the Olympic speed-skater and medical doctor-cum-humanitarian, whom she married in 1999, scarcely saw the ink dry on the pre-nup before he became her second ex in 2003. Meanwhile, in 2001, Belinda, at thirty-four, had replaced her first ex, Don Walker, as CEO of Magna, which at the time had 67,000 employees.

Whoever advises you on PR doesn't make your credibility his first priority, Frank. Your claim that you'd only reluctantly appointed Belinda as CEO at the board's insistence was a howler. Belinda's explanation – that Magna's culture had been like mother's milk in the Stronach household, so she was qualified to become CEO to sustain it – had more of a ring of truth than that guff about the board insisting on her. No one who's experienced the Full Frank, illustration and all, would have any trouble imagining you taking out the felt-tips at breakfast to go over things with Elfriede and the kids, and then doing it again at dinner.

Furthermore, in the view of most of Magna's biggest shareholders, the bags of gold you've been slugging home are evidence that the boards of Magna-related companies are more inclined to do what they think you'd want, than the other way around. It's the only reason I can think of that Magna directors are among the best paid in the country. Ed Lumley, for instance, got about $240,000 (U.S.) in all, after the compensation committee (that he heads) hiked directors' fees in 2004. As a director of Canadian National Railways, whose profit was about twice Magna's in 2004, Lumley got less than $70,000 (U.S.) and, in the same year, David McLean, CNR's board chair, got $133,000 (U.S.).

The measly $1.8 million (U.S.) you paid Belinda in her first year as CEO – less than two of the executives she outranked, and a lot less than you tossed at her cousin Werner Czernohorsky every time you gave him the heave-ho or he quit in a snit – seemed to suggest her apprentice status. The market concluded that Jim Nicol, the guy you made president and COO, would do the heavy hauling.

Mind you, it would have been hard for her to mess Magna up. It was Nicol's job to make sure it never happened, right? But a touch more confidence in Belinda might have helped at her first annual meeting, Frank. Your crack that "there is nothing to worry about for the next fifty years because I'm going to be here to a certain extent" looked like you'd already decided she needed a safety net. She had enough problems, what with having to present investors with another of those numbingly convoluted restructurings you're so fond of.

Things might have been different if she'd had a Magnalyzer available to help out. Remember the Magnalyzer, Frank? That tabletop contraption featured in the 1986 Annual Report that looked like the hybrid of a table-saw and a chess game. It was acclaimed for its decoder-ring powers to perform financial analysis using "the laws of physics to paint a picture that is worth 10,000 figures." Machined metal blocks that represented each Magna division, were weighted according to size. Each had a little flag on top to identify it. Profitable ones went on one side of the table top, losers on the other, and they were distributed according to geography. It conjured images of amazed executives standing around it in a clean-room somewhere saying things like, "I had no idea that manufacturing dipsticks meant

so much to Tesma." Sadly, we never heard about that particular innovation again. A victim of laptops, maybe?

But things come and go, nature of the beast, eh Frank? Take the
spincos. Before they were, I guess you could call it unspun, in 2005,
they were where all the action was. Tesma, under Fred Gingl, Decoma
under Al Power, and Intier, which Don Walker ran after buying into
it with his $11-million (U.S.) leaving-Magna package – were pretty
much stand-alone outfits. On the other hand, Magna Steyr in Europe
was a bit of an unknown. It hadn't been spun off yet and was run by
Siegi Wolf, who came across as, well, a bit nutty to outsiders. (To
some insiders, too, come to that. You might not know that some
attendees have claimed that Siegi scrambled to grab the chair next
to Belinda's at board meetings in the hope of being perceived as close
to the seat of power. It was a source of hilarity around head office.)

Belinda's stab at rearranging Magna into five supergroups –
Decoma, Tesma, Intier, Cosma and Magna Steyr – was another idea
that popped up. But before you got a chance to spruce Magna Steyr
up for its public debut, using some bits and pieces from Cosma, the
whole supergroup idea was gone.

So was Belinda, as it happened, in 2004. In her few years at the
top, her telegenic good looks, the friendship with Bill Clinton and
John Kennedy Jr., her dabbling in the fashion and pop music businesses – talk about good time-management! – added a little glamour
to auto parts. And she was smart enough to follow the first rule of
the job – do no damage.

True enough, *The National Post* in Canada and *Fortune* in the U.S.
both found that reason enough to embarrass themselves by ranking
her among the world's most powerful businesswomen. A little closer
look at the numbers and they might have wanted to recant. Sure,
operating revenue rose from $10.5 billion (U.S.) in 2001, her first
year, to $15.3 billion (U.S.) in her last. But profit dropped from $579
million to $522 million in the same period. Not that that was upset-
ting to you guys who depended on pre-tax profits for bonuses; the

pre-tax went from $900 million (U.S.) to $1 billion (U.S.), contributing to Belinda's $6.4-million (U.S.) payday in 2003. By my reckoning, by the way, that was a 250 per cent raise for her three years on the job. No wonder Siegi Wolf was keen to sit next to her. It couldn't hurt to be close by when the board was handing out that kind of money.

BELINDA GETS OUT OF THE FAMILY BUSINESS – AND INTO POLITICS

To give Belinda her due, she was quick to grasp that being CEO of Magna gave her access to higher places. What was it, do you think, that politicized her? Hanging around with all those ex-politicos you collect at Magna? Wishing she could actually enter Magna's "As Prime Minister" essay contest instead of just running it? Who would have bet she'd be toughing it out on "six large," as they say at the track, worrying about bumpers and door handles one day, then the next, becoming a political healer who unites the right in Canada? Yet there she was, persuading Stephen Harper, the Reform leader, to have a pow-wow with his counterpart Peter McKay of the old Progressive Conservatives to seek some common ground. First thing we know, a car-parts executive was taking curtsies for helping to create the new Conservative party.

Once blooded in politics, she quickly became acquainted with a fundamental tool of the trade: prevarication. In November 2003, she flat out wasn't interested in running for leader of the unified party. Magna, its customers, employees, and shareholders were paramount in her thoughts. Then, *wham*, in January, she called on the only language other than English that she knows, kissed all those Magna constituents *auf wiedersehen* (significantly, not *au revoir*, given her inability to answer the simplest question from a reporter in French, Canada's second official language), and she was in the thick of a campaign to become leader of the Conservative Party, never having been elected to anything before.

Belinda's political aspirations must have generated mixed emotions, Frank. When Nicol got tired of playing second fiddle to the boss's daughter, and left in 2002 to "reacquire his independence" (which he did for about a nanosecond before being hired as CEO of Tomkins PLC, a U.K. engineering conglomerate), you gave Belinda his job, making her president as well as CEO. But when, in 2004, she skipped her Manolo Blahniks out of the corner office to run for the Conservative Party leadership, the job she hadn't wanted a few months earlier, she left you, her seventy-two-year-old father, to cover her two jobs at Magna. Kids, eh Frank? Mine once had a morning paper route, and guess who wound up delivering papers when he was off with a friend's family for the weekend?

I know, I know, she wasn't really indispensable at Magna, so her jobs weren't that tough to cover. Her resignation caused scarcely a ripple in operations and Magna's share price actually went up in the days after the announcement. Her own stock went down though when, despite pouring millions into hiring top handlers and image consultants, Belinda lost the leadership battle to Stephen Harper, mainly because she displayed a high-school-level grasp of national issues, and inadvisedly clung to a platform of "baking a bigger economic pie," a concept she never quite explained. But she took it like a trouper, Frank. Next thing we knew, she was running in the 2004 federal election as a single soccer-mom in her hometown, Aurora. This time she won and became a Member of Parliament, sitting with the opposition Conservatives.

There was talk, I know, that you'd be pulling the strings, living your own failed political ambitions vicariously through Belinda. That didn't seem to be so, though, when you forecast a short political career for her. "My daughter will serve her country and then come back to the company, since she is not a career politician," was the way you put it to the Austrian press. I have to ask again about the PR person giving you counsel, Frank. You sounded jealous that voters who'd rejected you had accepted her. Belinda, on the other hand, came off looking spunkier than expected when, by her actions, she told you to take that job and shove it.

Which, come to think of it, is about what she told Stephen Harper in 2005, when he proved unenthusiastic about her support for same-sex marriage and the like. Tired of sitting in opposition where she would be unable to do anything to advance her liberal social agenda, she did what any former high-powered CEO would. She told her then boyfriend, the Conservative party deputy leader Peter McKay, that she was stepping out for a jiff on an errand, stuffed her House of Commons vote in her Gucci clutch, and swung by Prime Minister Paul Martin's house looking for a job. A few hours later, she returned to McKay and proudly informed him that she was the newly minted minister of human resources. Oh, yeah, and a Liberal.

It was good theatre, Frank, if devious politics. Belinda took with her to Martin's a pretty important vote, the deciding one that kept the Liberal government afloat a little longer. The Prime Minister, of course, hadn't given that a thought. He was purely interested in Belinda's intellectual heft, her high-level business experience, the bump in glamour her Prada outfits would bring to caucus meetings, her unflagging loyalty . . . well, maybe not that. A few days after the floor-crossing, Peter McKay was still in such shock at Belinda's double-ditching – him and the Conservatives at the same time – that he was reduced to interviews in gumboots, standing in his father's field of spuds in Nova Scotia, though he had the good sense to have a telegenic dog at his side.

Of course, things haven't quite unfolded as Belinda, or you, might have hoped. Although her vote bought the Liberals a little time, and she'd gone from opposition backbencher to cabinet minister, she scarcely had time to learn the names of her fellow Liberals when the scandal-ridden government fell and an election was called for February 2006.

Now Belinda had a new problem: how to persuade constituents who voted for her as a Conservative to elect her as a Liberal. It must have confused the folks at Magna, as well. In her first election, vice-chairman Fred Gingl had written letters asking employees, managers, and business associates to support Belinda's candidacy as a Conservative. Now he had to try to sell a turncoat Liberal candidate. But while Belinda came through and got herself re-elected (Dennis Mills tells me you actually knocked on doors campaigning for her – what a dad!), most of the rest of the country had had enough of the Liberals that Belinda had found so attractive. Canadians voted her old Conservative party – including her former lover Peter McKay – into power as the new government. Stephen Harper, Belinda's nemesis, who had "never really noticed complexity to be Belinda's strong point," became the new prime minister. And Paul Martin, her erstwhile Liberal patron, quit as Liberal leader, throwing open yet another political-party leadership race.

What to do, eh Frank? For a while, Belinda was bruited to be a possible contender for the leadership. At least until someone pointed out that since becoming a politician, she hadn't accomplished anything beyond grabbing headlines. She bowed out, disingenuously claiming she disagreed with the party's process for selecting its leader and felt she could beat the reform drum more effectively from the back benches. Ironically, she'd run for leadership of the Conservatives because she then felt she could reform that party in the top job. Go figure.

(As a kind of side issue, don't you find it interesting, Frank, that one of the contenders in 2006 for the top Liberal job is Bob Rae. He was the one who beat David Peterson to become Ontario's premier, and it was Peterson who set up Belinda's switch to the Liberals. And Rae, you'll recall, was once appointed to be an independent director of Tesma, but quit, according to observers, when he learned that "independent" didn't mean quite the same thing at Magna as it did at other companies.)

What will become of Belinda is still an open question. There have been rumours that she's experienced the ugly side of a politician's life, being bothered by a stalker. In any case, I'm just speculating here, Frank, but I don't see the top job at Magna going to her any time soon. Far be it for me to offer you advice, but if that's what you've got in mind, it's worth rethinking. If she were to quit politics now, she'd be confirming the view of many that she's little more than a ditzy dilettante who, as the old saw goes, was born on third base and thinks she hit a triple. A free pass home might not excite shareholders.

CHARITY BEGINS . . . WHERE IT GETS THE MOST PR

If Belinda is as uncomplex as Stephen Harper claimed, at least in parliament she only needs a single focus. You, on the other hand, have always displayed a Kiplingesque ability to compartmentalize your many interests and keep your head when all about you are losing theirs. True, it helped that a lot of the time you were the one performing the beheadings. In addition to Magna, you had the mess at MEC to deal with, for instance. Yet even while you must have already been plotting to put the skids to McAlpine, and while you were courting Tom Hodgson as his replacement as CEO, you found time for charity. The $8 million donated in October 2004 to the "Stronach Regional Cancer Centre – the Magna Building" at the Newmarket hospital where your kids and grandchildren had been born, was decidedly generous.

A small cavil, though: wouldn't it have been a little, well, classier, to give more prominence to Magna, whose shareholders were putting up the money, and a little less to the Stronach family, which was putting up nothing? The $100,000 Magna gave from its charitable pool to the tsunami relief fund was also generous, even if the third-world horror didn't seem to qualify for quite as much of Magna's money as the $750,000 you put out for the Austria Vienna football team.

But all of that paled against the biggest charitable gesture of all – the relief you offered to victims of Hurricane Katrina in New Orleans in September 2005. What a tale! As your friend and MEC vice-chairman Dennis Mills tells it, you were on the phone to him the instant you saw the devastation on television, giving him carte blanche to make your aid plan happen. He says you offered two hundred or so New Orleans evacuees the use of the living units at the new Palm Meadows training centre in Florida that were available until the training staff and horsemen moved into the units in November. You really caught the heartstrings of America with that, Frank, and lots in Canada, as well. You gave them another tug when you pledged to let the evacuees live rent-free for five years in new homes you would build for them on land you bought in Louisiana. "It was Frank's finest hour," Mills says.

Could be. But to me that's just Dennis being Dennis, your faithful wingman looking out for your best interests. I'd argue that it was an even finer hour for him. His *modus operandi*, at any rate, was all over the idea from the get-go. Unquestionably he was the perfect guy to take on a big-scale, feel-good project. Having put together extravaganzas like the Pope's visit to Toronto and the Rolling Stones SARS concert, who better to out-do the efforts of the U.S. government in coming up with a relief plan? As soon as he had your go-ahead (and Magna's money), he was farming out the work to Magna folks to execute the plan. He even found partners to share the costs. Within a few days everyone in North America was eulogizing you as a problem-solving philanthropist able to pull off what the catatonic U.S. government couldn't. On radio and television in both Canada and the U.S. it was all Frank, all the time. The only time it wasn't, it was Dennis, crediting you.

A little too generously, it seemed to me. As the story heroically played out, I couldn't help wondering where the money was coming from. History suggested it wasn't coming out of your pocket; the donation to the Newmarket hospital was just one example that you find Magna's charitable fund handier than a personal cheque when displaying public-spirited philanthropy. Media reports said that MEC was picking up the tab for the Katrina relief. But the trouble with that view was that MEC had been bleeding money for a few years, and was on its way to another losing year. So it could offer aid in kind – the Palm Meadows units – but it could ill afford to pay for buses, planes, houses, land to put them on, and all the rest of it.

But Magna and MID could. They have money. And no one in the U.S. knows the difference between Magna, MID and MEC anyway. And those who do, know you control all three. What I couldn't answer in my mind was, Why? You haven't done much to improve conditions for backstretch workers – grooms, outriders, hotwalkers, and such – who live in veritable squalor at some of your racetracks, notably at Pimlico. And neither you nor any Magna company had a history of improving housing on, say, Canadian native reserves. Given your apparent need to let the world know of any charitable work, we would have known. So why all of a sudden the change, and why in Louisiana and Florida?

Then it struck me: charity is a lot cheaper than lobbying. I feel a touch cynical about thinking this way, but let me try my theory of how the Katrina project went down, beginning with the motive.

THE KATRINA BACKGROUND

By mid 2005, slots had been approved for Gulfstream Park, but the Florida legislators still had to ratify their approval. MEC and its rival CDI, which also owned a track in the state, were worried that the legislature was balking and might even withhold support. MEC was expecting approval of 3,000 slot machines at Gulfstream and a state tax of maybe 40 to 45 per cent on them. Meanwhile, MEC had gone ahead with a $145-million (U.S.) rebuild of Gulfstream, including a room to hold them. You were hoping slots revenue would up the cash flow and pay for bigger purses, which would improve racing and increase betting. But still there was no approval from the state.

Mills, as MEC's vice-chairman, of course knew all this. He also knew that pro-slots lobbyists had soaked MEC for something north of $23 million (U.S.) between 2003 and 2005. Paul Cellucci, the former U.S. ambassador to Canada you hired as a full-time employee in 2005 to promote MEC's case in state legislatures, including Florida, was alone pulling down $765,000 (U.S.) a year. Cellucci's job is to get state governors onside – especially those of the Republican persuasion, like Cellucci.

Trouble is, though, you'd got mostly squat for all the dough. Your buddy Arnold in California sandbagged you by doing a deal with the state's Indian tribes. Maryland's new state government turned down the expected slots at Pimlico. In Florida, Jeb Bush, George W.'s brother, was dragging his feet on slots at Gulfstream, pressured by the anti-gambling religious right. He also might have resented the idea that MEC was buying approval for slots. The governor wasn't pleased that you spent $48,000 (U.S.) to fly four members of the state legislature on a two-day junket to Canada in July 2005 on what Cellucci called an educational trip. What were you thinking, Frank?

Anyway, things weren't bright for MEC when Katrina hit at the end of August 2005. I know Mills says *you* immediately called *him*. Somehow, I see Dennis catching the catastrophe in New Orleans on television (I don't picture you as a heavy TV-watcher) before the two of you spoke.

Whatever the case, I figure it was Mills, who's nothing if not lively of mind and silver of tongue, who also recognized a confluence of events – the ensuing New Orleans debacle, empty rooms at Palm Meadows, MEC's need for positive press in Florida – as the opportunity of a lifetime. You agreed, gave him the go-ahead, and a new hero was born – you.

Once Dennis swings into action, it's something to behold. Evacuees were bussed to your Florida training centre and you promised to house them, later, in new homes in Louisiana. The astonishing speed with which the media latched onto the story and broadened your canonization beyond Florida to all of North America was no accident. The Royal Bank of Canada and the Canadian Auto Workers union, who Mills found to support the project, were discreet in mentioning their role, if they did so at all. But Dennis made sure key media people got access to you, called columnists and invited them to interview you, and accommodated television crews.

When things seemed to be slowing down, a second wind from the Mills publicity machine pumped the story back onto the front pages. In Louisiana he'd engineered the purchase of land for "Canadaville," to which you committed $10 million (U.S.) over five years and on which you vowed to build factory-made homes. Never mind that insects and high humidity have driven conventional farmers out of business in the area you picked. In press releases and interviews no one found it the least bit improbable that the New Orleans residents you relocated from inner-city projects to double-wides rolled onto a hard-scrabble farm might actually turn a profit raising organic crops. Nobody so much as smiled when you declared the project not just a sustenance farm, but the foundation of a new organic-food industry for the state.

In fact, the whole Katrina thing became organic, a Dennis Mills production that became larger than life. People actually started to send *you* money to help out. For a change, journalists were singing your praises, and without using adjectives like "quirky" and "despotic" in their descriptions. One minute you were the devil incarnate, seeking to expand gambling. The next, you were Father Teresa, outdoing the most powerful government in the history of the world in looking after distressed citizens.

All of which, I admit, Frank, may have been done out of the goodness of your heart, and with Mills's altruistic energy. If so, I apologize. But I can't help thinking that linking the Katrina evacuee activity with approval of slot machines at Gulfstream was as much a corporate strategem as it was altruism. After all, it would take a curmudgeonly government indeed to deny gaming machines to MEC, given its transformation into some kind of Salvation Cavalry. Can you honestly say that you and Mills didn't notice or discuss the fact that committing $2 million a year to Canadaville was a lot cheaper, and generated a lot more positive publicity, than all the cash MEC shelled out for lobbyists?

And yet. And yet. Although Mills let the citizens of Florida know of your philanthropy in America's time of need, the state government somehow failed to grasp the humanitarianism, Frank. Maybe it remembered MEC's clumsy attempt to sway pro-gambling pols by taking them on that $24,000-a-day trip? And just possibly Jeb Bush didn't like the fact that your high-profile relief project made his brother look like an organizational doofus by comparison?

Whatever the reason, the plan kind of backfired. You built a room to hold an expected 3,000 slot machines, and raised purses for horsemen on the basis of the revenue anticipated from them. In passing here, Frank, I have to say you deserve kudos for the new Gulfstream. I'm not sure Dennis Mills's description of the new Gulfstream as the "Vatican of racetracks" is exactly how I'd describe it, but it's impressive. Except, apparently, to the state. Overlooking your status as hero of Katrina, when Florida finally okayed slots at the end of 2005, it only allowed 1,500 at Gulfstream. And it levied a 50 per cent tax that was 10 per cent higher than forecast. Now the horsemen are refusing to renegotiate the rich purses you promised, forcing you to seek arbitration. Do you sometimes get the feeling that Gulfstream is snake-bit? I mean, the target of two hurricanes that set back renovations, empty slots rooms, Horse Wizards that nobody uses, recalcitrant horsemen who won't give you a break. . . . What else can go wrong there?

THE ROAD AHEAD

In fact, there's a little too much bad karma among the Magna companies, these days, don't you think, Frank? MEC has been hemorrhaging so much money that it's dragged MID down with it. Greenlight Capital not only wants to restructure MID, but has charged you in court with oppressing minority shareholders for not permitting the change. In the spring of 2006, prior to the series of Magna company annual meetings, a proxy advisory company cited MEC's dismal performance and the roundelay of executive changes as reason that its shareholders should refuse to accept the re-election of the board. Sure, the move would only be symbolic since you control all the companies and appoint whom you want to the board. All the same, a loss in court on the oppression issue, combined with growing unrest by increasingly activist shareholders, strikes me as a hairball in the making.

Magna, the company that actually makes money, seems to carry on. But even it has some question marks. The car-parts business is only as good as its customers, which for Magna is still mainly North American automakers. But two of them, GM and Ford, are teetering financially. Delphi, the parts division that GM spun off on its own, is saddled with overpriced labour, who threatened in the spring of 2006 to strike if efforts were made to cut the pay and benefits of workers. Correct me if I'm wrong, Frank, but if Delphi went on strike, forcing GM plants to close for want of parts, wouldn't that put a serious crimp in Magna's very prosperous Formet hydroforming plant that supplies GM frames?

Finally, Frank, there's the succession issue underlying everything. It's kind of awkward to bring it up, but there will come a time when somebody has to replace you as chairman. If you've got someone in mind, we shareholders (who actually own the company) recognize that, barring a court decision, we're not likely to have much say about the choice. But we'd be interested in hearing what your exit strategy is.

Andy doesn't seem to figure in it. Neither does Belinda, unless she bails on yet another career — and then finds someone to run the place. Belinda's son, Frank? Good genes, being scion of two Magna

CEOs. Suitable first name, too. It's kind of unfair even to mention him while he's still a teen. But who would have expected that his mother would be appointed to the board at twenty-two? Somehow, I don't see any of the existing executives stepping up. Gingl, Walker, and Wolf have all had a shot at CEO. But it would be interesting if they were to battle for the chairmanship.

The one certainty, Frank, is that whoever succeeds you as head of Magna (and MID and MEC) will have to go some to come close to matching your achievement, energy, and innovative mind. Canada needs entrepreneurs like you. For all the zaniness you've periodically displayed, and despite your pecadillos and stubbornness – perhaps because of them – you've enriched Canadian business as no one else has for more than fifty years. I know you've sought to create a legacy to commemorate your life in business. Rest assured that you have done so, both in the buildings built to your painstaking specifications and in the industrial empire that is the pride of Canada, and probably of Austria.

Having inspected your life as closely as I've been able to, however, I hope this book contributes to that legacy in some small way. Somehow, though, I get the feeling that your remarkable presence is a long way from over. Give me a call some day and we can talk about the rest of your life.

Yours sincerely,
Wayne Lilley

EPILOGUE

The shareholder oppression lawsuit against MID that Greenlight Capital Inc. launched in the summer of 2005 went to court in December and concluded in March 2006. As this book went to press in the summer of 2006, Ontario Superior Court Justice John Ground had not delivered his ruling, so it was impossible to assess the impact the outcome might have. Nonetheless, the suit seemed to cast a general uneasiness over the intertwined Magna companies during the last half of 2005 and the first half of 2006.

The mood was not brightened by their annual financial results, reported at the end of March. MEC's 2005 revenue of $625 million (U.S.) was down from $703 million (U.S.) in 2004 and the net loss of $96 million posted in 2004 had swollen to $105 million. The company's management disarray wasn't inspiring, either. Tom Hodgson, who'd come on board as CEO less than a year earlier, had abruptly departed. Somewhat ironically, inasmuch as he was performing as both MEC's chairman and its interim CEO since Hodgson's exit, Stronach allowed that "there's no question we have to strengthen our management team."

Stronach did his best to turn MEC's annual meeting, the first of three Magna company meetings held on consecutive days in May, into a pep rally. MEC, he insisted, had bottomed out and was about to bounce back. To that end, he promised to deliver MEC from debt within a year – no small matter, in light of its $550 million (U.S.)

in long-term debt against only $460 million (U.S.) in shareholder equity. He told shareholders that MEC intended to continue selling off assets to raise cash. Excess real estate, MEC's two golf courses, and some smaller racetracks were all on the sales block. He also suggested that equity partners willing to join MEC as part-owners of the Gulfstream and Santa Anita tracks, and a possible "non-dilutive" equity issue were both being considered to raise some capital.

Investors, however, hadn't detected any of the promised bounce in MEC; in June, it was trading only marginally above its fifty-two-week low of about $5.64, hardly a time to go to market with a new stock issue. The asset sale hadn't exactly gone swimmingly, either. A $50-million (U.S.) deal to sell land adjacent to MEC's Florida training centre went south when the buyer backed out. Of greater concern was the $225-million (U.S.) sale of The Meadows, the Pittsburgh harness track at which slots had been approved after intense and expensive lobbying by MEC. While it had found a buyer, Pennsylvania regulators' approval of the ownership transfer wasn't expected until the fall of 2006. In the meantime, MEC was desperate for cash: it needed $50 million (U.S.) in July to meet payment of some secured debt, and another $100 million (U.S.) to pay off a bridge loan to MID that was coming due in August. At the MEC meeting, despite the dismal results – contributing to a total loss of $320 million in four years – not a single question came from the floor, an oddity at a meeting chaired by Frank Stronach.

But questions *were* raised by analysts once they had a chance to absorb the first quarter results, made public prior to the meeting. Although Stronach had conveniently neglected to mention in his address to shareholders the tight spot that MEC was in, a cautionary note tacked discreetly onto MEC's first-quarter report for 2006, issued at the meeting, warned that MEC would be hard-pressed to carry on as a going concern if it couldn't resolve a liquidity challenge that included a $112-million (U.S.) capital deficiency.

It was easier to put a positive spin on things at Magna International's annual meeting the next day. Revenue in 2005 had increased to $22.8 billion (U.S.), a new record. Still, that news had a sobering aspect. Profit had sagged to $639 million (U.S.) in 2005 from $676 million (U.S.) a year earlier, knocking nearly a dollar off Magna's earnings per share. The fact that the debt of Ford and General Motors, two of Magna's major customers, was considered below investment grade, demonstrated the travails of the auto industry and its suppliers. But Stronach saw the situation as an opportunity, not a problem for Magna. Unencumbered by the debt weighing down many of its competitors, Magna, he said, would be able to invest in innovation and new business. Stronach also had words of comfort for investors who were worried that Magna would begin sloshing money into troubled MEC, once the forbearance agreement expired on May 31. He assured them that Magna had no intention of underwriting money-losing MEC or of investing in any non-automotive ventures.

Although adamant that Magna would not buy a North American assembly plant to produce a car under its own name, he admitted to ambitions to develop an entire high-quality, low-cost vehicle, from prototype to finished product, which Magna would then turn over to an automaker to market. Following the Magna meeting, Fred Gingl indicated that Magna was also thinking about dipping its toe into direct-to-consumer sales with Magna-branded products such as child seats and roof racks that would be distributed through retailers.

The MID annual meeting, the last of the three, was a tame affair compared to the meeting in 2005 when Greenlight's David Einhorn had likened Stronach to Fidel Castro. MID's financial results from its real-estate business were fine; revenue was up 17 per cent to $151 million (U.S.) and income had increased almost 50 per cent to $76 million (U.S.) But when consolidated with MEC's, MID's numbers appeared to support Greenlight's argument for peddling off its 59 per cent stake in MEC. Revenue dropped to $784 million (U.S.) from

$825 million (U.S.) a year earlier. And MID's share of MEC's mountainous racetrack losses shaved its healthy $76-million (U.S.) profit from real estate down to a skinny $6.6 million (U.S.).

On the basis of that financial performance alone, MID shareholders had good reason for resenting MID's ownership of MEC. But MID was also a major MEC creditor. And while it might have seemed reasonable that it would bail out its wayward child, it could hardly do so without reinforcing Greenlight's claim that it was using its solid real-estate revenue to subsidize the iffy gaming-and-racing business. CEO Simonetti's message was mixed. In his address to shareholders, he seemed reluctant to reject unequivocally giving aid to MEC. But during a subsequent conference call with analysts, he backed away from the suggestion that MID would give MEC a sweetheart deal of some kind on its debt repayment. Moody's Investors Service, a credit-rating agency, was unconvinced. It placed MID under review and promised to downgrade its creditworthiness unless MEC was able to manage its problems without affecting MID.

As it turned out, Moody's didn't have to act on its threat. In mid-May, MEC reported that Pennsylvania had conditionally approved The Meadows sale and that it was confident the $225 million (U.S.) in proceeds would permit it to meet its debt obligations and resolve its liquidity crisis. The market, however, didn't agree wholeheartedly. At the AGM, Simonetti had justified shoring up MEC on grounds that it was a $400-million (U.S.) investment for MID. But MEC's stock price had dropped to a three-year low by the end of June, and NASDAQ was listing its entire market cap as just $255 million (U.S.).

But by far the biggest challenge facing MID was the outcome of the shareholder-oppression case. Looking ahead, no matter which way Judge Ground rules, MID has a problem. If MID wins its case, its share price may well drop as some frustrated investors sell off their stake in anticipation that nothing is going to change. If, on the other hand, the decision favours Greenlight, MID is certain to appeal. That will delay execution of any remedy required by the court but increase MID's legal costs, already at $5 million (U.S.) as of March, 2006.

For Stronach, a ruling against MID that limits his ability to use his supervoting shares to overpower shareholders would certainly be the worst case if it rippled through the rest of Magna's companies. In the past, he'd ignored protests from a majority of minority share-holders of Magna International who complained at his outsized con-sulting fees. But if a precedent were established at MID, it was not inconceivable that oppression challenges could be forthcoming by disaffected minority shareholders of MEC, a company that represents Stronach's passion. Worst of all the same thing might happen to Magna International itself, the company that reflects his innovative mind, his manufacturing genius, and his powerful will.

INDEX

OTHER TITLES FROM
DOUGLAS GIBSON BOOKS

PUBLISHED BY MCCLELLAND & STEWART LTD.

CHARLES THE BOLD *by* Yves Beauchemin; *Translated by* Wayne Grady
An unforgettable coming-of-age story set in 1960s and 1970s east-end
Montreal, from French Canada's most popular novelist. "Truly astonishing
. . . one of the great works of Canadian literature." – Madeleine Thien
Fiction, 6 × 9, 384 pages, hardcover

WHAT IS A CANADIAN? Forty-Three Thought-Provoking Responses
edited by Irvin Studin
Forty-two prominent Canadian "sages," including Roch Carrier, John
Crosbie, Joy Kogawa, and Margaret MacMillan, provide essays beginning
"A Canadian is . . ." The result is an important book for all thinking
Canadians.
Non-fiction, 6 × 9, 283 pages, hardcover

THE WAY IT WORKS: Inside Ottawa *by* Eddie Goldenberg
Chrétien's senior policy adviser from 1993 to 2003, Eddie Goldenberg takes
us behind the scenes to show how vital decisions are made at the top. The
book reveals secrets from the ultimate insider.
Non-fiction, 6 × 9, 382 pages, hardcover

THE VIEW FROM CASTLE ROCK *by* Alice Munro
The latest collection of short stories by Alice Munro is her most personal
yet, based loosely on her family history. "When reading her work it is difficult to remember why the novel was ever invented." – *The Times* (U.K.)
Non-fiction, 6 × 9, 368 pages, hardcover

SAILING AWAY FROM WINTER: A Cruise from Nova Scotia to Florida
and Beyond *by* Silver Donald Cameron
The author, his wife, and their dog, Leo, sailed from Nova Scotia down the
East Coast, all the way to the palm trees of the Bahamas. This is the perfect
armchair sailing adventure, with enough detail to set a person dreaming . . .
Non-fiction, 6 × 9, 336 pages, hardcover

RIGHT SIDE UP: The Fall of Paul Martin and the Rise of Stephen Harper's
New Conservatism *by* Paul Wells
Canadian politics were turned upside-down when the Conservative
Stephen Harper beat out the Liberal Paul Martin in the 2006 election. The
shrewd and irreverent Paul Wells tells the story of their duel for power from
2001 on. Canadian politics has never been so much fun.
Non-fiction, 6 × 9, 272 pages, hardcover

YOUNG TRUDEAU: 1919–1944 *by* Max and Monique Nemni; *Translated by* William Johnson
A disturbing intellectual biography of Pierre Trudeau that exposes his pro-fascist views until 1944, completely reshaping our understanding of him. "I was extremely shocked." – Lysiane Gagnon, *Globe and Mail*
Biography, 6 × 9, 384 pages, trade paperback

STILL AT THE COTTAGE *by* Charles Gordon
The follow-up to the classic *At the Cottage*, this is an affectionate and hilarious look at cottage living. "Funny, reflective, and always insightful, this is Charles Gordon at the top of his game." – Will Ferguson
Humour, 6 × 9, 176 pages, illustrations, trade paperback

SORRY, I DON'T SPEAK FRENCH: Confronting the Canadian Crisis That Won't Go Away *by* Graham Fraser
The national bestseller that looks at how well official bilingualism is working in Canada. "It's hard to think of any writer better qualified to write about language than Mr. Fraser. . . . He is informed, balanced, judicious and experienced, and a very clear writer." – Jeffrey Simpson, *Globe and Mail*
History, 6 × 9, 352 pages, hardcover

CRAZY ABOUT LILI: A Novel *by* William Weintraub
The author of *City Unique* takes us back to wicked old Montreal in 1948 in this fine, funny novel, where an innocent young McGill student falls for a stripper. "Funny, farcical and thoroughly engaging." – *Globe and Mail*
Fiction, 5½ × 8½, 272 pages, hardcover

THE QUOTABLE ROBERTSON DAVIES: The Wit and Wisdom of the Master *selected by* James Channing Shaw
More than eight hundred quotable aphorisms, opinions, and general advice for living selected from all of Davies' works. A hypnotic little book.
Non-fiction, 5¼ × 7, 160 pages, hardcover

ALICE MUNRO: Writing Her Lives. A Biography *by* Robert Thacker
The literary biography about one of the world's great authors, which shows how her life and her stories intertwine.
Non-fiction, 6½ × 9⅜, 616 pages plus photographs, hardcover

MITCHELL: The Life of W.O. Mitchell, The Years of Fame 1948–1998 *by* Barbara and Ormond Mitchell
From *Who Has Seen the Wind* on through *Jake and the Kid* and beyond, this is a fine biography of Canada's wildest – and best-loved – literary figure.
Non-fiction, 6½ × 9⅜, 488 pages plus photographs, hardcover